Japan's Changing Generations

Generations of young people in Japan have resisted the "adult social order" for the past fifty years; but for the most part, these young people grew up and entered that order. Today, however, in an era in which the Japanese social order has lost legitimacy, this may no longer be the case. Will Japanese young people today be swallowed up by the adult social order, or will they create a new social order, more flexible and pluralistic than that of their elders? In examining this question from many different angles, this book provides a generational roadmap into Japan's future.

Gordon Mathews is Associate Professor, Department of Anthropology, the Chinese University of Hong Kong.

Bruce White is Lecturer in Anthropology and Sociology at Doshisha University, Kyoto, Japan.

Japan Anthropology Workshop Series

Series editor:
Joy Hendry, Oxford Brookes University

A Japanese View of Nature
The World of Living Things by Kinji Imanichi
Translated by Pamela J Asquith, Heita Kawakatsu, Shusuke Yagi and Hiroyuki Takasaki
Edited and introduced by Pamela J Asquith

Japan's Changing Generations
Are Young People Creating a New Society?
Edited by Gordon Mathews and Bruce White

The Care of the Elderly in Japan
Yongmei Wu

Community Volunteers in Japan
Everyday Stories of Social Change
Lynne Y. Nakano

Nature, Ritual and Society in Japan's Ryukyu Islands
Arne Røkkum

Japan's Changing Generations

Are young people creating a
new society?

**Edited by Gordon Mathews and
Bruce White**

Routledge
Taylor & Francis Group

LONDON AND NEW YORK

First published 2004
by Routledge
2 Park Square, Milton Park, Abingdon, Oxon, OX14 4RN

Simultaneously published in the USA and Canada
by Routledge
270 Madison Ave, New York NY 10016

Routledge is an imprint of the Taylor & Francis Group

Transferred to Digital Printing 2006

Typeset in Times by LaserScript Ltd, Mitcham, Surrey

British Library Cataloguing in Publication Data
A catalogue record for this book is available from the British Library

Library of Congress Cataloging in Publication Data
A catalog record for this book has been requested

ISBN 0–415–32227–8 (hbk)
ISBN 0–415–38491–5 (pbk)

Contents

Contributors

Peter Ackermann is Chair, Department of Japanology, University of Erlangen-Nürnberg, Germany. He is the author of many articles and book chapters on the Japanese education industry, and on the structure of self and communication in Japan.

Satoshi Kotani is Associate Professor at Ōtsuma University, Tokyo, and author of the books *Wakamonoron o yomu* [Reading theories about youth] (1993) and *Wakamonotachi no henbō: sedai o meguru shakaigakuteki monogatari* [Changing youth: a sociological narrative about the generations] (1998).

Brian J. McVeigh teaches in the Department of East Asian Studies, University of Arizona. He is the author of many books, including *Nationalisms of Japan: Managing and Mystifying Identity* (forthcoming), *The Nature of the Japanese State* (1998), *Wearing Ideology: State, Schooling and Self-Presentation in Japan* (2000), and *Japanese Higher Education as Myth* (2002).

Gordon Mathews is Associate Professor, Department of Anthropology, the Chinese University of Hong Kong. He has written *What Makes Life Worth Living? How Japanese and Americans Make Sense of Their Worlds* (1996) and *Global Culture/Individual Identity: Searching for Home in the Cultural Supermarket* (2000), and edited *Consuming Hong Kong* (2001).

Laura Miller is Associate Professor, Department of Sociology and Anthropology, Loyola University Chicago, and is the author of numerous articles on Japanese language and culture, and gender representation in media. She is currently working on a book entitled *Beauty Up: The Consumption of Body Aesthetics in Japan*.

Shunta Mori is Associate Professor, Department of Regional and Cultural Policy, Shizuoka University of Arts and Culture. He is the author of numerous articles in Japanese on the effects of overseas university experience on Japanese life, as well as on cross-cultural senses of what makes life worth living.

Lynne Nakano is Associate Professor, Department of Japanese Studies, the Chinese University of Hong Kong. She is the author of the forthcoming book *Community Volunteers in Japan: Everyday Stories of Social Change.*

Tetsuo Sakurai is Professor at Tokyo Keizai University and author of many books, including *Kotoba o ushinatta wakamonotachi* [Young people who have lost mutual communication] (1985). He has also written the chapter "'Mondai' toshite no wakamono" [Youth as a 'social problem'], in *Shakaigaku ga wakaru* [Understanding sociology] (1997).

Ayumi Sasagawa is the author of the Ph.D. thesis "Life Choices: University-Educated Mothers in a Japanese Suburb," Department of Anthropology, Oxford Brookes University.

Moeko Wagatsuma is Research Associate, Department of Japanese Studies, the Chinese University of Hong Kong. She has a Ph.D. in Ethnic Studies from Warwick University, and has done research on single Japanese women in Hong Kong.

Bruce White teaches Anthropology and Intercultural Communication at Oxford Brookes University. There he authored the Ph.D. thesis "Local Paths to an Interstate Japan: Charting Generational Change and Identity," in the Department of Anthropology. He is co-founder of the Organisation for Intra-Cultural Development (OICD), an ethnographic research group focusing on identity and social action.

Series editor's preface

Members of the Japan Anthropology Workshop continually carry out detailed and insightful research in Japan, and they meet regularly to present papers about their research and to exchange views on the subjects of their study. The fruits of most of these gatherings have eventually appeared in print in a variety of different forms and formats, and we are proud of our collection. However, it sometimes takes several years for our deliberations to be made widely available, and in a country where change flourishes, this is regrettable. The inauguration of a series devoted specifically to the research of the Japan Anthropology Workshop is a step in the direction of speeding up this process, and offering an outlet for groundbreaking work as it proceeds. This book is our first example of success in this respect. The papers were presented at our most recent conference, and the authors have spent the intervening time revising and refining them, so that I think we now have a collection at the cutting edge of research on Japan.

Another aim of the series is to present studies that offer a deep understanding of aspects of Japanese society and culture to offset the impression of constant change and frivolity that so tempts the mass media around the world. Living in Japan brings anyone into contact with the fervent mood of change, and former residents from many other countries enjoy reading about their temporary home, but there is a demand also to penetrate less obvious elements of this temporary life. Anthropologists specialize in digging beneath the surface, in peeling off and examining layers of cultural wrapping, and in gaining an understanding of language and communication that goes beyond formal presentation and informal frolicking. I hope that this series will help to open the eyes of readers from many backgrounds to the work of these diligent "moles" in the social life of Japan.

This particular book includes the work of ethnographers from within Japan and from various places outside. Together they combine a deep internal understanding of close compatriots with a wide international context. Some of the authors have many years of experience and a reputation for excellent work; others offer the fresh approach of scholars starting out on their publishing lives. Their papers make for good reading, and they offer a broad range of understanding of the people of their focus. Finally, the authors are collectively well qualified to look to the future of the new generations they describe, and I am delighted that they have brought this groundbreaking book into our series.

Joy Hendry

Acknowledgments

Japanese names in this book are given in Japanese style, with surname first. The only exception is when a Japanese author is publishing in English, in which case the given name appears first.

This book's editors thank Joy Hendry for her help and encouragement in the creation of this book. We also thank Rebecca and Olivia Thompson for help in proofreading. We owe an extraordinary debt to Yoko Miyakawa for proofreading and for reviewing the book's transcriptions from Japanese, as well as for her superb translations of two of the book's chapters (Chapters 1 and 2).

We also thank Viki Li, of the Cultural Relations and Identities in East Asia Program at the Hong Kong Institute of Asia-Pacific Studies, CUHK, for formatting the typescript to match Routledge style.

Introduction

Changing generations in Japan today

Gordon Mathews and Bruce White

"The generation gap" in Japan today

In Japan these days, it is interesting to ask young people and older people what they think of each other. The question may be met with little response, or a positive response; but, very often, sets of mutually unflattering terms are invoked. Young people may be described by their elders as being "inconsiderate" (*omoiyari ga nai*), "self-centered" (*jiko chūshin*), and "spoiled" (*wagamama*); elders may be described by young people as being "old-fashioned" (*furui*), "stiff" (*katai*), and "inflexible" (*jūnansei ga nai*). "Young people today (*ima no wakamono*) have no desire to work hard"; "young people today don't know how to speak properly and how to relate to others"; "young people today have no common sense," elders may say. In turn, young people may criticize their elders for having no independent selves but only social roles ("My father only lives for his company; my mother only lives for her children. They have no lives of their own"), and for their lack of enjoyment of life ("Older people I know don't seem to enjoy life. I would never want to live like that").[1] These comments reflect stereotypes, to be sure; but the readiness and frequency with which they are offered illustrates a clear "generation gap" in Japan today between the young and their elders.

What are we to make of this? "The generation gap" may be partly a creation of mass media, with these mutually unflattering descriptions reflecting what young people and their elders have seen and read in print and on screen.[2] However, it also seems that these accusations reflect a real tension, relating to the precariousness of what might be termed "the adult social order" in Japan. The survival of that social order depends upon young people being willing to enter and re-create the world of their elders. When older people in Japan criticize young people for their selfishness, rudeness, and inability to communicate, they are in effect saying that young people lack the attributes necessary to sustain the social order that they themselves have spent their lives building and maintaining. When young people in Japan criticize older people for their inflexibility and inability to enjoy life, they are in effect claiming that their elders have been swallowed up by that social order.

This generational tension is not new to Japan. Over the past fifty years, Japanese commentators have continuously worried about "young people today"; but young people have, by and large, grown up to resemble their elders, and, in turn, are worried about later generations of young people. Today, however, many Japanese young people are choosing not to enter "the adult social order": not to hold stable jobs, as did their fathers, or to marry and have families, as did their mothers, but to follow paths of their own choosing. Many, although not all, of the chapters in this book argue that young people may be creating a new Japan through this very process: by making countless individual choices that serve to erode the social order in which their parents' generation has lived. But before proceeding with this argument, let us consider generational conflict within a broader, more universal perspective.

Generational conflict, life course, and history in human societies

Tension between young and old is apparent in a range of societies, both traditional and modern; it appears that generational conflict has existed as long as human societies have existed. Nancy Foner's *Ages in Conflict* (1984) examines how in non-industrial societies the old dominate the young in their control of authority, property, and, for older men, access to wives. The young may feel great resentment at this, but can only wait until they themselves grow old and have the opportunity to dominate future generations of young people. Foner argues that "inequalities between old and young are built into the very fabric of nonindustrial societies" (1984: 240). The generational conflict this creates is a matter of life course rather than of history. It is a tension between young and old that does not involve young people eventually creating a society that is different from that of their elders, a historically new society. Rather, as the young become older they become like their elders, and re-create the society of their elders, a process that reoccurs generation after generation after generation.

Foner argues that in modernity, the nature of generational conflict does not necessarily change: the old may continue to dominate the young, and, by implication, generational conflict may continue to be a matter of life course rather than of history. Nonetheless, it seems clear that in the contemporary world, technology gives a new set of meanings to generational conflict; in Margaret Mead's words, "the expectation [is] that each new generation will experience a technologically different world" (1970: 61). In her *Culture and Commitment*, Mead distinguishes between postfigurative cultures, in which children learn from their elders, cofigurative cultures, "in which both children and adults learn from their peers," and prefigurative cultures, "in which adults also learn from their children" (1970: 1). Today, societies across the globe are becoming prefigurative, she maintains, and thus "the generation gap is world wide" (1970: 68). Much of Mead's argument, written at the height of the worldwide youth revolts of the late 1960s, seems today to be exaggerated. However, the largely technology-based generation gap she describes clearly continues to exist today, with young people running rings around their elders in their mastery of the Internet and other technologies, technologies that arguably lead to fundamentally different ways of thinking between the young and their elders (see Tapscott [1998] for an analysis of the Internet and generational difference).

Foner and Mead explore two fundamental aspects of generational conflict in the world today. It is clearly a matter of life course, as Foner discusses, in terms of the ongoing battle between youth and age that recurs generation after generation; but it is also a matter of history, as Mead argues, especially in young people's mastery of new technologies that their elders may never comprehend. The young have a technological advantage over their elders that will continue as long as capitalism continues to generate new technologies. Aside from technology, societies go through historical transmutations that condition generations in ways that lead to generational gaps in understanding the world: consider the aspiring-capitalist child and staunchly communist parent in Russia in the early 1990s, or in China today. As long as societies retain continuity over the generations, generational conflict will be at least partially a matter of life course – each new generation will to some extent reproduce the society of its elders, with young people opposing their elders today but eventually coming to lead lives not so different from those of their elders. As long as societies change in significant ways over the generations, then generational conflict will also be a matter of history: young people opposing their elders today will create a society different from that of their elders. In most societies today, both of these perspectives have a degree of validity. If generational conflict is primarily a matter of life course, then it is somewhat less interesting analytically, in its unchanging recurrence. If it is a matter of history, however, it may be highly interesting: How are societies changed by the young as they enter into adulthood and reshape the world of their elders – the world they inherit?

Sociologists such as Pierre Bourdieu have extensively theorized about processes of social and cultural reproduction. For Bourdieu, the symbolic violence of "pedagogic action" – both family education and institutional education – infuses individual minds (Bourdieu and Passeron 1990), leading the young, through the workings of *habitus*, to re-create the society that has created them. The continuities we see in Japanese society and in all societies generation after generation provide evidence for this view: this is why Japanese social organization today in some crucial respects resembles Japanese social organization in centuries past (see Nakane 1970) and why Japanese countercultural groups have in crucial respects resembled Japanese corporations (see Steinhoff 1992).

On one level, then, young people largely create their world as they have been molded to create it, unwittingly reproducing the world of their elders because they know no other. However, it seems that aside from this, there is also always a degree of volition at work. After all, every generation of youth in the contemporary world has a choice of whether to reproduce, reject or reshape the world of its elders. Every society – every "adult social order" – always faces the possibility of "legitimation crisis" (to borrow Habermas's [1973] term), where its young people evaluate and make a decision as to whether or not to join that society. Does adult society seem worth entering? Is "the game worth playing"?

Some societies today – the United States comes to mind – are flexible in allowing pluralistic paths into adulthood, with multiple opportunities and "second chances": the individual in the United States can change job or career relatively easily and can go back to school and receive further training; the individual can also divorce relatively easily. This flexibility – although it may create societal problems – serves to diffuse the tension of entering "the adult social order," since one can do so on one's own timetable without necessarily endangering one's future. In comparison, Japanese society has been relatively inflexible. In the conventional lives of Japanese adults, men have been expected to live for their companies, which they must enter during a brief window in their twenties. Women – despite greater flexibility in the workplace of late – have been expected to live for their families, particularly their children. There has long been a minority of Japanese who have not followed this path, from day laborers, to freelancers, to those who run their own businesses; but this standard path has been the Japanese cultural ideal, one that Japanese have been expected to fulfill and that the majority has indeed fulfilled.

Socialization into adulthood in Japan has been a grueling process: from the demands in secondary school for constant study for examinations, to the demands that career-track workers devote their lives to their companies, to the demands that mothers abandon their own pursuits to devote themselves to their children. Young people have long chafed at demands of the adult social order; but as long as that social order worked effectively and created a rising standard of living, most young people felt little justification to do anything but follow the standard, conventionalized paths to adulthood laid out before them. Today, however, the Japanese economy has stagnated, and the Japanese social order seems ineffective; young people have more leeway in not following those standard paths. This is the crux of the Japanese generational divide today.

Generational conflict, life course, and history in Japan

Generational difference has drawn comment throughout the lifetimes of most Japanese alive today. Since the end of World War II, each new generation of young people has been targeted for its strange ways, from the *taiyōzoku* of the 1950s, seen as abandoning the discipline of their elders for their own hedonism, to protesters against the U.S.–Japan Security Treaty, and 1960s radicals reflecting the world tumult of youth in that decade, to *shinjinrui*, the "new breed" of the 1980s, claimed as being so different from their elders as to be no longer "Japanese," to *otaku*, technophiles swallowed up by the world of computers and other new media, and, in the late 1990s, *kogyaru*, young women with artificial dark tans and hair dyed bright blond (see Miller, Chapter 5, this volume). Of course most Japanese young people of these generations were not so flamboyantly opposed to their elders, or even opposed at all; but these young people drew conspicuous attention.

We have discussed how generational conflict may be seen as a matter of history or of life course. Many Japanese writers (e.g., Sengoku 1991; Sawaguchi 2000) tend to assume that "the generation gap" is a matter of history: that young people are different from their elders in ways that will lead to a Japan of the future very different from Japan of the recent past. This is the root of the pessimism with which they may view the Japanese future. As opposed to this, many foreign social scientists studying Japan have tended to see "the generation gap" as a matter of life course:[3] of youth rebelling, and then fitting into the adult social order, just as did their elders of an earlier era. Gordon (2000) relates how in the 1960s he was told that "younger workers are ... individualistic.... The old loyalty is disappearing"; but these younger workers became the corporate elders of today, making similar criticisms of today's younger workers. This leads Gordon to say, "'Plus ça change, plus c'est la même chose' (the more things change, the more they stay the same)." White (1993), in her comparison of Japanese and American teenagers, also downplays the historical significance of any Japanese "generation gap," in depicting Japanese youth and adults as being largely harmonious in their relations, finding conflict only in their occupying of different places in the life course – a depiction at odds with that of many Japanese commentators.

Both of these views – of Japanese generational difference as a matter of life course, and thus largely inconsequential, and of generational difference as a matter of history and thus very consequential – have a degree of validity. The life course approach seems to have been valid through most of Japanese postwar history: young Japanese critical of their elders have for the most part eventually become very much like their elders. Japanese commentators (e.g., Kotani 1998: 98) have often noted that the protesting students of the 1960s became the corporate warriors of later decades, and this is true for other postwar Japanese generations of wayward youth as well.[4]

Today, however, generational difference may be a matter of history, of young people forging fundamentally different paths from their elders. Current Japanese commentators worrying about "young people today" may most accurately describe the situation: the young may indeed be acting so as to help destroy the postwar Japanese social order. This does not mean that Japanese young people are rebelling *en masse* against their elders, engaging in street demonstrations and political protests: this is clearly not happening. There is no discernible "anti-establishment" political movement among young people, no organized efforts to create a better society; young people tend to accept without protest their apparently diminished prospects in life (see Kotani, Chapter 2, this volume). However, on the individual level, many of these young people are indeed acting to destroy the Japanese society of their elders. To understand this, let us examine the situation and problems of Japanese young people today.

The problems of Japanese young people today

"Problematic young people" depicted in Japanese mass media today range over a span of three decades, from unruly elementary school children to unmarried thirty-somethings living with their parents; what these groups have in common, for all their diversity, is that they have not yet become full-fledged members of "the adult social order." There is *gakkyū hōkai*, "classroom collapse," in which elementary school students reportedly stop paying attention to their teachers and chat among themselves or wander about doing what they please (see Kobayashi 2001). There is *futōkō*, "school refusal syndrome," whereby young students, particularly those of junior high-school age, stop going to school, and *hikikomori*, "shut-in syndrome," whereby young people in their late teens or twenties shut themselves in their rooms and refuse to come out, often for years on end, surviving on meals left on trays by their mothers (see Kyūtoku 2001; Shiokura 1999). There is *enjo kōsai*, "compensated dating," whereby high-school girls sell their company and often their bodies to older men, and *hikō shōnen*, juvenile delinquents, a concern reaching a peak in 2000 when a string of murders committed by 17-year-olds garnered extraordinary media attention (see Ōsawa 2001). There are *furiitaa*, temporary part-time workers – young people who don't take regular employment but work as store clerks and at fast-food counters, thereby avoiding "adult commitment" (see Gakken 2001; also Mathews, Chapter 7, this volume), and there are *parasaito shinguru*, "parasite singles," young people in their thirties who don't marry and start their own families but continue to live at home off the largesse of their parents (see Yamada 1999; also Nakano and Wagatsuma, Chapter 8, this volume). As this partial listing attests, the range of "youth problems" in Japan today – and the rhetorical tags that sociologists and the media give them – is remarkable in its breadth.

Some of these problems appear, from an outside perspective, to be mild. Writers discussing *gakkyū hōkai* sometimes express their shock over classroom infractions that would elicit only shrugs from teachers in the

United States and Great Britain. As for the heinous murders committed by 17-year-olds, juvenile murders in Japan have in fact declined in recent decades. But other of these "youth problems" appear quite significant. If, according to media reports, there are now almost two million *hikikomori* in Japan shutting themselves in their rooms – a problem not even recognized until the late 1980s – if there are three million *furiitaa*, forsaking the career paths of their fathers' generation, if there are ten million "parasite singles" not leaving home to start their own families, this may have significance far beyond the latest media craze (there are now 26.4 million people in Japan of 20 to 34 years of age [*Asahi Shinbun* 2002: 56], giving some idea as to the scale of these problems). The Japanese "generation gap" may in some respects be a media creation, but in other respects it may be quite profound, with potentially far-reaching consequences. The millions of young Japanese mentioned above are living in ways that may cut them off from the life paths of their parents: they may never enter "the adult social order."

The categories of young people listed above – the students who refuse to go to school, the *hikikomori* who refuse to leave their rooms, the juvenile delinquents, the graduates who don't take regular jobs but become *furiitaa*, the "parasite singles" – are of course different in their particulars, and represent a vast array of individual situations; but they do represent a collective refusal or inability to follow an established path to adulthood. A prominent theme in the anthropology of Japan has been how Japanese are socialized; many scholars have studied socialization processes from infancy through to school, through to employment and marriage – for example, Caudill and Weinstein (1986) on care of infants, Hendry (1986) and Ben-Ari (1997) on preschool socialization, Benjamin (1997) on primary school socialization, Rohlen (1983) on secondary school socialization, McVeigh (1997) on college socialization, Okano (1993) on the transition from school to work, and Rohlen (1974) and Dore and Sako (1998) on corporate socialization: these are all seminal works explaining how young people are molded into adult Japanese. These processes, as noted above, are arduous, but in these portrayals they tend to be successful in molding young Japanese to fit the adult social order. Today, however, we have entered an age of delegitimization of this social order, in which unsuccessful or spurned socialization may increasingly come to take center stage.

This delegitimization is not obvious. The casual visitor to Japan will see few signs of malaise beneath the sleekness of contemporary Japan – even the homeless in Tokyo, in their neat rows of tents in public parks, seem positively bourgeois. However, this malaise manifests itself in numerous ways in daily life, from the salaryman in a beleaguered company worrying about how long his job might last, to his wife frugally guarding their savings and bitterly wondering why she married a man who might soon no longer be able to support his family, to their children, facing severely limited job prospects and questioning the worth of working so hard to become adults, like their sad parents, in a society that might never reward them for that work. Why bother becoming a part of the adult social order in such a constraining, unrewarding world?

In tandem with the delegitimization of the adult Japanese social order over the past decade of economic downturn and social malaise, there is a pluralization of values taking place. Because "the adult social order" can no longer claim success, other, alternative paths to adulthood are opening up. Today, one need not necessarily marry and have children, or work for a big company; and even if one does, one can, more than in the past, have a degree of latitude in how one lives. Young people are not the cause of this loosening, but rather its beneficiaries, beneficiaries of the delegitimization of the adult social order; but by grasping these new chances and following these new paths, they are destroying the Japanese adult social order all the more. This is why "the generation gap" today, unlike that in Japan in previous generations, may foreshadow the shape of Japan tomorrow. Or it may not, as this book as a whole discusses, disputes, and explores.

The structure of this book

This Introduction has set forth themes that run through the book as a whole. Most particularly: Is "the generation gap" in Japan today a matter of history or of life course? Is it of fundamental importance in the creation of a new Japan, or is it finally not very significant, with the old Japan crushing all efforts to create a new Japan? The perspectives taken in the different chapters of this book run the gamut of views on this question. Like any argument that looks to map out a future defined by a new generation, this book is speculative. In order to give a fully nuanced picture of changing Japanese generations, multiple points of view are essential, which is what we have attempted to provide in this collection.

Part I explores "The Japanese generational divide," considering the Japanese "generation gap" in historical perspective. Sakurai, in Chapter 1, argues that the spirit of generational rebellion of late 1960s youth has become dormant, but has never entirely vanished; he traces the history of generational conflict since the 1960s and concludes hopefully that today's young people really are creating a new Japan. Kotani, in Chapter 2, is more gloomy. "Why are Japanese youth so passive?" he asks, and answers in terms of the cocoon of Japanese mass media as well as family structure today, in which parents and children experience not mutual conflict but mutual indifference. Finally, he concludes, the most intractable problem in Japan is not the youth but their conservative and inflexible elders. White, in Chapter 3, offers a more optimistic view: young people fundamentally differ from their elders in the diversity of values they are able to embrace and in their membership, unlike their elders, in a global culture – a change not just of life course but of historical significance, he argues.

Part II examines, over three chapters, "How teenagers cope with the adult world." Ackermann, in Chapter 4, considers how high-school students' social networks and private mediated spaces enable them to fend off pressure from the adult world and preserve their own senses of their lives. Miller, in Chapter 5, explores how teenagers, and young people as a whole, remake their own bodies in ways their elders never could have imagined, shaping their bodies into zones of freedom that adults cannot control. McVeigh, in Chapter 6, looks at how, beneath the "guidance" of Japanese universities, young people struggle but largely fail to preserve their own subjectivities.

Part III examines, over four chapters, "How young adults challenge the social order" – how young people in their twenties and thirties are entering, resisting, contesting, and changing the world of work and family in which their parents lived. Mathews, in Chapter 7, discusses how young people enter or resist career-track employment, while Nakano and Wagatsuma, in Chapter 8, consider young women who do not marry – both these chapters examine young people who refuse to enter the path to adulthood that their parents took for granted. The final two chapters carry these analyses further in the life course. Mori, in Chapter 9, considers how young Japanese educated in American universities face the Japanese corporate world upon their return to Japan, while Sasagawa, in Chapter 10, looks at how young mothers' self-centered conceptions of childrearing differ from those of their own mothers, who sacrificed themselves for family. These last four chapters explore how young Japanese moving into adulthood may be changing Japan through the sum of their individual actions. But this remains open to debate. The book's Epilogue, written by White and Mathews, returns to the pivotal question, are young people in Japan today creating a new Japan? Our generational considerations suggest that they are, but we do not know.

There are some lacunae in the topics covered in this book. Perhaps the most significant absence is the lack of discussion of generational conflict among secondary-school leavers and their elders. Four of the book's chapters deal with university students or graduates, but none deal with those who go from secondary school to employment, or who drop out of secondary school. This emphasis on the educated is partially justified, in that generational conflict with their elders seems most apparent among those who do not assume adult roles early in their lives, but who, through schooling, avoid those roles until later. It is also partially justified in that these young people, because of their relatively higher social status, may have more power to transform future Japanese society than their working-class fellows, and thus may be more directly relevant to the central question posed by this book. Nonetheless, this is a lacuna that is unfortunate, and that we hope will be more fully addressed in future research.

Will Japanese young people truly create a new Japanese society, or will they be subsumed in the postwar Japan created by their parents and grandparents? This book finally offers no unequivocal answer to this question. Not only do these chapters often disagree with one another; they are also often themselves ambivalent. But the one point upon which all these chapters unequivocally agree is that the future of Japan lies with the young. What kind of society will they create in the future?

Notes

1　These comments come from interviews with 105 young people and 52 elders about "the generation gap" in 1999 to 2000, and again in summer 2002 in Tokyo and in Sapporo. See Chapter 7, n. 1 for acknowledgments.
2　The mass media in Japan have made much of "the generation gap." The above-quoted comments about young people reflect mass media commentary about "young people" (there is less commentary about "old people," presumably because older people control the mass media). "Young people have lost the ability to communicate," argued Sakurai (1985); "young people have lost their work ethic and are no longer serious about life," claimed Sengoku (1991); "young people, with undeveloped frontal lobes, no longer know how to relate to others," argues Sawaguchi (2000), to cite three of the more notable volumes among hundreds of books in this genre.
3　There are exceptions to this, however: see the brief discussions in Sugimoto (1997: 64–73), Kelly (1993: 197–203), and Henshall (1999: 116–121).
4　Miller (1998: 51) notes that "almost all surveys testify that trends in the mentality of the young during the 1970s have survived their maturing, and are part of that generational cohort's values and belief system." This seems true – but there may, of course, be a difference between what people say in opinion surveys and how they behave in social situations. Perhaps both Miller and Kotani are correct, with Miller referring to private inclinations, and Kotani to the larger, more coercive world of social interactions

References

Asahi Shinbun (2002) *Asahi Shinbun Japan Almanac 2002*, Tokyo: Asahi Shinbun.

Ben-Ari, E. (1997) *Japanese Childcare: An Interpretive Study of Culture and Organization*, London: Kegan Paul International.

Benjamin, G. R. (1997) *Japanese Lessons: A Year in a Japanese School Through the Eyes of an American Anthropologist and Her Children,* New York: New York University Press.

Bourdieu, P. and Passeron, J. C. (1990) *Reproduction in Education, Society and Culture*, trans. R. Nice, London: Sage.

Caudill, W. and Weinstein, H. (1986) "Maternal Care and Infant Behavior in Japan and America," in T. Lebra and W. Lebra (eds) *Japanese Culture and Behavior: Selected Readings,* Honolulu: University of Hawaii Press.

Dore, R. and Sako, M. (1998) *How the Japanese Learn to Work*, London: Routledge.

Foner, N. (1984) *Ages in Conflict: A Cross-Cultural Perspective on Inequality Between Old and Young,* New York: Columbia University Press.

Gakken (ed.) (2001) *Furiitaa: naze? dō suru?* [*Furiitaa*: Why? What should we do?], Tokyo: Gakushū Kenkyūsha.

Gordon, A. (2000) "From the Director: Beyond the Crossroads – Talking About Change in Japanese Studies," *Tsūshin*, 6(1), Edwin O. Reischauer Institute of Japanese Studies, Harvard University.

Habermas, J. (1973) *Legitimation Crisis*, trans. T. McCarthy, Boston, MA: Beacon Press.

Hendry, J. (1986) *Becoming Japanese: The World of the Preschool Child*, Honolulu: University of Hawaii Press.

Henshall, K. G. (1999) *Dimensions of Japanese Society: Gender, Margins, and Mainstream*, New York: St. Martin's Press.

Kelly, W. W. (1993) "Finding a Place in Metropolitan Japan: Ideologies, Institutions, and Everyday Life," in A. Gordon (ed.) *Postwar Japan as History*, Berkeley: University of California Press.

Kobayashi, M. (2001) *Gakkyū saisei* [The rejuvenation of the classroom], Tokyo: Kōdansha.

Kotani, S. (1998) *Wakamonotachi no henbō: sedai o meguru shakaigakuteki monogatari* [Changing youth: a sociological narrative about the generations], Kyoto: Sekai Shisōsha.

Kyūtoku, S. (2001) *Koko made naoseru futōkō, hikomori* [To this extent, avoidance of school and of the outside world can be cured], Tokyo: Makino Shuppan.

McVeigh, B. (1997) *Life in a Japanese Women's College: Learning to be Ladylike*, London: Routledge.

Mead, M. (1970) *Culture and Commitment: A Study of the Generation Gap*, Garden City, NY: Natural History Press/Doubleday.

Miller, L. (1998) "Hidden Assets: Japan's Social Transformations for the Twenty-first Century," *American Asian Review*, 16 (3): 43–63.

Nakane, C. (1970) *Japanese Society*, Berkeley: University of California Press.

Okano, K. (1993) *School to Work Transition in Japan: An Ethnographic Study*, Philadelphia, PA: Multilingual Matters.

Ōsawa, T. (2000) *Hanzai shōnen* [Juveniles who commit crimes], Tokyo: Zanetto Shuppan.

Rohlen, T. (1974) *For Harmony and Strength: Japanese White-Collar Organization in Anthropological Perspective*, Berkeley: University of California Press.

—— (1983) *Japan's High Schools*, Berkeley: University of California Press.

Sakurai, T. (1985) *Kotoba o ushinatta wakamonotachi* [Young people who have lost mutual communication], Tokyo: Kōdansha.

Sawaguchi, T. (2000) *Heizen to shanai de keshō suru nō* [The kind of brain that leads people to nonchalantly put on their makeup while riding the subway], Tokyo: Fusōsha.

Sengoku, T. (1991) *'Majime' no hōkai: heisei nihon no wakamonotachi* [The destruction of seriousness: Japanese youth today], Tokyo: Saimaru Shuppankai.

Shiokura, Y. (1999) *Hikikomoru wakamonotachi* [Young people who have withdrawn from society], Tokyo: Birejji Sentaa Shuppankyoku.

Steinhoff, P. (1992) "Death by Defeatism and Other Fables," in T. S. Lebra (ed.) *Japanese Social Organization*, Honolulu: University of Hawaii Press.

Sugimoto, Y. (1997) *An Introduction to Japanese Society*, Cambridge: Cambridge University Press.

Tapscott, D. (1998) *Growing Up Digital: The Rise of the Net Generation*, New York: McGraw-Hill.

White, M. (1993) *The Material Child: Coming of Age in Japan and America,* New York: The Free Press.

Yamada, M. (1999) *Parasaito shinguru no jidai* [The age of "parasite singles"], Tokyo: Chikuma Shobō.

Part I
The Japanese generational divide

1   The generation gap in Japanese society since the 1960s

Tetsuo Sakurai[1]

The emergence of the postwar generation

After the end of World War II, the General Headquarters of the Allied Occupation took charge of large-scale reforms of Japanese society in its political, economical, administrative, and educational institutions. By the latter half of the 1950s, after the end of the occupation in 1952, a new generation of Japanese had emerged, severely criticizing the ideas and values of the older generation.

A key expression of this new generation was the novel *Taiyō no kisetsu* [Season of the sun] (Ishihara 2000 [1955]), winner of the *Akutagawa-shō*, a prestigious literary award, in January 1956. Written by Ishihara Shintarō, then a college student and now Governor of Tokyo, the novel was made into a movie in May of that year, and gained much popularity for its depiction of youths in rebellion against society, engaged in unbridled sex and violence. Just like the 1955 Hollywood film, *Rebel Without a Cause*, *Taiyō no kisetsu* portrayed young people's dissatisfaction with society and their unhappiness with the older generation.

The sociologist Katō Hidetoshi advocated in his *Chūkan bunka* [Intermediate culture] (Katō 1957) that Japanese people free themselves from the earlier cultural framework in which they had lived. Katō criticized the earlier culture that stifled individual freedom and stoically enforced work and study, and instead presented a new type of culture that would pursue comfort and convenience based on the younger generation's values.

In 1955 the ratio of students going to high school rather than entering the workforce after junior high school climbed to over 50 percent; one in every two members of the younger generation was able to enjoy life away from labor up until they were 18 years old. Consequently, the values of the new generation changed significantly compared to those of the older generation, who had gone to work at an earlier age, Katō argued. Based on this assessment, Katō concluded that to the earlier division between elite culture and popular culture a third form of culture could now be added:

"intermediate culture." This new culture, he held, was becoming the cultural mainstream, and high-school graduates were its major bearers. At around the same time, the young political scientist Matsushita Keiichi (Matsushita 1959) maintained that with the arrival of mass society in Japan, a new middle class was emerging, creating a new urban stratum of citizens detached from conventional party politics. Both Katō and Matsushita pointed out the emergence of a new social class, who were to bear the burden of Japan's postwar politics and culture. The youth challenging the older generation in films and novels was the symbol of this emerging new class.

Linked to the emergence of this new generation is the fact that, in the midst of Japan's economic recovery, standards of living were rising, and an increasing number of urban citizens began to enjoy the fruits of consumption. According to an opinion survey conducted in Tokyo and Osaka in 1961 (Shinohara 1972: 51), to the question "What does it mean to renovate your life?" 27 percent of respondents gave the answer, "Increased leisure activities (hobbies and entertainment)." This suggested that people's stoic attitudes toward life were changing.

In the 1960s, the younger generation in Japan and throughout the world began to express themselves in new ways – expressing what American sociologist Daniel Bell called "the sensibilities of the sixties" (1976: 120–45). Let me introduce two people who might be considered forerunners of "the sensibilities of the 1960s" in Japan.

On July 12 1961, *Asahi Shinbun* carried an article entitled "I tried to do what I wanted." The article consisted of essays written by two young men in their twenties. One was by Ozawa Seiji (born in 1935), now an internationally famous orchestral conductor. In January 1951 he went alone to Europe and won first prize in the Besançon International Conductors' Competition in France as well as in the "Youth Contest: Conducting with Karajan" in Berlin; in March of that year, he became a sub-conductor of the New York Philharmonic Orchestra (see his book about his experience: Ozawa 1962). In this essay (1961) he wrote:

> My habit of doing what I want to do finally made me get aboard a freighter bound for Europe. After running about in the muddle of Tokyo, I had managed to obtain a passport, and a motorcycle.[I went to Kobe] and at last embarked on a ship. I felt relieved only after everything disappeared from sight.... "What have I done?' I said to myself. But as I watched the waves, took naps, and played the 2000-yen guitar my brother had bought for me, I gradually felt emboldened. I thought, "Oh well, I can do anything I want to do if I try."

Another essay was written by Oda Makoto (born in 1932), who wrote the book *Nandemo miteyarō: sekai ichinichi ichidoru ryokō* [I'll go and see everything: a dollar-a-day journey around the world] (1961), which became a bestseller. Oda, a graduate student of Tokyo University, had won a Fulbright scholarship to study at Harvard for a year in 1958. The book is a record of his subsequent wandering through North and Central America, Europe and Asia on a shoestring. Oda's book contains severe criticism of American and European societies, a marked difference from the usual Japanese travelogues of this era, which tended to idolize Western societies. He begins his book as follows: "'I'll just go to America,' I thought. It was autumn three years ago. The reason was quite simple. I wanted to see the United States. In short, it was just that" (1961: 6). "In short, it was just that," Oda declared, but in those days Japan did not allow its citizens freely to go abroad. It was not until April 1964 that Japan liberalized overseas travel for sightseeing; in 1963 only 20,000 Japanese went abroad. The only option for those who wanted to go overseas was either to go on business or, as in the case of Oda, apply for a study-abroad program.

Oda did not have any "inferiority complex toward America," which had taken root in Japan during the Allied Occupation. Here lay Oda's novelty. He wrote of the following episode. Before leaving for America, he was made to take a lesson on table manners, arranged by the Fulbright Committee; he was warned not to put his elbows on the table while eating and not to use a toothpick. Certainly people did not do such things in the United States, he thought; but he saw people eating with their elbows on the table in Paris, and using toothpicks after a meal in Spain. An American girl whom he met in Paris said to him that since her childhood she had been told not to eat with her elbows on the table, but now in Paris she ate with her elbows on the table like Parisians, and realized that what she had been doing (back home) was stupid and that she had been behaving like a hillbilly (1961: 15–16).

Oda symbolized a new generation in that he was able to adopt the perspective of "cultural relativism" in postwar Japanese society, where American culture enjoyed overwhelming dominance. Both Oda and Ozawa were the forerunners of the young generation of the 1960s, a generation that had no hesitation in expressing itself. Another youth who symbolized this generation was Horie Kenichi. Horie, at age 23, successfully sailed by himself across the Pacific Ocean in his small yacht of 5.8 meters in length. Sailing alone for 94 days, he finally arrived in San Francisco, without passport or visa. The voyage, which lasted from May through August of 1962, was the first of its kind in the world. Like Oda and Ozawa, Horie was a youth who tried to pursue his own individual desires, refusing to give in to the opposition of people around him (Horie 1962). He was part of a new generation that broke away from the established common sense of Japanese society, rooted in a loathing of deviation and stressing the importance of cooperation.

Inter-generational conflicts in the 1960s: the revolt against "motherhood"

In the 1960s, the baby boomers born after World War II became teenagers. They had grown up in an environment of new media, particularly television. TV broadcasting had begun in February 1953, and by 1962 the diffusion rate of TV sets had reached about 80 percent; TV had become a ubiquitous medium (Sakurai 1994). In the mid-1960s, American television programs were broadcast in Japan only a few months after they had been shown in the United States, and American culture was having a major impact on Japan's teenagers. In November 1963, a satellite relay system was established between the United States and Japan. The first news relayed to Japan via a satellite from the United States was that of the assassination of President Kennedy. I was 14 at the time, but still remember vividly the great shock I felt from the broadcast.

The feature-length comic book (*chōhen manga*), created by Tezuka Osamu in the immediate postwar years (Sakurai 1990), took root firmly among children, who were never to outgrow them; the comic book was part and parcel of the culture of this generation. In the mid-1960s, the readership of comic books had expanded to include college students, a fact the older generation was quick to criticize. However, the comic books in the 1960s were no longer for children, but rather had evolved into a new adult-oriented medium for creative expression following a variety of different themes, giving rise to a weekly comic magazine with a circulation of more than a million.[2] The huge market created by comics attracted many talented young artists and writers, and consequently provided the foundation for the spread of Japan's film and TV animation throughout the world, these media being based on comic-book culture (Kinsella 2000).

In the field of music as well, the young generation blossomed. In the 1960s, young people, deeply immersed in music since their childhood, became engrossed in British and American rock and folk music. Many began to form their own bands and play their own music. The Beatles' performance in Japan in 1966 had a great social impact, revealing a clear generation gap between the young, who rapturously embraced their music, and the old, who rejected it as nothing but "noise."

In the 1960s, Japanese society underwent enormous transformations of demography. The percentage of people engaged in primary industry – agriculture, fishery and forestry – was 32.7 percent of the total workforce in 1960, but decreased to 19.4 percent by 1970, a decline of 40 percent in this period. The ratio for those engaged in agriculture was 26.8 percent of the total workforce in 1960 and just 15.9 percent in 1970. As if in proportion to this change, the movement of the population into cities accelerated. The population of the three largest urban regions (the Minami Kantō Region with Tokyo as its center, the Nishi Kinki Region with Osaka as its center, and the Tōkai Region with Nagoya as its center) occupied 48.6 percent of Japan's total population by 1970 (Iida *et al.*1976). Industry expanded as well: the number of cars produced in Japan was 810,000 in 1961, but increased to 5.29 million by 1970 (and to 11.04 million by 1980) (*Asahi Shinbun* 1980). In addition, the ratio of students going to universities and junior colleges rose from 10.3 percent in 1960 to 38.4 percent in 1975. The number of students in those institutions increased dramatically, from 756,926 in 1961 to 1,684,296 in 1970 and to 2,248,903 in 1975 (Monbushō 1981). However, universities failed to change their structure in the face of a rapidly swelling number of students, and still maintained their old system of education.

In considering the student rebellion at the end of the 1960s, we must take into account the fact that the system of higher education was unable to deal with these cataclysmic changes in Japanese society. The May Revolution in France in 1968 was triggered in part by students' dissatisfaction about the management of dormitories. Similarly, Japan's students' revolt began with their demand for a repeal of a punishment meted out by mistake at Tokyo University and an inquiry into accounting irregularities at Nihon University. Their criticism of universities, combined with the anti-Vietnam War movement and political controversy over the revision of the Japan–U.S. Security Treaty, grew into a large-scale movement, involving many non-political students who were discontented with university education.

The style of the social movements of the young generation that grew up in a cultural environment of comic books, rock music, and television was different from that of earlier movements. They self-mockingly described themselves as "with *Asahi Jaanaru* [Asahi journal] in the right hand, and *Shōnen Magajin* [Boy's magazine] in the left hand." *Asahi Jaanaru* was a high-quality editorial weekly, whose main readership consisted of left-wing intellectuals, and *Shōnen Magajin* was the most popular comic weekly. The students were asserting themselves as ordinary youths who would not tolerate injustice and deception, rather than as elite revolutionaries, as in the past.

Thus, the student rebellion at the end of the 1960s should not be considered a revolutionary movement of elite students. Instead, it should be seen as the younger generation's cultural revolt against an older generation that had grown up in a wholly different environment. One of the characters the students drew as a symbol on their banners was the cat "Nyarome" from a gag cartoon by Akatsuka Fujio. This light-heartedness of the students was probably incomprehensible to the older generation that had engaged in the sober and stoic student movements of the 1950s.

Although the postwar baby-boom generation rebelled against the older generation almost simultaneously with revolts of the young in many other countries, the students' revolt in Japanese society had different characteristics from those in France, Germany, and the United States. Whereas in those countries the revolt against the older generation could be in a sense described, in a Freudian fashion, as an impulse to "kill the father," in Japan it involved an impulse to "kill the mother."

From Oedipus to Electra

The mental structure of Japanese people is sometimes explained by the concept of *amae* (indulgence), which may be described as one's long-term mental reliance on one's mother (Doi 1971, 1994). Interrelationships of indulgence between mother and child in infancy shape the foundation of the intimate relationship based on mutual reliance among adults in Japanese society, it is sometimes claimed (Kawai 1976; Kimura 1972). In his work *Childhood and Society* (1964 [1950]), Erik Erikson points out that American mothers' "disapproving attitudes" in coldly pushing their children away shaped the spirit of Americans, who as settlers survived in the wild without relying on anybody (1964: 288–96). In contrast, in Japan the mother's almost excessive love for the child formed the foundation of intimate relationships among Japanese people, who make every effort not to hurt one another's feelings.

For young people of the postwar baby-boom generation, however, the traditional "mother who tries to wrap the child in excessive love" threatened their independence. In the latter half of the 1960s, when baby boomers were approaching entrance into university, mothers who made every effort at securing their children a place in a prestigious university came to be labeled "*kyōiku mama*" ("education moms") and were mocked by the media. Children who had been fed up with their mothers' excessive love and control came to call them, though with a certain kind of affection, "Mamagon," in imitation of a monster in "Urutora Man" (Ultra Man), a science-fiction TV drama of the day.

In 1968 a poet wrote that in order to escape the "motherhood" (*haha naru mono*) buried in Japanese unconsciousness that prevented all deviation from social norms, Japanese must symbolically "kill the mother" (see Sakurai 1985: 87–9). A poster for a campus festival at Tokyo University at the time of the students' revolt bore these words: "*Tomete kureruna, okkasan*" (literally, "Don't stop me, Mother!" or "Mother, don't disturb my independence!"), words that may be interpreted as students' self-mockery (Sakurai 1985: 89–90).

The students' anger over the injustice and deception of the university authorities turned to rage over the "motherly and ambiguous human relations" of Japanese society. The students felt enormous indignation toward the faculty and university administration, who refused to clarify where responsibility lay and to respond to their inquiries. The authorities' decision to forcefully remove the students who had barricaded the university led to violent confrontations between students and riot police all over Japan.

In the end, forceful removal of these students brought the universities back to "normalcy," but spiritual confusion and a sense of despair over university authorities' oppressive behavior lingered on among students.

The narcissistic generation

After universities were "normalized," the terms *shirakeru* (indifferent) and *shirake* (indifference) came into vogue. The terms originally depicted the sense of disappointment the young generation felt toward the older generation that had failed to listen seriously to their complaints: educational reforms they had demanded were never taken up and the authorities' control over education from elementary school to university became further tightened. These terms then came to be used to describe the mental state of lethargic youth who felt enthusiastic about nothing and indolent about everything. Kasahara Yomishi, a famous psychiatrist, coined the term "student apathy" to depict this mental state prevalent among university students (Kasahara 1984; Kasahara and Yamada 1981).

Social scientists argued that this mental state reflected the state of students' human relations: they formed relationships with weak mutual communication, as if shutting themselves up in a capsule, without becoming involved deeply with each other (Nakano and Hirano 1975). In 1977, the Japanese psychiatrist Okonogi, using Erikson's concept of "moratorium," suggested that Japanese young people were avoiding or rejecting growing up (Okonogi 1978). Kasahara (1977) presented the idea of "extended adolescence," arguing that in an age when the average life span has greatly increased, the old idea of growth is no longer valid. He argued that the period of adolescence, which used to end at around 22 years of age, might now extend to 30.

This emergence of young people afraid of being hurt by others, shutting themselves up in their capsules and trying not to be deeply involved with others (Kurihara 1981), was not limited to Japan. In the United States, Christopher Lasch published *The Culture of Narcissism* (1991 [1979]), in which he wrote that America had developed into a "bureaucratically controlled society," where people were losing a sense of reality and turning their backs on tangible human relations (1991: 31–51). Surrounded and controlled by electronically created images, people were avoiding direct human relations, and the "narcissistic personality" was becoming widespread, Lasch argued. Similarly, in France the sociologist Gilles Lipovetsky argued in *L'ère du vide* [The age of emptiness] that the self wrapped in narcissism today was an "empty mirror" (1983: 55–87), receiving and reflecting a massive amount of information and analysis without responding.

It was during this period that the novelist Murakami Haruki became popular (see Aoki 1996; Sakurai 1992). In his first novel *Kaze no uta o kike* [Hear the wind song], there is a line from a book by Derek Hartfield, a fictitious author who writes: "life is empty" (Murakami 1979: 152). Murakami's novel became a bestseller, reflecting the condition of an age when narcissism had began to prevail. The basic theme of his early novels was "incommunicability." The protagonist of *Kaze no uta o kike*, predisposed to autism, had been taken to a psychiatrist when he was a child, and was told, "Civilization is communication. If one cannot express something, one does not exist" (1979: 33). Later the protagonist came to the conclusion: "What the doctor said is correct. Civilization is communication. When there is nothing left to express and communicate, civilization ends. Click ... OFF" (1979: 35).

Human relations in which people try in vain to understand each other is the theme of Murakami's novel; thus his characters have no names and are known only by symbols such as "rat," "208," or "209." Was this symbolism modeled on actual changes in society? Let me give one example from a book by psychiatrist Ōhira Ken analyzing those who were pathologically dependent upon "things" – the kind of people who emerged in the 1980s in Japan. Ōhira writes (1990: 113–16) of a 29-year-old secretary working for a foreign-affiliated company who identified her friends by the brand name of their scarves. When she became friends with someone, she bought a scarf by the brand of which she remembered the new friend; or when someone gave her a scarf, she wrote down its brand name, such as Verde Monte, instead of the name of that person in her telephone book. This woman unconsciously selected brand names as a symbol in her attempt to avoid intimate relations with others.

The 1980s brought a host of new social phenomena. Another of these was long telephone conversations among high-school and college students. According to a 1986 survey by Nippon Telephone and Telegraph Corporation, female high-school students spent an average of 28 minutes on the telephone each day. A 1989 survey by the NTT Development Office showed that male college students made 6.7 telephone calls a week, while female college students made 7.4 calls a week. It also found that the time spent on one call was 9.6 minutes for male college students and 11.8 minutes for female college students (Yoshimi *et al.* 1992: 150).

Although the rate of junior and senior high-school students who possessed their own telephone was only 2.5 percent in those days, the rate for college students was much higher, with 27.5 percent of male students and 22 percent of female students possessing their own telephone (Yoshimi *et al.* 1992: 157). The telephone was becoming a tool to shape the social networks of individuals without the need for face-to-face interaction.

The emergence of a new community based on *"dengon daiyaru"* ("message dialing") which NTT began operating in 1986 continued this trend. It worked as follows: by repeating a simple set of numbers, say 1234 for a contact number, and repeating the same procedure with a secret number, people could obtain a code number. By using such a code number, total strangers could begin sending arbitrary messages to each other. This mode of communication was often abused by men trying to seduce women, but there also emerged people who felt that meeting someone on a telephone circuit was more real than meeting someone in person.

Mass media in the 1980s labeled such young people "*shinjinrui*" ("new species of human being" or "new breed"), in that they were a generation highly conversant with new technology, more interested in visual culture than in print culture, and who rejected old hierarchical relations. In the latter half of the 1980s, a new term arose to describe a certain type of young person, "*otaku*." The word *otaku* in Japanese is a second-person pronoun used to address with respect a person with whom the speaker does not have a close relationship. However, it acquired a new meaning when young fans of animation and comics began to use this term to address each other at gatherings of enthusiasts. *Otaku* became a term to refer to young people who were so engrossed in animation, comics or video games that they turned their backs on any pretense that relationships with others were important (Barral 1999).

In 1988 and 1989, there was a serial murder case involving little girls in Japan. The suspect turned out to be a young man obsessed with animation. Due to media reports that "a young man who shut himself up in his room with hundreds of animation videos committed perverse crimes," the term *otaku* came to depict a young generation completely divorced from the social and moral world of their elders.

Again, the narcissistic tendency to avoid close contact with others was not a social phenomenon limited to Japan, but a phenomenon common to the young generation in advanced industrial societies as a whole. For example, Douglas Coupland's much-talked-about novel *Generation X* (1991) depicts a generation characterized by nihilism and ennui in the midst of an all-enveloping consumer culture. It has to be pointed out, however, that because of rapid social changes since the 1960s, the generation gap has been far wider in Japan than in the United States and Europe, and the hostility of the older generation toward the younger generation has been much more severe in Japanese society.

The future of inter-generational conflicts

The diffusion of the Internet in the 1990s extended the culture of narcissism into the world of net-chatting. According to Shane (2001), between 1998 and 2000 the time Americans were connected to the Internet increased from an average of 4.4 to 7.6 hours a week. He points out that the increase in the number of Internet users is creating "a community of me," a closed community that generates little fostering of human relations (2001: 118–42). Similarly, according to a survey of 1500 Japanese men and women aged 16 to 69 in January and February of 2001 (Dentsū 2001), 46.1 percent of respondents used the Internet at home or in the office, or via mobile phone

(65 percent of 15 to 19-year-olds and more than 70 percent of those in their twenties used the Internet). The average time spent on the Internet at home was about 4.6 hours a week, an increase from 3.8 hours found in a survey of August 2000. The rapid spread of mobile phones also contributed to the expansion of this anonymous community. The number of mobile phone subscriptions exceeded 10 million in 1995, and by the end of February 2002 it surpassed 68 million. The subscription to mobile phones with an Internet function such as i-mode exceeded 50 million by this time.

The prevalence of this technology has meant that the young generation is developing new responses to human interaction: when they receive a call on their mobile phone, they check the number of the caller on the screen before deciding whether to answer or not. Such an option enables them to refuse calls from someone with whom they do not wish to communicate, and to talk with only those whom they "allow in." In other words, mobile technology enables them to construct a kind of exclusive space of their own. Young people's desire to communicate openly with only a select list of people with whom they feel a psychological identification has been seen by the older generation as the expression of a mentality that refuses to be criticized and reproached by others (Matsuda 2001: 126–37).

Is the generation of narcissism, described by the older generation as creating a closed "community of me," to blame for preventing the emergence of a common culture? Perhaps the answer depends on what kinds of skill and outlook might herald such a culture. For with the emergence of the Internet, the old forms of expression have greatly changed. Unlike such media as newspapers, magazines, and TV, which require much money if one seeks to dispatch information, the Internet has created the opportunity for individuals to dispatch information easily and inexpensively. The generation that grew up surrounded by audiovisual media has, without doubt, begun to acquire a new media literacy.

Today, the children of the baby-boom generation, born between 1947 and 1949, have begun to express a "new youth sensibility" in various fields. The baby-boom generation strongly criticized Japanese society, which was closed to the outside world during the Edo period (1600–1868), an isolation that continued to influence Japan in the twentieth century. They criticized Japanese human relations that tended to avoid giving a clear "yes" or "no"; many traveled outside Japan; and many took for granted that they should assert themselves. While many members of this generation, following the collapse of the student revolt of the 1960s, came to take on standard conservative roles within Japanese society, such as those of salaryman and housewife, this sense of freedom and self-expression was never snuffed out altogether, and influenced how they raised their children. Today's young adults are the products of these desires and concerns, the expressions of a need for greater freedom made real through improving the opportunities for the next generation.

Nakata Hidetoshi (born in 1977), who has played with Perugia, Rome, and Parma of Serie A teams in the Italian Soccer League, and Ichirō (Suzuki Ichirō, born in 1973) of the Seattle Mariners, the American Major League baseball team, are both children of the baby-boom generation. They possess the ability to express and assert themselves openly, an ability that older Japanese did not have. Because they are not intimidated by foreigners, unlike older Japanese still fettered by an isolation mentality, they can assert themselves and establish their own positions on their teams.

Nakata is known to stress the importance of communicating with his fans via his own website (http://nakata.net), keeping his distance from TV and newspapers. The way he relates to mass media is very different from that of conventional sports heroes. Being fully aware that mass media never report the true picture of who he is, Nakata speaks directly to his fans by posting his opinions on his website. He pleads with his fans to respect his privacy, explaining how rude it is to take his picture without his permission. He affirms that what were reported to be his words in the mass media were not in fact his, and points out the danger of media reports. He also criticizes the arbitrary conjectures of sports media and explains in detail about the games he participated in, in terms of his view of team strategy, why he did what he did, and so on. Thanks to Nakata's influence, many Japanese soccer players now have their own home page (Nakata 2000).

Similarly, Ichirō, who has been playing for the Seattle Mariners since 2001, had been confronted with closed-minded sports media while in Japan; indeed, Japanese baseball is well known to be the most closed-minded of all professional sports in Japan. At the time of the Sydney Olympics in 2000, many corporations owning baseball teams refused to cooperate by sending their major league players to the Olympics to represent Japan. When the Japanese pitcher Nomo Hideo (born in 1968) moved to the Los Angeles Dodgers in 1995, he was condemned by Japanese mass media and baseball corporations as a traitor to Japan. But Nomo's success not only enabled other Japanese players to join American baseball teams, it also made young players in Japan conscious of the possibility of leaving the old-fashioned world of Japanese baseball to play in the American Major Leagues.

The decline in the number of viewers of baseball game broadcasts has been remarkable (see Sankei web 2001). Those who watch baseball broadcasts tend to be in their fifties; viewers in their twenties are few in number. In contrast to this, soccer broadcasts attract those in their twenties and thirties. It seems that baseball symbolizes the sport of the closed-minded older generation, whereas soccer symbolizes the sport of the younger generation conscious of the outside world. Young soccer players – Ono Shinji (Holland), Nakamura Shunsuke (Italy), Inamoto Jun'ichi (England), Suzuki Takayuki (Belgium), Takahara Naohiro (Germany), Hiroyama Nozomi (France) – have gone overseas to play, generating in Japanese teenagers a longing to join foreign soccer teams. In fact there are already instances where 13- and 14-year-old Japanese boys have joined soccer youth teams in Spain. The World Cup held in South Korea and Japan in 2002 further intensified this tendency.

Japan's isolation mentality of the past is clearly about to change. It is inevitable that Japanese society, which was closed to foreigners, must also change. The number of registered foreign residents in Japan was 1,281,644 in 1992 but increased to 1,778,462 in 2001 (Hōmushō [Ministry of Justice] 2002). Even in Japan it is becoming common to coexist with people from various ethnic groups.

Let us consider, in this context, the words of Oda Makoto. Oda, who, as we have seen, studied in America in 1958, has said that Japanese students going overseas, including himself, seemed like "the third generation" of an upstart family. The first generation, in Oda's view, was that which shouldered the modernization of Japan after the Meiji Restoration; many of its members studied abroad from the 1870s to the 1890s in various European countries. In a metaphorical sense, they built their homes in a Western style because of the necessity of keeping company with foreigners upon their return, and private teachers were taken in to teach their children English and other European languages. But there was a large split between the inside of the house, where this generation did not change at all, and the outside, which wholly imitated the European style. This division inside and outside, heart and appearance, becomes the second generation's starting point.

The collections of European literary works and pictures that the first generation had brought back from Europe served as the cultural stock for the second generation, but it would soon come to doubt the earlier generation, which it felt had not really understood Western culture. The first generation had not understood at all the concepts of freedom and equality, but had merely been practicing Western etiquette. The second generation, which studied abroad in the 1920s and 1930s, absorbed European culture eagerly and correctly; but they came back to Japan and, like the generation before them, became completely entangled in the division between inside and outside, heart and appearance.

The third generation, which was born in the 1930s and studied abroad in the 1960s, has never known the former generations' distress; that is, the cultural split between a Japanese spiritual inside and a Western material appearance. The third generation is the generation that covets and reads Western literature, present in the second generation's bookshelf since the third generation's infancy. Moreover, they could enjoy all the literary works translated into the Japanese language. The third generation experiences a sense of closeness to Alexandre Dumas and Victor Hugo, Vincent Van Gogh and Pablo Picasso, much more than to Kanō Tan'yū (1602–74), the famous Japanese artist, and the novelist Ihara Saikaku (1642–93) of the Edo Period. The third generation was probably less proficient at English than the first and the second generations. This is because all the things that both the first and the second generation had to learn in their original languages can be learned in Japanese by the third generation. Nonetheless, the third generation, unlike earlier generations, can talk about Western ideas and literature without any reservation. Therefore, suggested Oda, a third-generation member himself, "Could we in the third generation understand the Western world by understanding the malaise of the West as our own malaise?" (1961: 334–8).

Extending Oda's generational metaphor, we may then consider the baby-boom generation, born after World War II, as the fourth generation. This generation developed under the new political and social system set forth in the occupation reforms. This generation was educated under the new school system of postwar education reform, and developed methods of expression that were markedly different from earlier generations who had grown up under a system dominated by authoritarian principles. Under the old system, harmony (*wa*) was respected, but the culture of dispute was brought into Japanese society by the fourth generation, who caused the uproar of the 1960s. They expressed their emotions without boundaries, playing guitars and putting together bands, enthusing over the songs of Bob Dylan, the Beatles, and the Rolling Stones. And they enjoyed American television comedies and comics, very different from the older generations' asceticism and lack of humor. The children of that generation will be the fifth generation, whose members are the famous athletes Ichirō and Nakata, as we have seen, and who go into the Western world without any sense of incongruity.

A big difference in this fifth generation is its involvement with the Internet. This generation is becoming independent of dominant media such as newspapers and TV, controlled by the older generation following the authoritarian seniority system. Consider, for example, a company called Magmag which publishes net magazines (http://www.mag2.com). The story of this company begins with a meeting of two young men in 1996. Fukami Eiichirō (born in 1969) (see http://www.gozans.com; http://www.writing-space.com), after quitting his job with a computer software company, created a system (EX-E-mail system) to distribute private magazines via e-mail. When he ran an ad recruiting business partners for commercializing this system, the only person who answered was Ōkawa Kōichi (born in 1970) (see http://www.united-digital.com). Magmag was launched on 7 January 1997 with fifteen magazines and 10,000 registrants. The system works this way: once you register and send in your magazine article, Magmag distributes it free of charge to those who wish to read it. If a reader doesn't like a magazine, he or she simply requests that it should not be sent.

This system of publishing private net magazines on the Internet has expanded enormously. By the end of November 1998 magazines published through Magmag exceeded 5,000, and registered readers reached 7 million, making Magmag the largest magazine publishing company in the world. By the end of November 2002, it published a total of 24,074 magazines, with 25.46 million registered readers (Magmag 2002) – figures that are unprecedented. Magmag publishes a variety of magazines, some with a circulation of a few dozen and others with a circulation of hundreds of thousands. This would have been impossible without the automatic distribution system provided through the Internet.

The multifarious content of these magazines has revolutionized Japanese forms of expression. Following the success of Magmag, other Internet magazine companies such as Meruma! (http://www.melma.com) sprang up as well. Eighty percent of the publishers of Internet magazines are said to be in their twenties and thirties, meaning that the young generation now has access to opportunities for self-expression that were unavailable to their elders.

A new culture is being created by the children of the countercultural generation of the 1960s. In the twenty-first century, Japan's inter-generational conflicts since the 1960s will finally come to an end, with a defeat for the culture of an older generation predisposed to isolationism. Generation after generation, Japan's new generations have been waging a battle against Japan's isolationism. With the fifth generation, the young people of today, that battle will have finally been won, and Japan will truly become a part of the world at large.

Notes

1 This chapter was written in Japanese by Sakurai, and translated into English by Yoko Miyakawa.
2 The circulation *of Shūkan Shōnen Magajin* [Weekly Boys' Magazine] was 1 million in 1966, and reached 1.5 million in 1970.

References

Aoki, T. (1996) "Murakami Haruki and Japan Today," in John Whittier Treat (ed.) *Contemporary Japan and Popular Culture*, Honolulu: University of Hawaii Press.
Asahi Shinbun (1980) "Nihon no sekai-ichi kakutei – jidōsha seisan" [Confirming Japan as number one in the world in automobile production], 14 December.
Barral, E. (1999) *Otaku: Les Enfants du Virtue*, Paris: Editions Denoël.
Bell, D. (1976) *The Cultural Contradictions of Capitalism*, New York: Basic Books.
Coupland, D. (1991) *Generation X: Tales for an Accelerated Culture*, New York: St Martin's Press.
Dentsū (2001) "*Dejitaru laifu zenkoku chōsa*" [Nationwide survey of digital life], *Dentsū hō* [Dentsu report], 23 April.
Doi, T. (1971) *Amae no kōzō*, Tokyo: Kōbundō.
—— (1994) *The Anatomy of Dependence*, Tokyo: Kodansha.
Erikson, E. H. (1964 [1950]) *Childhood and Society*, New York: W. W. Norton.

Hōmushō [Ministry of Justice] (2002) <http://www.moj.go.jp/Press/020611-1.html>.

Horie, K. (1962) *Taiheiyō hitoribotchi* [Alone in the Pacific], Tokyo: Bungei Shunjū.

Iida, T. *et al.* (1976) *Gendai nihon keizaishi* [The economic history of contemporary Japan], 2 vols, Tokyo: Chikuma Shobō.

Ishihara, S. (2000 [1955]) *Taiyō no kisetsu* [Season of the sun], Tokyo: Shinchōsha.

Kasahara, Y. (1977) *Seinenki* [Adolescence], Tokyo: Chūō Kōronsha.

—— (1984) *Apashii shindorōmu: kōgakureki shakai no seinen shinri* [Apathy syndrome: the psychology of youth in highly educated society], Tokyo: Iwanami Shoten.

Kasahara, Y. and Yamada, K. (eds) (1981) *Kyanpasu no shōjōgun: gendai gakusei no fuan to kattō* [Symptoms on campus: the anxieties and mental struggles of contemporary students], Tokyo: Kōbundō.

Katō, H. (1957) *Chūkan bunka* [Intermediate culture], Tokyo: Heibonsha.

Kawai, H. (1976) *Bosei shakai nihon no byōri* [The pathology of maternal society: Japan], Tokyo: Chūō Kōronsha.

Kimura, B. (1972) *Hito to hito no aida: seishin byōrigakuteki nihonron* [Between man and man: a psychopathological theory of Japan], Tokyo: Kōbundō.

Kinsella, S. (2000) *Adult Manga: Culture and Power in Contemporary Japanese Society*, Richmond, UK: Curzon.

Kurihara, A. (1981) *Yasashisa no yukue: gendai seinenron* [The future of tenderness: an essay on contemporary youth], Tokyo: Chikuma Shobō.

Lasch, C. (1991 [1979]) *The Culture of Narcissism: American Life in an Age of Diminishing Expectations*, New York: W. W. Norton; trans. Ishikawa, H., *Narushishizumu no jidai*, Tokyo: Natsume Shobō.

Lipovetsky, G. (1983) *L'ère du Vide: Essais sur l'individualisme Contemporain*, Paris: Gallimard.

Magmag (2002) <http://www.mag2.com/magdata/magmag.htm>.

Matsuda, M. (2001) "Paasonarufon, mobairufon, puraibeetofon" [Personal phone, mobile phone, private phone], *Gendai no esupuri* 405, Tokyo: Shibundō.

Matsushita, K. (1959) *Gendai seiji no jōken* [The conditions of contemporary politics], Tokyo: Chūō Kōronsha.

Monbushō [Ministry of Education] (ed.) (1981) *Wagakuni no kyōikusuijun, shōwa 55 nendo* [The situation of national education, 1980], Tokyo: Monbushō.

Murakami, H.(1979) *Kaze no uta o kike* [Hear the wind song], Tokyo: Kōdansha.

Nakano, O. and Hirano, H. (1975) *Kopii taiken no bunka: kodoku na gunshū no matsuei* [The culture of fake experience: the offspring of the lonely crowd], Tokyo: Jiji Tsūshinsha.

Nakata, H. (2000) *nakata.net 98–99*, Tokyo: Shinchōsha.

Oda, M. (1961) *Nandemo miteyarō: sekai ichinichi ichidoru ryokō* ["I'll go and see everything": a dollar-a-day journey around the world], Tokyo: Kawade Shobō Shinsha.

Ōhira, K. (1990) *Yutakasa no seishinbyōri* [The psychopathology of affluence], Tokyo: Iwanami Shoten.

Okonogi, K. (1978) *Moratoriamu ningen no jidai* [The era of "moratorium people"], Tokyo: Chūō Kōronsha.

Ozawa, S. (1961) "Boku no ongaku henreki" [My itinerancy in music], *Asahi Shinbun*, 12 July.

—— (1962) *Boku no ongaku mushashugyō* [My knight-errantry in music], Tokyo: Ongaku no Tomosha.

Sakurai, T. (1985) *Kotoba o ushinatta wakamonotachi* [Young people who have lost mutual communication], Tokyo: Kōdansha.

—— (1990) *Tezuka Osamu: jidai to kirimusubu hyōgensha* [Tezuka Osamu: an expresser crossing swords with an epoch], Tokyo: Kōdansha.

—— (1992) "Murakami Haruki no 80 nendai" [The 1980s and Murakami Haruki], in *Bōdaresuka shakai* [A society becoming borderless], Tokyo: Shinyōsha.

—— (1994) *TV: mahō no media* [TV: magic media], Tokyo: Chikuma Shobō.

Sankei web (2001) <http://www.sankei.co.jp/edit/anke/kekka/0618yakyu.html>.

Shane, E. (2001) *Disconnected America: The Consequences of Mass Media in a Narcissistic World*, New York: M.E. Sharpe.

Shinohara, H. (1972) *Gendai nihon no bunka henyō* [The cultural changes of contemporary Japan], Tokyo: Renge Shobō.

Yoshimi, S., Wakabayashi, M. and Mizukoshi, S. (1992) *Media toshite no denwa* [Telephone as media], Tokyo: Kōbundō.

2 Why are Japanese youth today so passive?

Satoshi Kotani[1]

Young people in Japan are, objectively speaking, in a miserable situation. There is no guarantee that they can find a decent job even with a college degree. There is no prospect for Japan's getting out of its long economic stagnation, dubbed as "the lost decade" since the 1990s. Economists predict that the lifetime income of young people today will certainly be lower than that of their parents' generation. Who is to blame for this disastrous state of affairs? Politicians, bureaucrats and managers of big corporations: the top elite in Japan, of course! However, they refuse to take responsibility for their failures. This is the kind of situation where it would not be strange if young people started large-scale riots. But in Japan today, nothing happens; young people don't even stage demonstrations to protest their miserable prospects. Why? Why don't young people vent their anger against adults, who are making the young pay for their own failure? Why don't they try to change Japanese society, as youths have tried to do in the past?

Depoliticization of youth may to some extent be a worldwide trend. The world in the post-Cold War era is dominated increasingly by the ideology of neoliberalism, emphasizing individual rather than societal responsibility for social injustice. It may be that not only in Japan but in the world at large, young people today are politically and socially more passive than young people in the past. However, in many foreign countries, young people's collective protests have not yet died out. In Hong Kong, students hold a protest rally on the anniversary of the Tiananmen Incident every year. In 1998, demonstrations of young people against a government plan to charge for middle-school education broke out in France, and more than 500,000 high school students took part. I believe that if the young people of these countries had been in the situation of Japanese youth today, they would have protested.

Japanese youth were not always so passive. The baby-boom generation in Japan, namely those born in the latter half of the 1940s, is called "*dankai no sedai*" ("the mass generation"). They are now the target of *risutora* ("restructuring": redundancy or dismissal) in their organizations, and, probably because of this, are in low spirits today. But at the end of the

1960s, this generation was spectacularly active as the torch-bearer of the student movement and counterculture, just like young people throughout the world in those days. Many in the generation of parents of today's youth belong to the "post-*dankai*" generation, born in the first half of the 1950s. This generation, which reached puberty after the collapse of the student movement, is reputed to lack vitality. Its members did not want to commit themselves to any ideals, and were called "*shirake sedai*," or "the indifferent generation." I myself belong to this generation, but in my school days, students' demonstrations and strikes were not that unusual. Even from the standpoint of the *shirake* generation, the passivity of youth today seems strange.

"Youthphobia":[2] the astonishment of a Finnish reporter

Some readers may be skeptical about my assessment of Japanese youth and may wonder if young people are expressing their discontent with society in other ways. We can find some evidence for this. In 1997 a shocking crime occurred in Kobe. A 14-year-old boy killed an elementary schoolchild, and placed his decapitated head in front of the main gate of the junior high school he attended. The juvenile offender sent to media organizations crime statements signed by Sakakibara Seito, a name that, written in Chinese characters, resembled the names of heroes of animated films. Sensational reporting of this crime by mass media helped to set in people's minds the image that juvenile crimes were rapidly increasing and becoming more brutal in Japan. In 2000, sensational and heinous crimes by 17-year-olds occurred one after another. That the juvenile offenders of these crimes invariably admired the boy Sakakibara clinched the fear that adults felt toward juvenile crime. In 2001 the minimum age punishable under criminal law was lowered from 16 to 14. Conservatives continue to claim loudly that the cause of juvenile crimes lies in the poor quality of Japanese education. There is a widely accepted consensus in Japan that the schools are responsible not only for the intellectual training of children but also for their moral development. Thus, this conservative claim has had considerable support.

In contrast to the general image, however, murders by juveniles are in fact substantially lower in number than in the past.[3] Thus, why are adults in Japan so fearful of heinous crimes by youth? Of course mass media that excessively report sensational juvenile crimes are much to blame. But the biggest factor contributing to the spread of this erroneous image of youth is the fact that adults entertain strong apprehensions about the status quo and future of Japanese society. Projecting their own anxiety, adults have created dreadful monsters out of youth: this is "youthphobia."

However, the image of Japanese youth in the eyes of foreign observers may belie this dark picture. In 2001 I was interviewed by a Finnish reporter, who told me that he had come to Japan with the presupposition that, due to Japan's economic stagnation, the streets would be full of "desperate" young people indulging in alcohol and drugs and behaving violently. But he found that his presupposition was completely false. Polite Japanese young people accepted his interviews with smiles. "Aren't there any 'desperate youth' in Japan?" he wondered.

One Sunday a Japanese journalist took him to Harajuku in Tokyo, a youth area lined with "*kawaii*" [cute] shops frequented by teenage girls. Harajuku is also known as the place where young people dressed in strange costumes have gathered and performed collective dances every Sunday since the 1980s. When he saw these young people in unusual clothing engaged in their strange performances, he thought intuitively that he had found the "desperate youth" in Japan. Judging by their weird costumes, he mistook these groups for a "Japanese version of punk." He approached them nervously and asked some questions, which they answered earnestly. They were not staging a performance as a protest against society, they said; as the leader of the group explained, "We don't feel lonely here because we are with our friends. That's why we come here every Sunday." After the performance they picked up all their trash. Punks in Europe and the U.S.A. would probably set fire to their trash! Even the youth in Harajuku, who look exactly like punks in appearance, are after all "polite and diligent" Japanese.

As observed by the Finnish reporter, despite its ten-year economic stagnation, Japanese society has not yet reached a state of desperation. In the 1970s and 1980s, Japan's manufacturing industry dominated the world market. At that time, Japan was "the sole winner" of global economic competition. As a result, Japan has accumulated an astronomical amount of wealth which was invested to speculation in the 1980s, pushing up prices of stocks and land, and giving birth to the so-called "bubble economy." In 1990 the bubble burst; Japan has not yet recovered. However, the wealth accumulated over this period largely remains. The total amount of individual monetary assets in Japan is an extraordinary 1,400,000,000,000,000 yen. Amidst this wealth, youth in Japan have not recognized the severity of the situation they are in – the fact that Japan is in decline, and that they themselves may lead far less affluent lives than those of their parents.

Japanese youths and their parents' wealth

Japanese young people can avoid facing reality because of the wealth of their parents. The sociologist Yamada Masahiro recently coined the term "*parasaito shinguru*" ("parasite single") (Yamada 1999). *Parasaito shinguru* refers to unmarried young people who enjoy comfortable lives by living with their parents after graduating from university, depending upon their mothers for household chores, and using their own salaries as pocket-money. Japan's prolonged recession is making employment opportunities for young people scarce, increasing the number of people who become "*furiitaa*," (young people who do not have regular jobs, and live by doing temporary work). Without regular jobs they cannot earn much income, but by living with their parents they can use their disposable income to enjoy their own moderate consumption. "*Hikikomori*," a phenomenon whereby young people shut themselves up in their rooms, cutting off all social contact, is another serious problem in Japan today. There are many reasons why young people become *hikikomori*; but in order to withdraw, they first need their own room, generally within the households of their parents, who provide them with food. The number of young people who are *parasaito shinguru*, *furiitaa*, and *hikikomori* is now enormous;[4] there is no doubt that the affluence of parents allows this dependency.

There is nothing new about the dependency of youth. When I was in college, *Moratoriamu ningen no jidai* [The era of "moratorium people"] (Okonogi 1978) became a bestseller. In this book, Okonogi depicts Japanese youth who refuse to leave home. Indeed, the dependency of youth is a theme discussed continuously since the end of the 1970s, when affluence took root in Japan – that is, since the parents of young people today were young themselves. I am a product of that age; but in the era when I was young, forces countering the dependency of youth were still at work. Parents' wallets then were not so fat – they could not afford to let their children depend upon them for long. Furthermore, there was the sense of a wide gap between youth and their parents' generation in Japan until the 1980s. The parents had been educated in militaristic ideology in pre-war Japan and had experienced the war and the poverty of immediate postwar Japan; their children grew up and received a democratic education in affluent postwar Japan. To escape the control of their old-fashioned parents was one of the inducements for young people to seek independence.

However, in the 1990s the whole situation changed, with the emergence of the children of the *dankai* generation, dubbed "*dankai* junior." Born in the late 1940s, the *dankai* generation had moved into large urban areas, riding the tide of rapid economic development, and setting up nuclear families in the suburbs. Many members of this generation shunned an authoritarian relationship between parent and child, instead advocating "*tomodachi oyako*" ("parent and child as friends"). This unconventional form of family relationships was termed "the new family" in the 1970s. Both parents and children of the "new family" have internalized the values of postwar education. In their youth, members of the *dankai* generation were also highly interested in fashion and cars, and listened to the Beatles and read comics. In that they have both shared the pleasures of consuming goods and information, there has been no large gap between *dankai* parents and children, giving birth to "*tomodachi oyako*." Indeed, this has become established as the dominant mode of parent–child relationship in Japan. Youth can live in ease at their parents' house, and parents are as understanding as their friends. Japanese youth who live in a comfortable environment have thus lost any motive to become independent.

Japanese parents' way of life seems totally centered on their children; we may call them "addicted to their children." Although they advocated a "new family," the *dankai* generation never built a "husband-and-wife-oriented family" along European or American lines. Instead, they have lived by such maxims as "*ko wa kasugai*" (the child is the clamp that binds together husband and wife). This is because only in Japan, among advanced countries, has the gender-specific division of labor not collapsed since the 1970s. Those of the *dankai* generation were "corporate warriors"; the husband went out to work, sometimes to the brink of "*karōshi*" (death from overwork), and the wife stayed at home to nurture the family. In such a relationship, little can be shared by husband and wife except their children. If the child leaves home, the reason for remaining husband and wife may become tenuous. Thus, underlying the structure that prevents young people's independence is a condition of "mutual dependency" between parent and child.

"The whole country is like Disneyland"

In recent years, young people in East Asian countries such as South Korea and Taiwan have become captivated by Japan's popular culture and by a consumer society flooded with fascinating products. A South Korean student once told me that "the whole country of Japan is like Disneyland." His words aptly describe the circumstances of Japanese youth.

Japan today remains extraordinarily affluent. The clothes my students wear, at a woman's college, are dazzling; their favorites are Gucci, Prada, and Louis Vuitton. It is not uncommon to see students dressed from head to toe in such brand-name products. Of course they are not economically independent, but when they take a part-time job, all their income can go on buying such clothes. Japan is saturated not only with material goods, but also with media. Japanese youth are media addicts, and feel uneasy unless they are connected to media: they often keep the TV on all the time at home and listen to their Walkmans while walking or riding the train. Indeed, their relationships with one another are largely maintained through media. TV programs are important topics of their conversation, and, above all, their communications would fall apart without mobile phones, through which they exchange e-mail as well as voice messages. Various media surrounding young people function as magic boxes giving pleasure. Drowning in a sea of pleasure, young people do not notice the severe situation in which they have been placed. That is why they are so placid and passive about their situation.

We have seen how Japanese youth live their lives dependent upon the wealth of their parents, and are indulged in material goods and media that never stop offering them a sense of pleasure. However, if Japan's economy deteriorates further and they can no longer depend on their parents, what will they do? Will some turn to deviant acts? Will others be so outraged at the government's inability that they will resort to large-scale protest? It seems to me that the chances of this happening are very small. Further deterioration of the economy will certainly deprive young people of some of their pleasures as consumers. However, various media, which have become as much part of young people's lives as the air they breathe, will probably remain the same regardless. Wrapped in the cocoon that the media spin, young people will probably remain passive. Japan's highly developed media, to paraphrase Marx, is an "opiate" for young people who have forgotten how to be angry.

The failure of the Japanese student revolts

The student revolts of the late 1960s did not last long in Japan, just as in Europe and the United States. However, in terms of actual political results, there was a great difference between Japan and other countries. The pattern of political action established by youth – that is, protest by those on the margins of society – has penetrated European and American societies since the 1960s, bringing about the transformation of these societies. In the United States, various forms of affirmative action were taken to alleviate discrimination. In West Germany, the entire nation resolved to tackle the issues of war responsibility and of environmental protection that young people had proposed. Of course we cannot claim that all those changes were direct products of youth protest, but in these countries, progressive changes were introduced into society after the late 1960s. In France, the incident of May 1968 was not a "riot" but a "revolution," and May revolutionaries are still the heroes of ordinary people and often occupy important positions in the government (Adachi 2001: 72–5). All advanced countries except Japan have realized the ever-increasing participation of women in public affairs and greater sexual equality. This did not come about in Japan, where even today the gender-specific division of labor remains strong, politicians still repeat speeches glorifying World War II, and environmentally unfriendly public works are still carried out.

Why this difference between Japan and other industrialized societies? In the background of the 1960s students' revolt in Japan was a generational conflict between students and their parents. The parents' generation, saddled with memories of the war and urged on by a fear of scarcity, worked hard and enabled the economic development of postwar Japan. However, youth, who grew up in postwar affluence and received a permissive education, had doubts about the economy-centered way of life of their parents. Their doubts and resentments toward the older generation exploded into violent protests in the late 1960s. In this point there is little difference between Japan and Europe and the United States. What differed were the subsequent conditions of their economies. After the oil shock of 1973, the economies of Europe and the United States were faced with severe stagnation, which caused "adult men" to lose prestige. This decline in prestige and loss of confidence of males steeped in econocentrism led to a rise in the social influence of the feminist and environmental movements. Hobsbawm called those dramatic changes caused by the decline of "adult men" in highly developed Western societies of that era a "cultural revolution" (1997: 52).

The economy of Japan, on the other hand, continued to grow in the 1970s and 1980s, and during those years Japanese adults never lost confidence.[5] In an inter-generational tug-of-war, the adult world won an overwhelming victory over youth. At a time when the gender-specific division of labor was being discarded in Europe and the United States, in Japan many women in the *dankai* generation became full-time housewives, since prospering Japanese companies could pay enough salary to male employees to support their wives and children. Even more than before, men became "company workers," and women "wives and mothers" – this role model for Japanese adults further solidified its unshakeable status in Japan. The militants of the student revolts found employment and "converted"; this generation became the driving force for Japan's economic development. The riots that involved many Japanese universities thus left no trace in real politics in Japan.

Resistance against the parental generation was a cause of students' revolt in every country, but young radicals in the United States had a strong sense of identity with the political traditions of their country. America's New Left, the Students for a Democratic Society (SDS), had nothing to do with Marxism at its foundation. Its famous *Port Huron Statement* indicated a unity with the tradition of American democracy, symbolized by Jefferson, Thoreau, and Whitman (Gitlin 1987; trans. Hikita and Mukai 1993: 158). Disappointed by the powerlessness and hypocrisy of their liberal parents who, despite believing in American democracy, could not stop the barbarism in Vietnam, these young people chose a path of radical direct action. In the case of young people in Europe, which has traditions of liberalism stemming from Christian philanthropy and social democracy, we can point out a similar tendency (see, e.g., Naruse's comments on Philippe Aries' support of the 1960s youth revolts in France [1985: 273–6]).

But in Japan, young people did not have a tradition of democracy; liberalism had not taken root in Japan. Young people indignant at the evils of capitalism had nothing but Marxism to fall back upon.[6] In 1968, a group of radical New Left factions advocating revolution came into being in Japan, gathering the support of many young people. However, in a Japan that had already become affluent, the Marxist tenet that the poor would rise up and overthrow the capitalist system lacked a sense of reality. Faced with the impossibility of revolution, young people in Japan who had nothing but Marxism with which to criticize the establishment had only two options: to convert and become "corporate warriors," or to deny reality and to try to hasten the arrival of a revolution through terrorist acts. Needless to say, a majority of youth chose the former. A few who chose the latter met a miserable end. In 1972, after murdering fourteen of their comrades in a spiral of ideological paranoia, the remaining few members of *Rengō Sekigun* (the "Allied Red Army") died in a gun battle with police.

Europe and the United States had radical groups similar to *Rengō Sekigun*, such as the Weathermen. However, in Europe and the United States, the torch of liberalism existed as a real political force; liberal adults took seriously some of the assertions of young people, resulting in the realization of some progressive social reforms.[7] In Japan, which had no tradition of democracy and no political ideologies except obstinate conservatives versus idealistic leftists, "the revolt of youth" could only end in emptiness.

Youth in an era when Japan was the winner

In the 1970s, the "indifferent generation" (*shirake sedai*) emerged, the generation of the parents of youth today. The *dankai* generation held an ideal, but the revolt of these youth came to an ignominious end. As a result, the "indifferent generation" came to harbor a sense of aversion toward any commitment to ideals.

While becoming politically and socially passive, young people of this generation became increasingly active in media-making and consumption. The "*shinjinrui*" ("new species of human being" or "new breed") generation that emerged in the 1980s acutely expressed this tendency. Born into an environment flooded with media, they astounded adults with their ability to use various information apparatuses, including the personal computer, which had just come on to the market. They were also active as pioneers of an urban consumptive lifestyle, symbolized by a liking for high-class brand-name products. *Shinjinrui* disliked the tight web of human relations that dominated Japan's corporate society; they may be seen as working to deconstruct that system. But at the same time, this generation made the ideal of social change held by the *dankai* generation a butt of ridicule.

In the era when Japan was the winner in the world economy, Japanese corporate society was firmly entrenched, and for middle-class men in particular it was difficult to think of any other life than that of a salaryman. The rank of companies to which an individual could possibly apply was decided by the unified yardstick of academic ranking as measured through secondary school and university examinations. Thus a feeling of resignation – "My life has already been decided" – was fixed in young people's minds. Young people expressed two different reactions to this situation. One was a move toward conservatism: they felt at home in an affluent society. That the Liberal Democratic Party, Japan's conservative ruling party, received the largest support from among students of Tokyo University in a 1978 survey symbolized this trend. Because Tokyo University, the greatest university in Japan, had long been a hotbed of left-wing thought, this survey result was a shock. It seemed that the higher the students were in their academic ranking, the more their sense of being beneficiaries of the system grew, and the more conservative they became. The emergence of "*shinjinrui,*" as discussed earlier, who felt that the feast of goods and information produced by advanced capitalism was a paradise, can also be considered a product of society becoming conservative.

Another, alternative reaction to Japan's affluence was the emergence of youth who regarded a life as a salaryman to be a prison. The corporate society that young people (overwhelmingly male) entered was a world of tough labor and severe competition. The youth in this generation were raised with care in an affluent society; they were hesitant to enter harsh corporate society. Kasahara (1977: 69–70) vividly describes students who, despite their high intellectual ability, became incapable of attending class due to some minor failure they experienced. These young people, who may be the forerunner of *hikikomori* today, as discussed above, were of course a small minority. However, the fear of being hurt in a world ruled by competition was widely shared by young people in those days.

In the late 1980s, young people labeled "*otaku*" came to attract wide attention. *Otaku* are those who are obsessed with infantile hobbies such as collecting animation, comic books, and videos of special-effect programs.[8] Barral (1999) recognizes in *otaku* the twisted idealism of youth in the 1980s, who seemingly despised ideals. Japanese parents never talked with their children about political and social ideals; they only forced them to study. The first generation of *otaku* that emerged in the 1980s was disgusted with the emptiness of their parents' way of living, and shut themselves away in the memory of an idealized childhood.[9] *Otaku* resembled the *dankai* generation in that both detested an adult way of life devoid of ideals. What is different is the site where this protest against the adult world took place. For the *dankai* generation, it was on campuses or on the streets; *otaku*, on the other hand, shut themselves in their rooms and their idealized inner childhoods. Many *otaku* have on the surface adapted themselves to society, and live normal adult lives during the day. Kurihara (1996: 292) has called the tendency to avoid dedicating oneself to one's company whole-heartedly while externally adapting oneself to corporate society the "twofold consciousness" of young people.

This form of adaptation to society was young people's protest against the Japanese corporate world. But this protest was passive; and indeed, during the twenty years when Japan was the winner in the world economy, Japanese youth had already become passive politically and socially. They were bound by a sense of resignation.

A series of incidents involving the religious cult *Aum Shinrikyō* that came to light in 1995 greatly shocked Japanese society. Trading on the cultivation of "supernatural power," *Aum* was a religious order of *otaku* with a worldview that resembled animated cartoons, in which chosen warriors would save the world from destruction. The executives of this religious order were what Barall called "the first generation of *otaku*," youth born in the 1960s. Among them were many young scientists who had finished graduate courses at Japan's prestigious universities. They chose the path of becoming scientists with the ambition of contributing to the happiness of mankind, but in doing scientific research in corporations and universities, their dreams were dashed. They turned to Asahara Shōkō, the leader of *Aum*, who claimed he could transcend the limits of modern science, and revered him as a "guru." Their scientific expertise resulted in the production of a poison gas, sarin, which *Aum* used to kill people in the Tokyo subway attack in 1995. In an era of Japanese economic prosperity, corporate society and its adult role models were as firm as a rock, and young people had no other means of protest but to shut themselves up in a world of fantasy, such as *Aum*. Here lies the root of the tragedy of *Aum*. It became a closed organization cocooned in a fantasy world, and followed in the footsteps of *Rengō Sekigun* in destroying itself after much terrorism and murder.

The political and social passivity of Japanese youth has thus developed over decades since the era of Japan's economic prosperity. Indeed, today's youth have taken on parental models of passivity. Has passivity been inherited over the generations? Or might young people somehow transcend this passivity?

The new form of "the generation gap" in Japan today

Today, it is almost as if "the generation gap" has disappeared in Japan. Not only has *tomodachi oyako* – "parent and child as friend" – become the dominant mode of relationship between parent and child, but also parent and child today resemble each other in their political and social passivity. A "meltdown of the barrier between generations" is occurring. Programs in which heroes transform themselves into supermen and fight against evil monsters should be enjoyed by children; yet today, not only *otaku* youth but also mothers go wild with excitement over these programs (mothers' interests are directed at the handsome actors who play the heroes). Those who enjoy performances in weird costumes at Harajuku are not only young people, but include mothers in their thirties. Children's culture, youth culture, adults' and old people's culture – such categories no longer mean anything.

As was the case for youth in the 1960s, young people's resistance against society begins with their resistance against the parental generation. When young people feel that society is oppressive, they often project the image of their oppressive parents on to society. If their relationship with their parents is harmonious, they won't feel discontented with society. In this sense, the absence of a "generation gap" may be the biggest factor making young people so passive. Differences in sensibility and consciousness should exist between two generations that grew up in different ages. However, the idea of "parent and child as friend" destroys this opportunity for inter-generational conflict. The apparent absence of a "generation gap" may indicate a fundamental absence of communication: this is the case today in the relationship between generations in Japan.[10]

In the 1990s, the sociologist Miyadai revealed that high school girls engaged widely in prostitution under the name of "*enjo kōsai*" ("compensated dating") (1994). The fact that even "daughters of good families" with high academic ability were trying their hand at dangerous sexual games shocked adults, but it is even more shocking how little parents recognized what their own children were doing. If children made money through *enjo kōsai*, they must have shown changes in appearance, such as starting to wear expensive clothes. Why didn't Japanese parents, who were supposed to have a keen interest in their children, even notice such changes?

Adults in Japan often believe that spending money on their children is proof of their love. In Japan it is common for parents to pay for children's education until graduation from college. The total expenditure needed for children's education from elementary school through private university is said to be between 20 and 30 million yen. Fathers, forced to work and commute long hours, are seldom home. Mothers too are busy working part-time to earn money for their children's education. Even junior high school students don't come home before 10 p.m., after doing extracurricular activities at school and going to cram schools in preparation for high school entrance examinations. Japanese families with adolescent children have mostly become "empty nests." Even when all family members are at home, they are absorbed in TV, mobile phones and the Internet, making communication within the family hollow. Herein lies the root of the loneliness of youth at Harajuku; yet Japanese parents are generally not aware of the loneliness of their children. They believe they fulfill their responsibility as parents as long as they spend money on their children and their children attend school regularly. Parents in Japan are surprisingly indifferent to the actual conditions of their children's lives.

After all, parent and child are finally not friends, but parent and child – there is something artificial about "parent and child as friend." In such a relationship, they may never express their true feelings to one another; instead they perform the roles of "understanding parent" and "lovely obedient child." Even within the family, the most basic human group, Japanese youth are forced to perform their roles.

Can the activism of youth be revived?

The notion that society cannot be changed was already apparent among young people in the 1970s, as we have seen. However, since then the situation has worsened. The psychologist Ozawa laments that young people today, when faced with difficulty, tend to search within themselves for the cause of their problem and try to change their mental states, rather than talking with people around them to change the situation. This leads to young people taking excessive interest in clinical psychology and counseling (2002: 39–41). Rather than arguing whether or not society can be changed, the existence of society itself is left out of the thinking of young people today.

The Finnish reporter I described earlier praised the politeness of Japanese youth, yet their manners in public places are poor. They talk during class at university, and apply their make-up while riding the train or subway. Indeed, for them, "everything but friends is just scenery," in an excellent phrase coined by Miyadai (1997: 130) to describe the psychology of young people today. Young people cannot feel the reality of other people. Their heroes are athletes such as Nakata Hidetoshi of soccer and Ichirō of baseball, who value their own self-expression more than their contribution to their team. But there is a huge gap between the self-assured lives led by Nakata and Ichirō and the far more diminished lives of ordinary Japanese youth. The world of sports and games, which was the realm of children's autonomy and spontaneity until Japan's high economic growth, is now under adult supervision. No wonder young people who grew up in such an environment lack the ability to actively form a group – they are no more than consumers of the flood of goods and information in an affluent society.

However, not every youth is satisfied with being merely a passive consumer. After the 1995 Hanshin earthquake, young people from all over Japan spontaneously gathered in Kobe and conducted volunteer activities. They showed remarkable coordination and creativity, and proved to be of tremendous help to the victims. Since their experience in Kobe, young people have begun to take part in volunteer activities. This represents an expression of political and social activism, very differently conceived from young people's protest movements based on political ideology in the past. Such contributions may perhaps suggest different, more positive ways in which young people perceive their place in society.

I notice inconsistencies in my daily contact with students. Most students take part-time jobs, which serve as a means of earning money to support their consumptive activities, but at the same time they often talk excitedly about their experiences at work. They are in charge at work, and are helping their employers and customers. They have their own "place," albeit a temporary one, and feel happy about it. Is the "loneliness" that young people at Harajuku talk about partly to do with not being needed, not being given any role to play? Perhaps what is needed to reanimate the dynamic of change in Japan is more inter-generational opportunities to share visions of Japan's present and future.

Since the Hanshin earthquake, volunteer activities have come to attract the attention of conservative politicians. The main pillar of the education reform policy recently proposed by the Ministry of Education, Science and Culture is to make volunteer activities compulsory.[11] But of course "compulsory volunteer activities" is an oxymoron. Young people become volunteers in their search for spontaneous activity; once volunteer activities become compulsory, young people will lose interest. It is as if adults are seeking to destroy the vitality of young people. To create a place in the world for young people, adults should abandon the idea of guiding and educating youth. Adults too are sunk in despair: their way of life, totally committed to economic growth, has collapsed. They themselves are clueless about what to do. So, why not ask young people for help, and work together as equal partners?

Young people are Japan's real hope in helping it to continue to change and adapt. Conservation and regeneration of the natural environment left neglected in the midst of economic development, or local currency movements born as a means of protecting ordinary people caught in the fury of the globalized economy – these activities require the strength and enthusiasm of young people (Sasaki 2002: 208–10). Cooperation in these fields will bring about cross-generational communication, which in turn must give rise to tension and conflict between generations – a "generation gap." It seems possible that from such relationships a "new Japan" can emerge, although I am not too optimistic. My misgivings are directed not to youth – who, despite all I have written about their passivity, seem to have more flexible and adaptable models of understanding than their elders – but rather to the adult generation. Are they really able to cast off their sense of resignation that "society cannot be changed"?[12] If they can, they may find that young people will perhaps offer new approaches to living in and imagining Japan that until now have been hidden from view.

Notes

1 This chapter was written in Japanese by Kotani, and was translated into English by Yoko Miyakawa.
2 "Youthphobia" is a word coined by Nakanishi Shintarō, a professor at Yokohama City University (Nakanishi 2000).
3 The number of male juveniles prosecuted for murder exceeded 400 a year in 1960, but in 1997, the year of the Kobe murder, seventy-one prosecutions took place, only one-sixth of the 1960 figure (Ayukawa 2001: 156).
4 The number of *parasaito shinguru* is commonly estimated at 10 million (Yamada 1999: 57). The estimation by the Welfare and Labor Ministry puts the number of *hikikomori* at 2 million, while a trial calculation by *Recruit Works Institute* (http://www.works-i.com/article/db/wn43_60.html) estimates the number of *furiitaa* at 3.44 million. About 60 percent of *furiitaa* are thought to be living with their parents (*Furiitaa kenkyūkai* 2001: 83).
5 Throughout the 1980s, Japan's conservative politicians continued to repeat their racist rhetoric of boasting of the superiority of the Japanese. In 1985, Prime Minister Nakasone argued that the superiority of Japan was rooted in the fact that

Japan consisted of Japanese only, not intermixed with other (inferior) ethnic groups. This shows their arrogant confidence in Japan as the sole winner in the world economy.

6 From 1955 until the end of the Cold War, Japanese politics was under a two-party system, where the Liberal Democratic Party, endorsing capitalism, and the Japan Socialist Party, embracing Marxism, competed for political office. However, this was a deformed system, and a change of government from one party to another never took place until 1993, for just a year. This indicates that in reality Marxist ideology has had no power in Japan. This also suggests the difficulty of changing the social system, given the deep-rooted conservatism of Japanese society.

7 I may be idealizing the 1968 generation of Europe and the United States. After all, the 1968 generation, a product of affluence, also succumbed to economism in these countries. Rosen finds a typical member of the 1968 generation to be Bill Clinton. Clinton entered the political stage posing as a liberal, but what he actually did was to spread the belief in the almighty market in society (Rosen 2001: 70).

8 What triggered this attention was a serial murderer of young girls in the Tokyo suburbs at the end of the 1980s. The culprit, a young man of 26 years old, possessed several thousand videos in his room; he recorded on video his mutilation and murder of the girls.

9 One of the first generation of *otaku* said to Barral: "we grew up in a society that had appearance but no content, just like a parody.... We decided to fill the vacuum in our own way. What was available then was ... the world of our childhood.... In this graceful period, what occupied our imagination was heroes in comic books and TV dramas.... I think that a majority of young people of our generation don't trust anybody except a few friends from their childhood and heroes of animation they saw when they were children" (2000: 7).

10 Seki (1995: 12) points out that for all human societies, the succession of experiences across generations is a fundamental problem. "Without relearning through the alteration of generations, human society, without an instinctive basis, will repeat mistakes and destroy itself. A society consisting of understanding adults and gentle and obedient children faces a threat of destruction."

11 In 2000, the National Conference on Education Reforms, the Prime Minister's private advisory body, came up with a plan in its final report for a "draft system for volunteers," under which every 18-year-old is required to engage in volunteer activities for a year. Since then, making volunteer activities compulsory has become a leading proposal of the government-led education reform.

12 Tanaka Yasuo, who belongs to the *shirake* generation and who, as a novelist in the 1980s helped start the "brand-name boom," is now setting forth remarkable reform policies as the Governor of Nagano Prefecture. Ōtsuka Eiji, of the same generation and a long-time editor of an *otaku* magazine, is now actively publishing his political statements, one of which is an anti-war declaration immediately after the September 11 terrorist attack. It is possible to interpret their behavior as a sign that at least some members of the parental generation of today's youth have cast off their resignation in an effort to change their society and the world.

References

Adachi, I. (2001) *Shitte isōde shiranai furansu* [What everyone thinks they know about France but don't], Tokyo: Heibonsha.

Ayukawa, J. (2001) *Shōnen hanzai* [Juvenile crime], Tokyo: Heibonsha.

Barral, E. (1999) *Otaku: Les Enfants du Virtue*, Paris: Editions Denoel; trans. Niijima, S. (2000) *Otaku japonika: kasō genjitsu ningen no tanjō* [Japanese otaku: the birth of humans in virtual reality], Tokyo: Kawade Shobō Shinsha.

Furiitaa kenkyūkai [temporary workers' research group] (ed.) (2001) *Furiitaa ga wakaru hon!* [A book for understanding temporary workers], Tokyo: Sūken Shuppansha.

Gitlin, T. (1987) *The Sixties: Years of Hope, Days of Rage*, New York: Bantam Books; trans. Hikita, S. and Mukai, S. (1993) *60 nendai amerika – ikari to kibō no hibi* [1960s America: days of rage and hope], Tokyo: Sairyūsha.

Hobsbawm, E. (1994) *The Age of Extremes: The Short Twentieth Century 1914–1991*, London: Abacus; trans. Kawai, H. (1997) *20 seiki no rekishi* [The history of the twentieth century], vol. 2, Tokyo: Sanseidō.

Kasahara, Y. (1977) *Seinenki* [Adolescence], Tokyo: Chūō Kōronsha.

Kurihara, A. (1996) *Yasashisa no sonzai shōmei* [Testimony of the existence of gentleness], Tokyo: Shinyōsha.

Miyadai, S. (1994) *Seifuku shōjotachi no sentaku* [The choices of girls in uniform], Tokyo: Chūō Kōronsha.

—— (1997) *Maboroshi no kōgai* [The illusion of suburbs], Tokyo: Asahi Shinbunsha.

Nakanishi, S. (2000) "Seishōnen bōryoku to gendai nihon shakai" [Youth violence and contemporary Japanese society], *Kyōiku* [Education], July, Kyōiku kagaku kenkyūkai [research group on education as science], Tokyo: Kokudosha.

Naruse, K. (1985) "Yakusha atogaki" [Translator's commentary], in *Nichiyō rekishika* [Sunday historian], Tokyo: Misuzu Shobō.

Okonogi, K. (1978) *Moratoriamu ningen no jidai* [The era of "moratorium people"], Tokyo: Chūō Kōronsha.

Ozawa, M. (2002) *Kokoro no senmonka wa iranai* [No need for mind specialists], Tokyo: Yōsensha.

Recruit Works Institute (2002), Online. <http://www.works-i.com/index.html>.

Rosen, B. (2001) *Masks and Mirrors: Generation X and the Chameleon Personality*, Westport: Praeger.

Sasaki, K. (2002) *Oya to kyōshi ga sukoshi raku ni naru hon* [A book to make parents and teachers feel a little easier], Tokyo: Hokuto Shuppan.

Seki, H. (1995) *Kyōiku – shi to aragau seimei* [Education: life against death], Tokyo: Tarōjirōsha.

Yamada, M. (1999) *Parasaito shinguru no jidai* [The age of parasite singles], Tokyo: Chikuma Shobō.

3 The local roots of global citizenship

Generational change in a Kyushu hamlet

Bruce White

This chapter demonstrates how young people from the Kyushu town of Amatetsu[1] construct a diverse and plural community around them that bears little resemblance to the geographically specific *kumi*[2] groups to which their parents and grandparents belong. This respective local experience polarizes and informs the generations' conceptions of themselves as part of a wider Japanese collective, giving life to a new cosmopolitanism as the young seek to define themselves against the old.

This chapter draws on thirty-six months of fieldwork in the town of Amatetsu, eighteen of which were spent in the small hamlet of *yon-gumi*. The town of Amatetsu (population approximately 10,000) sits in the center of a triangle between the cities of Fukuoka, Kurume, and Oita, on the southern Japanese island of Kyushu. It is divided into forty-eight *kumi* – of which the hamlet of *yon-gumi* is number four. These household groups traditionally collaborate, keeping their respective zones (including shrines) clean, preparing their members for neighborhood and town-wide festivals, and collecting money for local taxes, tri-yearly celebrations, and sometimes certain forms of insurance.

Yon-gumi is a hamlet typical of its rural southern Japanese setting, comprising predominately older people who make a variety of efforts to maintain spaces for face-to-face interaction derived from once highly cooperative ways of life. In *yon-gumi* there are regular community meetings [*chōnaikai*][3] and a variety of celebrations, all of which I attended during my fieldwork, and all of which help the hamlet's members to keep abreast of town and hamlet gossip and maintain local house-to-house relations. For the duration of my fieldwork, I occupied one of *yon-gumi's* nine family houses in the middle of the small quiet street around which the community was centered.[4]

In attempting to chart the generational divisions of local memberships and global worldviews and identities, one of my main research methodologies was to draw on focus groups comprising different generations of the same family. These were designed to elicit attitudes toward community membership and to gauge generational relations – as well as the knowledge which one generation had about the other – of my informants. The focus group sessions were taped, and notes were written up on the gestures and emotional contexts of the exchanges soon after the focus sessions had finished. The same process was applied to interviews I conducted with members of *yon-gumi's* nine households, as well as to the younger people I talked to in various settings outside the town. I include some of this emotional and contextual content in a number of the representations here, to provide a comprehensive picture of the respective social realities of the informants.

The following interchange is an extract from one of many such encounters, and introduces some of the core generational divisions among the people of the town, in terms of their senses of belonging within local and global frameworks.

The two men – father and son – sat in my *tatami*-mat room drinking tea. Hideo (20) looked blankly at his father (49) while the older man continued talking. I had asked Hideo's father, Mr. Kawaguchi, whether he identified more with the small hamlet in which the three of us lived, or with the wider town of Amatetsu.

> "Yes, well, I *loathe* this hamlet and the life that goes with it. I have never liked the fact that people are all aware of other people's business. I don't know why I put up with running the community meetings; maybe it's just that no one else would. But it's strange. To answer your question, I suppose I do feel first and foremost a member of *yon-gumi* rather than the bigger town of Amatetsu, and that gives me a sense of responsibility to the hamlet."

"See, now that's weird, Dad, don't you think?" interjected Hideo. "Like, I don't feel part of this ... hamlet ... or whatever you call it. I am first and foremost from Amatetsu ... in fact, probably I would say I belong to Fukuoka prefecture before I would think of myself as an 'Amatetsuian' or whatever."

"Yes, well," said his father after a brief pause, "you young people are free of some of the obligations that my generation has had to put up with. You just go about your business with little care for those around you."

Mr. Kawaguchi sighed and turned to face me.

"I don't know whether this freedom that young people have is a good thing or a bad thing, you know. I mean I would have *loved* to be able to get on my motorbike," he said, glancing at his son who owned a loud and large 250cc:

> "I'd love to be able to ride off, disappear off to some place of my choosing. But I suppose I didn't have such an opportunity for independence. Yet I wonder, looking at the young, whether they have

lost something, some sense of what it is like to feel part of a community at all."

Hideo remained silent throughout his father's short pronouncement, his head bowed in a posture which reflected apparent respect along with a sort of resignation. He then said:

> "You see, Dad, you always think the worst of me and my friends, but you simply don't understand the world in which we all live. We like what we do – we are interested in the same things and we talk together about our interests. We *do* understand how to live in a community; it's just a different community from the one you know."

These differences between Hideo and his father represented some key generational divisions in the ways in which social life in the Kyushu town of Amatetsu was being experienced and constructed by its members. Hideo's father was both envious of his son's freedom, his ability to run a life independent of a need to oblige others in the locale, and critical of the degree to which such an independent lifestyle was depriving his son of some necessary lessons in how to co-exist with others. Meanwhile, Hideo clearly felt that while his community was built upon a different premise – a kind of community of interest rather than of necessity – it was as valid as his father's or even more so. Contained in these experiences and interpretations were patterns of change that had come to inform and characterize the real and abstract worlds of *yon-gumi*'s various generations: what it meant to be a member of a local community, of a cultural and national collective, and, most obviously, a member of a particular generation with particular concerns and opportunities.

Generational change in *yon-gumi* and beyond

These patterns of generational change, and the generational identities they produce, seem to have revolved most closely around increasing desires for improved social freedom. Indeed, for the older members of *yon-gumi*, social freedom, independence, and social and imaginative mobility – and the lack of opportunities to obtain them – were key themes that ran throughout their recounting of community life.

Commenting on the way social sanctions worked to curtail freedom in the community, Mrs. Kora (65) remembered:

> "It's not so bad now, but I remember when everything one said and did was out in the open for people to criticize. You couldn't even feel like you had your own life – not that I suppose you even expected to in those days!"

Although some of the older residents (men in particular) talked about the community's (past) communal way of life with nostalgia, others, predominantly women, spoke of the degree to which social sanctions made life difficult for them. The majority of the older residents of *yon-gumi* recognized that it was the tight-knit sanctioning way of life that has served to divide generational relations and caused the community to begin to "implode" – there now being a common opinion that few young people are interested in continuing hamlet activities and maintaining its identity.

In attempting to understand the foundations of change in Japanese communities, a variety of anthropologists have seen the forces of modernity and mobility as central to local social transformation. As far back as the 1930s, Embree (1939) observed the powerful effect that money was having in changing many of the old forms of labor exchange and bringing about new frameworks for social relations based on wealth and status. He also saw how these economic effects coincided with a shift from local to national loyalties, as efforts to engender nationalism took hold. Three decades later, in the 1960s, Johnson (1967) observed how, despite the fact that nationalism and the effects of industrialization had turned communities further "inward" by increasing social sanctions, the postwar community was essentially no different from its pre-war predecessor: "Both hierarchical and egalitarian hamlets have frequently retained their exclusive, or closed, nature" (Johnson 1967: 171). But in the village of Kurusu by the 1970s, according to Smith, a generational sea change was emerging as younger people began to desire more independence than the traditional systems could accommodate:

> The constraints of a hamlet-centered life have little appeal to the young, and their elders seem powerless to communicate to them their own sense of its value and its promise. Indeed, by their own example they have placed its most fundamental principles in jeopardy.
>
> (Smith 1978: 248)

The older people's "own example" was to involve a reinforcement of social sanctions that restricted certain freedoms. These older people pushed further toward enclosing the community life in its own borders – efforts that went against the grain of what younger people wanted in the 1970s: more independence and individual choice. It is not a phenomenon confined to Smith's Kurusu.

For Hideo's father and his "middle" generation, this push to maintain an inward "enclosed"[5] solidarity became increasingly incompatible with their emerging desires for independence. These "baby boomers" – now the parents of contemporary Japanese youth – began to want to separate themselves from the sanctions and expectations of the community. In rural *yon-gumi*, this middle generation seems to have been partially successful in achieving this independence: over 50 percent of the middle-generation residents now reside in nearby cities, removed from the need to manage or maintain local hamlet relations. But for those who remain, like Hideo's father, there are the frustrations that come with maintaining local systems seen as restrictive. For others still in the community, like Mr. Seijō (48), there is the notion that the disadvantages of not being able to find spaces to express desires for independence in his own generation can be offset by ensuring opportunities for the next generation. As he put it, "Imposing constraints on the way that my children choose to live their lives is not my idea of being a good parent."

The familial roots of collective change

In the exchange between Hideo and his father, and the comments from other community members, as well as in the broader patterns of generational change in *yon-gumi*, we begin to see that it is from within the contexts of our familial experience that we negotiate new subjectivities and solidarities *vis-à-vis* older generations (see also Mannheim 1952 [1929]). This local, familial, experience – and the generational contexts through which it is made real – may represent a powerful force for social change in the way collective cultural and national identities are conceived in the world.

Both Geertz (1983), and, later, Carrithers (1996) have seen that our identities are made real through combining the local detail of our lives with the abstract structure and collective representation of our social relations.[6] Therefore we can be seen as constantly attempting to make our social realities reflect our collective imagination and vice versa, and so we are involved in an unceasing cyclical movement of evaluation and expression. I follow these theoretical understandings by attempting to fit these perspectives to one that sees the generation as a key locus through which the local details (familial systems and relations) of our lives are transformed (see Bertaux and Thompson 1993; Spencer 1990).

If we see that broad socio-cultural changes in collective identity are directly linked to the familial contexts of our lives, then it follows that as local relations change generationally in response to a variety of factors but consistently to increasing modernity and mobility, so too do our larger ideas of who we are as members of cultures, nations, and global collectives.

In order to explore these links further, let me turn again to the worlds of Amatetsu's young people: How are they seeking out solidarities which build the very concepts of freedom and mobility into the fabric of their real and abstract collectives? One of the first things to observe here is that only rarely are the "communities" of the Amatetsu young expressed within the town itself.

Alternative solidarities

Nobu and Daisuke were in their early twenties when I met them in a bar in the city of Fukuoka – a forty-minute drive from Amatetsu. It soon emerged that these two young men saw Amatetsu as a place from which to launch themselves into worlds beyond. To them, the community did not represent the boundaries of social existence but the foundation from which to build a dynamic and meaningful cosmopolitan set of relationships and locations.

> "It's not that 'community life' there is so bad, exactly. But there isn't much for us, so to speak, 'young people,' who get turned on by totally different things. I mean I was at a reggae concert on the beach in August dancing with a Japanese girl with a three-foot-tall Afro – I couldn't see my old man doing that at a *chōnaikai* [community meeting]!"

Daisuke laughed and shook his head. "I don't wish them any disrespect, but there is a real sense of outdatedness – of a gap between what my world is about and what those *oyaji* [older men] think and do and say."

I asked the two men if they could characterize these differences. "Well," laughed Nobu, inserting his pack of cigarettes and lighter into his top pocket and taking a wet cloth off the bar to wipe his head, "you could do this...." Daisuke laughed at this performance of *oyaji* behavior – older men often keep cigarettes and a lighter in a top shirt pocket and use a hot towel to wipe sweat from their heads and this is seen by the young as very "uncool." He continued:

> "Seriously, it's more about what we as a generation have and what they don't.
>
> "Like, we are here now in this bar, right? We are here from the town of Amatetsu. Now, me and Nobu come here a lot – we like the music they play and we are good buddies with the DJ Tomi and some of the other guys who play here. And occasionally some friends of one or another of us will head down from Tokyo or Osaka to see a set, or just to hang out. In turn those guys – and many of us – have links with people further afield, from other countries maybe. This means that basically our 'community' is kind of linked to thousands of others – and I suppose that is what makes us so different from our parents, and certainly our grandparents, back in Amatetsu. I mean, they have, like, the *kumi*, their work community and maybe some old friends that they go for a drink with, but that's it!"

Nobu agreed, and then added the following:

> "I suppose they get that from the way they were brought up to think of everyone as a collective. My dad often goes on about obligation to others in the community and all that. We do have groups but they are different from the groups that older people understand. I don't know how exactly ... I can only say that there is a sense of the world we live in being sort of ... connected."

In their explanations of their world, in the way that they spoke – a kind of hybrid of Kyushu dialect and Tokyo vocal presentation that sounded highly contemporary – in their very appearance and the way they carried and presented themselves, Nobu, Daisuke, and the majority of the other young people I came to know from Amatetsu were undeniably connected to influences beyond their locales. Not only were their day-to-day lives characterized by wildly different forms of social relations and interactions, but the wider Japan of which they imagined themselves a part was radically different too. This was a world linked and bound to many networks – sets of relations formed around stylistic and transient trends. This was a polar opposite to a solidarity based on an enclosed, exclusive, collective model. Theirs was a diverse world connected.

A diverse world connected

This connecting together reflects stylistic trends that embody a huge variety of forms, from musically defined interest groups to lifestyle choices that dictate what events people go to (concerts, festivals, etc.), the types of friends they have, and even the types of attitude they hold. In this, young people from Amatetsu may be seen to embody what many commentators have called (in various guises) a society of mass popular consumption (Clammer 1997; McCreery 2000; Powers *et al.* 1989).

It is a mistake to see communities of consumption in a negative solidarity-robbing way. We can suggest, rather, that not only does mass popular consumption prevent "one from being excluded from the club" (Clammer 1997: 168), but also actively creates a club of its own; a club built from interconnecting strands of common group interests and individual expressions of identity. And perhaps most importantly, it creates a club whose salient feature is its ability to evolve and change in response to individual needs to *move*. Indeed, the notions of dynamism and fluidity are central to the community of consumption, structuring the very concrete interactions that occur under its conceptual umbrella.

In many ways, then, the "community of consumption" has become an alternative for traditional hamlet solidarity in the minds of many Amatetsu young. They are able to conjure memberships and solidarities as they go –

able to use the community of consumption to achieve a non-geographically specific membership with others, in a community that has a need for social and imaginative mobility at its heart. In so doing, the community of consumption represents a new ordering of and exposure to diversity, something which Clammer says is giving us subjectivities "unprecedented in human history" (1997: 154).

However we choose to interpret and characterize these new community memberships and explain their existence – and we could talk about them in terms of being part of an increasingly diverse popular culture (see Martinez 1998) – we reaffirm that it is on the local levels of social life, in their families and communities, that young Japanese are interacting and approaching each other in ways totally unfamiliar to their parents and grandparents. There is a marked generational contrast between how particular types of community activities are created and undertaken; alongside this, there is a playing out of community memberships as plural, dynamic, and open entities exposed to and connected with the outside world.

Considering that he had effectively just been told by his son, Hideo, that he was ignorant about the way in which the young lived, Mr. Kawaguchi, in continuing the exchange we saw at the start of this chapter, displayed an unusual – and uncharacteristic – degree of calmness and control. Perhaps he saw that there was something he was missing here.

"What is so special about hanging out with your friends and shooting the breeze? Wouldn't be nice if we could all do that, hey?" He laughed and turned to me again. "I suppose I do think that these young folk have something that we didn't, you know. They are freer than we were, and I suppose," he turned to look at his son, "that I am pleased that they seem to look at the world through fresh eyes. That's something we never quite had the opportunity to do. Like, you listen to all that weird Indian music, don't you Hideo?" Hideo grunted in affirmation. "We wouldn't have done that. Your generation has a confidence about meeting the outside world that is so different from the way we were brought up that maybe sometimes we don't understand what you're about."

Japanese and "the making and unmaking of strangers"

There have been countless articles written about how "the Japanese" distinguish themselves as unique or different in relation to foreigners. Not only is much of the native *nihonjinron* literature alive with references to senses of Japanese uniqueness and distinctness (Befu 2001), but the "objective" commentators on Japanese society have variously remarked on the particular ways in which Japan has understood itself in relation to others in the world.

Reischauer has commented on the contradiction that the Japanese are "among the world leaders" but "perceive themselves as being so distinct from the rest of humanity as to be unique" (1988: 395). Nakano identifies an instability in the historical narrative of Japaneseness in the world, seeing that Japanese suffer from "a kind of inferiority complex which results in their still being reluctant to take a vigorous part in world affairs, simply because they do not belong to the main ethnic groups who built the modern system of contemporary world order" (1995: 69). Katō, with a sense of desperation, sees "many people in this country even go[ing] so far as to divide all human beings into two major categories: Japanese and non-Japanese. Cosmopolitans are rare and cosmopolitan ideas and values are unwelcome" (1992: 313).

The dynamic nature in the way young Japanese in Amatetsu interact with *each other* in their "exposed" communities[7] is changing the way in which they approach non-Japanese people and how they imagine Japan as situated in a world of nations. This link between local diversity and a new way of conceiving Japanese society has been predicted:

> It is this diversity *among* teens themselves, in family life, buying power, sexual and interpersonal experience, political and personal ideas – that will indeed be the basis of new thinking on the nature of Japanese society.
>
> (White 1994: 221)

But just what kind of new thinking is this internal diversity creating? And how can we see that it is a product of familial experience and changed local realities?

One of the ways in which we can clearly see the divisions of collective identity in operation across the generations is by focusing on the conception of Japan within a wider Asia. There is a long history of building cultural and national narratives out of interaction with other Asian countries. Despite a long history of building a relationship with China as a significant and informative other (see Ohnuki-Tierney 1993), by the time Western powers arrived on the scene, Japan had become embroiled in a kind of identity crusade – an attempt to raise its own self-image by separating itself from other Asian countries (see also Yoshino 1992). Throughout the twentieth century, some Japanese cultural narratives attempted to raise the relative position of Japan on the world stage by depicting other Asian peoples as inferior in a variety of ways. In one example, the Tokugawa nativist Hirata Atsutane held Japanese rice to be akin to worshipping the Shinto deities and repaying their blessings, whereas Chinese rice was "begun by the mandate of men ... [and] those who eat it are weak and enervated" (Ohnuki-Tierney 1993: 104, quoting Harootunian).

For the majority of younger Japanese in Amatetsu, narratives of cultural nationalism, which somehow separate off Japan as superior to other Asian countries, seemed inextricably linked to the world of the older generation, and did not represent key understandings that related to their identities as Japanese.

Hiro, a young man in his mid-twenties, said:

> "My father . . . sees other Asians as . . . well, inferior to Japanese, to put it plainly. He is, I suppose, still living in a colonial Japan, where the ideas that 'we' took 'them' over, dominated and converted them into 'second-class' Japanese still hold strong. But for me, and I think for many people around my age and younger, that idea has begun not to make much sense. . . . Like I don't see people from, say, Korea, as somehow 'below' Japanese people in any way. Perhaps they have slightly different cultures, but people, after all, are people.

> "I went out with a girl in high school who was a second-generation Korean. Do you know that her family had drilled into her that it was crucial that she never let on that she was of mixed nationality? I didn't find out for *seven years*! It was thought that she would suffer from bullying if people knew, and that she would be discriminated against. . . . That's terrible, really, but you know, like all these power-trips that people go through, I think that my father's old-fashioned view of Japan comes from a sort of deep insecurity about Japan's place in the world. Maybe the reason that we – I mean my generation – don't think like that anymore is because we don't feel the same pressures to get Japan on an equal footing with other nations of the world."

Hiro's view of his place as a Japanese in Asia was that he was *Asian*, a member of Asian – not exclusively Japanese – civilization (as was the consistent answer from my young informants when I asked them if they considered themselves to be an integral part of Asia or whether Japan was somehow separated from that category). It was understood implicitly that some of the older generation obtained their Japanese identity from viewing the world through social-Darwinist eyes, believing that some "races" are superior to others and employing a "ranked-power" model for understanding self *vis-à-vis* other countries in a hierarchy (see Watanabe 1990). By contrast, Hiro's identity was constructed using this as an oppositional other for the development of his "contemporary" narrative of cultural identity. He did not employ that model, but another, which puts everyone on an equal footing in a world where "people are people."

Holding different ideas about other Asian countries and including themselves fully in the category "Asian" are not the only ways in which many young people from Amatetsu are reworking ideas of Japan in the world. "I don't have that much interest in going around the sights of Europe, or visiting the Statue of Liberty," said Jun, a street-wise 20-year-old. "India's where it's at. Just look at the amazing music it's producing of late –

sort of fusion stuff: 'the traditional and the modern man' – excellent! It's really getting popular in some of the circles I move in now."

Consuming and celebrating some of the products of other Asian peoples is one important way in which young Japanese are beginning to change how the outside world is perceived in Japan; this is fed back into an evolving notion of what it means to be Japanese. The fact that Japanese culture has been and is being commodified by other Asian countries (see Ching 1996) helps in this sense of exchange. Increasingly, young Japanese travelers, exchange students, and backpackers visit Korea, China, Taiwan, Thailand, Cambodia, Vietnam, the Philippines, and Indonesia. This new exchange of information and experiences between Japan and its Asian neighbors has spurred huge domestic interest. Television programs documenting back-packer travels around Asia (*Gekiteki-kikō [Shinya-tokkyū] '96–'98*) and the books upon which the travels are based focus on interactions between Japanese and other Asians, and have been hugely popular with younger people.[8] Likewise, new Japanese cinema seeks increasingly to incorporate other Asians into its representations of Japan, thus helping to break down racially homogeneous ideologies (Gerow 2002).

The increased ability to interact freely across national borders without some of the baggage of received collective identities stressing homo-geneity becomes evident when Japanese of different generations travel together. A three-day trip to Korea which I took with a Japanese family from Amatestu – mother (58), father (60), and son (25) – revealed the degree to which the older people found their Japanese identities working against natural interaction with the Koreans we encountered. The parents were unable to respond naturally to encounters with Koreans, or to initiate any kind of interaction themselves, whereas Hiroyuki (the son) was constantly seeking out companions. After three days, Hiroyuki finally said to me, "Isn't it terrible that my parents seem so closed-minded? They're living in a completely different world – I just can't put up with it much longer!"

The younger Japanese of Amatetsu seem able to envisage foreigners in a psychological matrix of diverse relations, with confidence that at some significant point a connection between themselves and "the other" may be found. It is as if they have honed the skill of establishing a connection with anyone they meet. This seemingly well-practiced "skill" or "technique," I argue, is the mainstay of younger Japanese dealings *with each other*. Again we see how the local social lives of the older people – reflecting their enclosed forms of solidarity – are mirrored in their interactions with "the other," and how the templates of diversity that younger people have developed are transposed to the new forms of developing collective identity, based on common diversity.

Local citizen, global identity

> It is only by recognising the internal presence of foreignness that one
> can avoid projecting on to the foreigner all that we find dangerous or
> unpleasant in ourselves, and it is only with the knowledge that we are
> "foreigners to ourselves" that we can attempt to live with others – so
> that, by recognising the "foreigner" within us we are spared detesting
> him in himself.
>
> (Kristeva, from Morley 2000: 222; see also Freud 1988)

In their exposure to local diversity – to "foreignness" within – younger
people in Amatetsu are developing the ability to incorporate diversity
without. In many ways, the conceptualizing of Japan in an Asian and world
framework has been realized through a process of linkage and connectivity
mirroring the diverse solidarities of young people's local communities.
There has been a physical and imaginative reaching out to assemble
common points of identification both in real interaction and in the abstract
reordering of the "ranked power" collective model held by members of older
generations.

While the construction of younger people's communities of consumption
is doubtless influenced by the variety of transnational cultural "products"
increasingly available worldwide (see Mathews 2000),[9] it is important to
emphasize that this understanding of themselves in the world has come
primarily through experience in *locales* – through increasing exposure to
internal diversity and transitions that challenge the thinking of older
generations. It is in the local realm that younger people are locating
themselves within diversity, and this local diversity then comes to inform
their vision of themselves as part of wider collectives. This process of young
people experiencing local diversities, Amit-Talai shows, is bringing new
forms of consciousness to the fore in many countries around the world:

> Youth cultural production occurs at home, at school, at work, at play, on
> the street, with friends, teachers, parents, siblings and bosses, draws
> elements from home-grown as well as transnational influences, and
> intertwines with class, gender, ethnicity and locality with all the
> cultural diversity that such a multiplicity of circumstances compels.
> Such multi-culturalism imparts to youths, as to adults, a degree of
> consciousness that goes beyond any one situation, an awareness that
> each moment is embedded with a range of cultural possibilities.
>
> (Amit-Talai 1995: 231)

This "degree of consciousness" is what most distinguishes young people
from Amatetsu from their elders. Here, young people demonstrate that this
multi-contextual consciousness infiltrates and orders collective cultural and

national identities. It creates a way of positioning oneself in the world which can respond to and include diverse others, and as such is seen as incompatible with identities that have as their premise a model of homogeneity[10] (see Gerow 2002).

In a reaffirmation of the circular nature of the identity-making process, these concerns to represent diversity on the collective level are also fed back to the familial arenas. Here younger people are quite literally bringing home some of the ideas, techniques, narratives, and identities that they are constructing in their diverse communities, thereby influencing the thinking of their parents and grandparents. Noriko, a 22-year-old from *yon-gumi*, put it as follows:

> "Well, my Dad's a sweetie but sometimes he needs a bit of educating. Like it came up the other day that my sister liked some guy off the TV from Morocco. My Dad just said, off-hand, that she'd better not be thinking of marrying a foreigner. We weren't shocked but we challenged my Dad: 'What's wrong with marrying a foreigner?' And after a while we basically got down to the fact that it was OK in his terms to marry a white person, but that he discriminated against darker-skinned people. Well, that was it – we had no choice but to set to work on him: 'What, so you're going to decide the quality of a person from his skin color?' and stuff like that. Eventually what could he do? He had to take our point of view – his was just indefensible – and now he thinks we're really clever!"

While of course not all the young people in Amatetsu had quite the same ability to talk to and educate their parents in this way, it was common for younger people to introduce some element from their worlds into their parental home. Commonly, computer technology gave their elders new access to information and was introduced by the younger generation. This bringing back of information and identities helps create spaces for inter-generational communication and exchange, and to the credit of old and young in *yon-gumi*, it seems that some of these "exposed" memberships have been adopted by older people, who are now taking small initiatives to redevelop their notions of community and to breathe new life back into their local neigborhoods.

Conclusion

The generational transitions that have occurred in *yon-gumi*, Amatetsu, and beyond have resulted in a young generation which grounds a diverse social reality in an abstract collective construct of Japaneseness that is representative of that reality. For the parents of Amatetsu's young, the middle-aged baby-boomer generation, there seemed little opportunity to make their desires for independence concrete through alternative solidarities and communities. The emergence of the community of consumption, of popular culture, however, has provided a framework through which diverse local memberships can now be made and maintained. It is in this world of locally experienced solidarity, constructed through pluralism, that many young people from Amatetsu now choose to locate their sense of community. And it is the perceived benefits of this solidarity that young people are feeding back to their elders in order to reorientate them to contemporary opportunities to find expression and place in an increasingly diverse Japanese society.

Continuing a trend to see Japanese cosmopolitanism as a rarity in a Japan rooted in an old and unchanging conservatism, Befu (2000: 40) remarks that "one might entertain the hypothesis that Japanese society is able to retain its relatively conservative social structure and value system because the very people who suffer most from these institutions and could challenge them tend to leave." I hope to have shown here that far from liberal cosmopolitan-minded Japanese leaving their native land, they are present in the villages and towns of even the most remote and provincial of regions. Indeed, it is in these very locales that people find themselves coming to terms with some important generational divisions, and from here that new interpretations of Japanese society are given life.

In a world of increasingly diversifying locales, youth-driven collective identities founded on the principles of diversity seem increasingly relevant to us all. By understanding the processes which have led to these identities – the micro-level inter-generational negotiation and adaptation to new social freedoms and opportunities, and how these become salient in particular places at particular times – we can continue to plot the course of transnational culture and familiarize ourselves with the emerging and possible identities of our immediate futures.

It was the end of my interview with Mr. Kawaguchi and Hideo and, as always during my interviews, some of the things that had failed to air themselves while the tape-recorder was running, now – with the hitting of the stop button – came out.

"It's funny, you know," said Mr. Kawaguchi with a chuckle. "I suppose we've learned from Hideo. I mean, you taught me how to use the Internet and all that, and your mother loves it too." He paused for a moment and then reached out to ruffle his son's hair – which Hideo clearly found embarrassing. It was an action that cleared the air between them, though, and beneath his embarrassment I could sense in Hideo a relief and renewed confidence in and affection for his father.

"Yes," Mr. Kawaguchi said to me conclusively. "Hideo introduces us to new worlds, and we're grateful for it. We wouldn't want to be miserable old sods who never changed with the times now, would we?"

Notes

1 Amatetsu is a fictional name, as are those I give to my informants throughout.
2 *Kumi,* or "team," is a subsection of a hamlet or town usually consisting of up to fifteen households.
3 *Chōnaikai* meetings occurred once every two months, and were the major form of community meeting. Every three months there would be a free party for all *yon-gumi* residents (money used from the monthly 2500 yen which all households paid) providing beer and sake and food.
4 My fieldwork in Amatetsu was conducted between 1998 and 2001. I lived in *yon-gumi* from 1999 to 2000. This fieldwork was supported by the Japanese Ministry of Education.
5 I use the word "enclosed" to signal Johnson's (1967) observations of hamlets retaining an exclusive membership, and being unwilling to accept and incorporate strangers and outsiders. One of my informants, Mrs. Mada (85), who came to *yon-gumi* during the war, left fifty years later because she still felt as though she had not been accepted into the community, despite raising six children there.
6 This perspective has been given various names. Perhaps the most popular is the notion of the hermeneutic circle (Dilthey; see Geertz 1983), which illustrates that meaning is derived from an interpretative method which is engaged in constantly playing out local detail with a global or collective structure. Carrither's (1996) argument is complementary: identities are made "concrete" through a combination of real and abstract forums for cultural expression.
7 I use the word "exposed" to represent the cultural pluralism inherent in young people's communities as opposed to the "enclosed" nature of the hamlet identities maintained by the older people (see n. 5). I use the title of Bauman's paper (1997) as inspiration for this section title.
8 There are a number of these books on this theme by Sawaki Kōtaro, published by Shincho-bunko.
9 The forms of "club-like" solidarity we see in the local arenas are here expanded to define and determine the way that Japaneseness is placed within a relativized global setting. There are strong parallels here to Mathews' (2000) discussion of "the cultural supermarket."
10 See Steele (1995) for a parallel discussion on how Yanagi Sōetsu used peripheries to destabilize homogeneous cultural centers.

References

Amit-Talai, V. (1995) "Conclusion: The 'Multi' Cultural of Youth," in V. Amit-Talai and H. Wulff (eds) *Youth Cultures: A Cross Cultural Perspective*, London: Routledge.

Bauman, Z. (1997) "The Making and Unmaking of Strangers," in P. Werbner and T. Modood (eds) *Debating Cultural Hybridity*, London: Zed Books.

Befu, H. (2000) "Globalization as Human Dispersal: From the Perspective of Japan," in J. S. Eades, T. Gill, and H. Befu (eds) *Globalization and Social Change in Contemporary Japan*, Melbourne: Trans Pacific Press.

—— (2001) *Hegemony of Homogeneity: An Anthropological Analysis of Nihonjinron*, Melbourne: Trans Pacific Press.

Bertaux, D. and Thompson, P. (eds) (1993) *Between Generations: Family Models, Myths and Memories*, Oxford: Oxford University Press.

Carrithers, M. (1996) "Concretely Imagining the Southern Digambar Jain Community, 1899–1920," *Modern Asian Studies*, 30 (3): 523–548.

Ching, L. (1996) "Imaginings in the Empires of the Sun: Japanese Mass Culture in Asia," in J. W. Treat (ed.) *Contemporary Japan and Popular Culture*, Richmond: Curzon.

Clammer, J. (1997) *Contemporary Urban Japan: A Sociology of Consumption*, Oxford: Blackwell.

Embree, J. (1939) *Suye Mura: A Japanese Village*, Chicago: University of Chicago Press.

Freud, S. (1988) *Essentials of Psycho-Analysis*, London: Penguin.

Geertz, C. (1983) *Local Knowledge*, New York: Basic Books.

Gerow, A. (2002) "Recognizing 'Others' in a New Japanese Cinema," *The Japan Foundation Newsletter*, 29: 2: 1–7.

Johnson, E. (1967) "Status Changes in Hamlet Structure Accompanying Modernisation," in R. Dore (ed.) *Aspects of Social Change in Modern Japan*, Princeton: Princeton University Press.

Katō, S. (1992) "The Internationalization of Japan," in G. Hook and M. Weiner (eds) *The Internationalization of Japan*, London: Routledge.

Kristeva, J. (1991) *Strangers to Ourselves*, New York: Columbia University Press.

McCreery, J. (2000) *Japanese Consumer Behaviour: From Worker Bees to Wary Shoppers*, Richmond: Curzon.

Mannheim, K. (1952 [1929]) "The Problem of Generations," in *Essays on the Sociology of Knowledge*, London: Routledge & Kegan Paul.

Martinez, D. (ed.) (1998) *The Worlds of Popular Culture: Gender, Shifting Boundaries and Global Cultures*, Cambridge: Cambridge University Press.

Mathews, G. (2000) *Global Culture/Individual Identity: Searching for Home in the Cultural Supermarket*, London: Routledge.

Morley, D. (2000) *Home Territories: Media Mobility and Identity*, London: Routledge.

Nakano, H. (1995) "The Sociology of Ethnocentrism in Japan," in J. C. Maher and G. Macdonald (eds) *Diversity in Japanese Culture and Language*, New York: Kegan Paul.

Ohnuki-Tierney, E. (1993) *Rice as Self: Japanese Identities through Time*, Princeton: Princeton University Press.

Powers, R., Kato, H. and Stronach, B. (eds) (1989) *Handbook of Japanese Popular Culture*, Westport: Greenwood Press.

Reischauer, E. (1988) *The Japanese Today: Change and Continuity*, Tokyo: Charles Tuttle.

Smith, R. (1978) *Kurusu: The Price of Progress in a Japanese Village, 1951–1975*, New York: Dawson.

Spencer, P. (ed.) (1990) *Anthropology and the Riddle of the Sphinx: Paradoxes of Change in the Life Course*, London: Routledge.

Steele, W. (1995) "Nationalism and Cultural Pluralism in Modern Japan: Soetsu Yanagi and the Mingei Movement," in J. Maher and G. Macdonald (eds) *Diversity in Japanese Culture and Language*, New York: Kegan Paul.

Watanabe, M. (1990) *The Japanese and Western Science*, Philadelphia: University of Pennsylvania Press.

White, M. (1994) *The Material Child: Coming of Age in Japan and America*, London: University of California Press.

Yoshino, K. (1992) *Cultural Nationalism in Contemporary Japan: A Sociological Enquiry*, London: Routledge.

Part II

How teenagers cope with the adult world

4 How Japanese teenagers cope

Social pressures and personal responses

Peter Ackermann

The power of indirect social pressure

There is an intensive discourse in Japan that aims to bring attention to, seek reasons for, and propose methods of dealing with misconduct (*hikō*) among youth.[1] Largely due to this discourse, outside Japan the impression is easily gained that the country's youth are in a complete state of disarray. Given this discourse, my interest is in youths themselves: not merely how they perceive their lives, but especially how they perceive their lives in the face of what the elder generation – the generation promulgating the intensive discourse on misconduct – is saying about them.

In 2001 I spent several months in the small Japanese cities of Tsu, Yamaguchi, Hōfu, and Kurume. Within the limits of possibility,[2] I gathered through questionnaires the views of about a hundred young people on their feelings about language, about cell phones, about their grandparents' generation, and about their own futures. These disparate topics could serve, I felt, as a window into the minds of young people, enabling me to see how they responded to the social pressures of the adult world. Before exploring what they told me, let me focus on the concept of "social pressure."

Socialization – "growing up" – always implies having to deal with the pressure of expectations from people older than oneself. Such expectations might go hand in hand with force or coercion, exercised by concrete "official" persons such as parents or teachers. This kind of overt pressure is relatively easy to observe;[3] it is therefore important to pay special attention to "social pressure," i.e. to expectations that are not so much spelled out as just "present in the air," felt to be limiting or channelling the scope of action one might take. Because individuals are often unconscious of such pressure, I was not surprised that the majority of young people questioned did not relate this pressure explicitly to an older generation perceived to be spelling out expectations. Consequently, these young people were not intent on irritating, shocking, resisting, or criticizing their elders. Rather, their desire was to maintain and defend their privacy, close friendships, and inner images of a happy life, as an everyday and unspectacular way of defending against social pressure.

Let me give four examples of this indirect kind of social pressure – the kind of pressure that "can be felt in the air" and against which it is difficult to rebel. There are, first, the very terms with which young people are classified. In German, there is a clear differentiation between "child" (under 14) and "youth" (14 to 18). Japanese language usage is less clear on this point. Some authors make a similar distinction, referring to youths as *seinen* or *seishōnen* (youths, young people), or *kōkōsei* (senior high school boys/girls). However, a surprising number of books and articles – particularly those lamenting youthful misconduct – speak of young people who are well past puberty as *kodomo* (children). This may be the expression of a specific expectation – that the 17-year-old identifies with the same social status and concomitant self-image as the 12-year-old. This kind of pressure would not exist if discourse differentiated systematically between "child" and "youth."[4]

Second, there is the reiteration of values which brought success in the past that the older generation wants to pass on to the next, irrespective of the views the latter may have and irrespective of how the world may have changed. In Japan, influential segments of the now-older generation – the generation in its prime roughly from about 1970 to 1985 – are keenly aware of the country's worldwide success. The huge number of instruction books produced during this time explaining the nature of institutions and enterprises to prospective employees spell out expectations in an unmistakable language, emphasizing above all the devotion of the individual's entire physical and emotional energy to the network of persons at one's place of work. At least two elements may be seen in this discourse that no longer carry much weight in the affluent society of today. One is a high level of consensus epitomized in the call *kyō yori mo yoi seikatsu!* ("Tomorrow's life should be better than today's!") (Sofue 1987; Nissei 1994). The other element is the awareness of Japan's success and its internationally high level of reliability, safety, and order. This also led to a high level of consensus, focusing on the possibility of being "better" – more harmonious, more efficient, more sensitive, more reliable, more polite – than other, and especially Western, societies. It may be only natural that a generation, having seen its consensus-based values bring about success, should feel legitimized to claim their superiority over all others. However, such values constitute a subtle and constant pressure on the younger generation growing up in a world that has changed.

Third, there is the fact that in Japan today, ideas concerning an individual's responsibility within the social network are heavily shaped by official, government-related positions: there exists a more or less official stance shared by powerful and influential organs within the state, such as the ministries, or important industries. Thus a high degree of legitimacy is given to arguments that uphold this stance, which may be described as "pressure to maintain harmony" – "harmony" not in the positive sense it connotes in English, but in the neutral sense of "strict order." Let me take a closer look at this harmony.

Numerous guidelines for correct behavior in organizations and institutions, as well as manuals for schoolteachers, begin with a definition of what it means to be human. To be human, we read, is to live within a social network, outside of which the individual cannot exist; one's duty is the maintenance of this network so as to enable others to lead a wholly human life.[5] In Japan the young generation is exposed to this line of thinking to a considerable degree. In effect, if the social network is the basic precondition for an individual's life, then if an individual suffers, this cannot be attributed to the social network but always to the misconduct of individuals. This places enormous responsibility and stress upon the individual, who must not point to "others" or to "society" as the source of one's problems. It is always the individual who upholds or destroys the social fabric. On a practical level, socialization at home, at school, or at one's place of work can thus easily rob a person of possibilities for discussing contexts and external structures and leave only introspection – and feelings of guilt – as the locus through which to frame a problem.[6]

In his studies of Japanese approaches to deviant behavior, Metzler (2000a, 2000b, 2001; see also Foljanty-Jost and Rössner 1997) concludes that there is a strong tendency to limit discussion to the micro-social level, i.e. to take an isolated view of the person who is guilty of misconduct and to shut out macro-social considerations (Metzler 2000a: 10–11). Non-deviant, "good" behavior, according to Metzler, appears in a majority of cases to be defined from the point of view of the social network. Deviance, on the other hand, is defined as egoistic behavior that cannot be brought into line with the demands of society on the individual (Metzler 2000b: 18).

Fourth, a considerable degree of pressure on the individual is rooted in the vision of an ideal, well-functioning social structure. This ideal is put forward in a surprisingly aggressive fashion in books, articles, and television programs, where it is contrasted to a reality that falls short. If the ideal is that of a well-functioning, harmonious society, then reality is characterized by decay, collapse, erosion, danger, and chaos. This reference to an abstract system of norms against which the individual must constantly measure oneself can exert a considerably higher amount of pressure than when reality is seen for what it actually is.

There is a tendency for Japanese writers to take this ideal state of "harmony" as a point of reference against which the individual must measure oneself, and a corresponding disregard for the complexities of social reality. Two examples illustrate this process well. Kamata (2001), dealing with the breakdown of the family, postulates the ideal of a harmonious family which is made impossible by the "brutal structure of present Japanese society." For Kamata, the Japanese father works himself to death for his family – "*kazoku no tame ni*" (2001: 55–6). However, Kamata's image of a harmonious Japanese family, where the husband, spending long hours at his company, yearns to return to his wife and children, does not seem to take into account the actual interpersonal dynamics in many real Japanese families. Why does

Kamata not even as much as hint at problems such as tensions between husband and wife, or the blind ambition and career orientation of so many husbands? Surely an analysis of what actually shapes the interactions of individual family members would suggest that reality is far too complicated to be reducible to a vision of an ideal "harmonious family."[7]

Similarly, Ogi, a well-known commentator on educational matters, describes the breakdown of an idealized concept of Japan as follows (2000: 120–33):

> The family is no longer a place where one feels security. If children thought of the family this way they would not commit suicide. The family has become a place where there is no more communication among its members.
>
> The individual homes in the local district have no contact with each other any more. Therefore the morals, the habits, and the common sense of the local community can no longer be transmitted to the children through the home. The children feel no more pressure from the local society and walk along the streets proudly smoking cigarettes, gather in front of convenience stores until late at night, or calmly put on makeup on the train. Children who do not feel the gaze of other people have lost their sense of morality.

Can Japanese readers of these texts, who must know very well that times cannot be turned back, feel anything other than guilt that they are not behaving according to "proper Japanese norms"? If these texts were structured around arguments that discussed the dilemmas many present-day families faced, it would be possible to understand why a plurality of life patterns have arisen. However, as the arguments revolve around contrasting a negative reality with a positive ideal, and appear to be telling the young generation that – for reasons it cannot help – it has lost its sense of morality, it seems difficult to see how the young generation can develop a positive view of itself. Who, then, is really creating "the generation gap"?

How young people resist pressure

My research in 2001 focused on the quieter processes by which young people resist the pressures of the adult world. How do these young people respond to social pressure created by a discourse that laments so vociferously the disappearance of old ways and "good morals"?

As I did not wish to influence the direction of responses I received, I consciously did not refer directly to social pressure, and to the discourse reflected in the media and in publications placed conspicuously in bookstores and evidently widely read. I also did not refer directly to the current adult generation – these students' parents and teachers – and its efforts to shape young people; given widespread discussion of the gap between youth and their elders in Japan today, I felt that students might simply repeat for me a set of stereotypes. Rather, I asked more indirect questions, centered on (1) feelings about the use of language, and especially of verbal communication, particularly between different generations, (2) feelings about the use of the cell phone as a means of maintaining or increasing contact outside the control of the elder generation, (3) feelings towards the grandparents' generation – the generation of elders "no longer threatening," and the latter's relation to young people, and (4) these young people's visions of their own future, when they themselves become adults. Let me discuss each of these areas in turn.[8]

Language

The responses I received from young people tended to emphasize their feelings of tenseness concerning language use. Not infrequently, they saw language as a means to conceal rather than enhance communicative exchange. These characteristics seem to contribute to a marked distance between the generations. Some of their responses ran as follows:

> "Language is not necessarily used to get someone else to understand your feelings. Sometimes I use language to *prevent* another person from knowing my feelings and my values, for instance when I lie, or say something close to a lie.... Language is used to get people to understand you, and therefore demands a very careful and cautious attitude (*taido*).... Language is also used to keep an adequate distance between one human being and another.... *Angō* (ciphers, codes) and *kotoba asobi* (word plays) are expressions common just to the insiders of the group to which one belongs, and they serve to keep secrets, strengthen intimacy, and keep distance from other groups. Language is a means to show distance in personal relationships."

> "*Wakamono kotoba* (expressions used by young people) are made up of values and opinions that only one generation has in common, and used only by this generation. Such communication can be difficult for other generations to understand. This is particularly so when one wants to exclude other generations from one's communication.... *Wakamono kotoba* are used to separate oneself from the elder generation, and to make concrete the common consciousness of one's own generation."

> "If you 'feel the body' of someone, i.e. are 'touched' by someone's physical appearance or voice, you become *tense* and take on a posture. It's different if you can contact someone by e-mail – it's much more relaxing than if you meet or talk to someone."

These responses reveal considerable communicative stress. Such stress may be a general characteristic of the Japanese language, because of the status hierarchy intrinsic to the language, but this stress seems to be experienced very acutely by young people: language, to them, is a way of keeping outsiders, and particularly the older generation, apart from one's own realm of discourse. Yet even among one's own generation, tension may be pervasive in face-to-face communication, as the third response above implies. Discussions with teachers in Yamaguchi and Mie prefectures showed that an important source of stress at school had its roots not in classroom study but in extra-curricular activities (*bukatsu*), where slightly different age groups of pupils create harsh hierarchies among themselves.[9] This reveals how youths themselves may re-create the social pressure they experience at the hands of the adult world. One recourse to the tension of day-to-day communication is the cell phone.

Keitai *(cell phones)*

Keitai are a ubiquitous tool in the communicative processes of young people. How far, I wondered, is the massive use of *keitai* – either for e-mail or for telephoning – bringing about a new kind of communication and new kinds of networks to establish identity in the face of the external pressures of the adult world? I organize my findings into several categories, each reflecting the awareness of a gap between the values one was taught (the "ideal," as it were) and the reality to which young people must, and are, adapting.

A first group of answers suggests a very keen awareness of "good," "proper," "polite," and "decent" attitudes, and shows a high regard for, and a high level of reflection upon, social pressure that requires well-defined standards of behavior. These young people seemingly have no intention of widening the generation gap – they see *keitai* as having negative effects on "proper behavior":

> "Things have become convenient. *Keitai* makes possible fast, immediate information. However, it is important to keep manners. It worries me that, unlike when using a regular telephone, you do not say hello to their family any more when you call your friends...."

> "Life has changed since the introduction of *keitai*.... I always have to have the thing with me, otherwise I feel uncomfortable. It makes you restless, jumpy [*ochitsukanai*]. Even at the bedside you must have it. This is strange, really. Formerly people used to speak face to face, or put their thoughts into writing. It scares me to think that this is no longer so."

"When they have a *keitai,* people in trains and elsewhere start talking without paying any attention to those around them.... It's strange to see people walking along the road talking into their *keitai.**"[10]

A second group of answers focused on fears of isolation – an attitude that contrasts with the experiences of the older generations who, when they were small, usually spent more time playing with other children than is the case in recent years.

"*Keitai* gives you a feeling of *anshin* (peace of mind, the sense of having been reassured); *keitai* gives you the feeling you have many friends."

"Thanks to mails you become acquainted with people with whom you would otherwise not be on close terms (*nakayoku*). You can contact people any time (*itsudemo*), anywhere (*doko ni ite mo*), casually (*kigaru ni*). Feeling ties with others gives you a sense of *anshin*. However, seeing people face to face can now make you feel tense."

"When you meet people, you immediately exchange *keitai* numbers and feel, 'I have many friends.'"

"Since I have a *keitai* I don't feel lonely and isolated (*kodoku*). If I'm alone I can catch someone. Someone will be there for me (*aite ni shite kureru*). On the other hand, now I think less for myself. I look less into myself (*jibun jishin o mitsumenaosu*). I think less of the future and about life. I know this is not good, but I can't say no when people call me.*"

A further group was very outspoken about the wish to be left alone and have private time for oneself. This emphasis on privacy and on structuring one's own time I hold to be an important aspect of the "generation gap," because "privacy" can easily get in the way of the rules for "polite, social behavior." In addition, stress on privacy contrasts with the widespread fear of loneliness:

"*Keitai* means you are subject to stress from outside. You get all sorts of advertisements and invitations from broadcasting companies, newspapers, religions.... It's really disagreeable being called without considering whether it suits me.*"

"*Keitai* is a good thing if you get lost. But it is also a pain.... Because of *keitai* you become tied, controlled, managed from outside."

"Human beings can't live alone, some say [echoing the 'official discourses' we earlier discussed], but I think also the opposite can be true.... I don't like it if this time for oneself alone is interrupted by *keitai*.*"

"I like to have time for myself. I noticed this for the first time when I got a *keitai*. I had no privacy any more. It's like being a dog on a leash."

The next group of answers stresses a qualitative change in the nature of interpersonal relationships as compared to past generations, a change created by the new technology of *keitai*:

"Now I can end a relationship by just not answering the mail. As the tie to the other person 'just has the degree of a mail acquaintance' (*meiru teido no naka*), that person is not so hurt..."

"Formerly, when I called, I had to ask the parents of my friends to pass on the telephone. Now I can contact my friends by mail whenever I want to. When I call someone at home the person I want answers, so I don't need *keigo* [formal polite language] any more."

"The pattern of making friends has changed. I can talk to people casually. By using mail it is easy to converse back and forth. I can also say things that I could not if I had to use my mouth...."

"Seeing people face to face can now make you feel tense. Through *keitai* you can tell people directly what you want to tell them, even though this is somehow strange."

Finally, several answers related *keitai* explicitly to a profound change in the relationship to parents, and to the generation that the parents represent:

"I have my own room, where I have my TV, my telephone, everything I need. I don't have to go into the living room.... Even though I'm at home, I can communicate with whomever I want to, I don't have to ask my parents to use the telephone.... Formerly parents knew everything about who you mixed with, but now they know nothing. Thanks to *keitai* my freedom has increased, I can easily contact all sorts of people...."

"Long distance calls in the middle of the night have increased; life has become irregular. Parents no longer know that you are telephoning; you can do and say what you like.... *Keitai* is like an invisible wall between parents and children."

Generally, *keitai* seem to facilitate an extraordinary new set of connections that young people experience in a way quite removed from their parents. Through *keitai*, young people bypass their parents, to be in direct and constant contact with the world of their peers, a world that makes them feel connected to others but that also causes some to feel a loss of privacy for oneself. In general for young people, *keitai* strengthen the social pressure from peers, and weaken the social pressure imposed by elders, who are largely excluded from young people's *keitai* world.

Young people and their grandparents

If we assume that the relationship between the generation of young people and the generation of the parents is changing, not least because of *keitai*, then we may ask whether this change is reflected in feelings towards grandparents. Grandparents are worth considering because they are the older generation past, but are not at present usually in a position to directly pressure young people. By considering grandparents, we can see how young people view past generations apart from the social pressure of the adult world that they experience on a daily basis.

It was surprising to me that many answers given by my respondents were vague, and showed that contacts with grandparents were sparse and often limited to one meeting a year. On the other hand, a few answers did portray very fond recollections. What I had not expected, however, was the surprisingly intense association of the grandparents with the topic of "war."[11]

> "The topics my grandparents talk about are their childhood, and the war. When they talk of the poverty during and before the war, this is very instructive for me.... My grandparents, who lost brothers and friends during the war, taught me a lot about how to think about human life. They have lived from an epoch of poverty up until today.... It's very important to hear from them of times when education did not take place in a context of merchandise and money.*"

> "I learn from grandmother about 'what you should know in life' (*seikatsu no chie*), i.e. how to make laundry clean without the material losing its colors, how to keep foodstuffs over a long period of time, etc. Also, my grandparents told me about the war. Grandmother worked in a factory. Grandfather ... lost friends. I can only meet my grandparents once a year."

> "My grandparents lost many things during the war: friends, family members, their pride, things they treasured. I learned the terrible reality of an education that taught about the goodness of conquering other countries, and also of not getting education because children had to work."

"My mother's parents were very peaceful and I often went to play at their house. They had a little field and planted all sorts of vegetables. They were never angry, and even when we made holes in their field we were told: 'You really played quietly, causing no trouble for grandma and grandpa, you are such good children' [*minna ojiichan ya obaachan no jama ni naranai yō ni shizuka ni asonde itan da ne. hontō ni ii ko da ne*]. My grandparents read me a lot of picture books, and talked of their youth and their experience of the war."

As in the last quotation above, grandparents may seem to represent a nostalgia for a more peaceful past; they may also be seen as the purveyors of a non-threatening, unobtrusive wisdom, not bearing the social pressures of parents and teachers in the adult generation now in power. More often, they were seen as victims of the past that they had no choice but to live through, of a war and a poverty that young people today can hardly imagine. Both because of the decline of the three-generation family – many of these students did not live with their grandparents – and because the grandparents' youth seemed so far removed from the world of today, grandparents seemed to have little moral authority in directing the young: their world was truly a world apart from that lived by today's youth.

Young people's senses of the future

We have seen how, through their grandparents, young people relate to the past, but what now of the future? How do youths' visions of their future reflect the pressures they are exposed to? Do these visions suggest conflict with the elder generation? Or indifference? Or perhaps a self-reliance of the young generation, to an extent where what is being said about it, and what is expected of it, leaves but a weak impression?

Students were asked, "How do you see yourself at age 30 to 35?" When looking at replies, we should take note of differences between males and females. The females were outspoken, even resolute, in their visions of a self-determined life that did not tolerate pressures from social norms and outside criticism. True, these were only dreams and not reality; but their assertiveness was striking.

On the other hand, it was difficult to obtain well-formulated answers from males, and what they said was marked by uncertainty over how to react to pressures from outside and from the elder generation. Some answers from males ran as follows:

"Usually one does *shūshoku* (finds career-track employment) ... and then enters a company. But if you say what you can do, you may purposely not be given that job or position. It is basically the company that decides."*

"I'm now 18. Will Japan still exist in the future? Maybe not. We are in an economically bad situation and dark things are happening.*"

"I don't like to think about views of the world and human beings. I want to do work in which I can express the world in my mind, such as writing novels.*"

"My wishes can't be integrated into plans for finding a job. I like music, film, tennis. I'd like to study complicated rhythms, but nobody understands this wish.*"

The pessimism, and indeed, escapism of these young males is striking: there is no confident striding into the adult future, but a desire to hide from the conventional adult world. Many of the answers by females concerning the future portrayed a more assertive will to respond to pressures from society:

"The nicest thing for me is if I am able to work. I won't be married; I'll be working energetically. I have always wanted to work abroad, as a reporter, not in a company.... In Japan, people work too much and too restlessly (*sewashiku hatarakisugiru*). So people are dead tired. I can't live in such surroundings. Everything is too fast.... I want to be by the sea or in the mountains, live with cats and dogs, live with someone I love and share work with him...."

"I want to be someone who can live alone. So I must work maybe as a career woman in a bank abroad. But I also want to make a family, marry someone I like, have children, finish work early in the evening, prepare dinner, and spend the weekend with the family. The surroundings in which I live should not be dirty and littered (*gomigomi*) like in Japan. I want to be somewhere with a lot of nature."

"I want a happy family, live by the seaside or in the mountains, be in nature. I will live happily with my husband and children and not be chased by time. I want to be able to watch the passing of the seasons."

"I will be married and have more than two children.... I want to be at home when my children come home. Sometimes I'll make cakes; in the holidays we'll go places; for breakfast and supper we'll all be together."

Of the more than one hundred answers, only two mentioned a concrete partnership, using the expression *koibito* [lover]. Indeed, many of these young women had little concrete idea of career or marriage plans – what they stated seems more often to be a matter of personal fantasy than of a concrete plan.[12] Nonetheless, these young women generally had a positive outlook towards their future that young men lacked. Why? A female student who was asked to interpret this referred immediately to pressure:

> "There is high pressure on male students.... Men are not supposed to give up their job, no matter how unbearable it is. They are not supposed to change their working place much. This may lead them to withdraw into themselves, so they shrink and grow timid."

Perhaps these young men had already internalized this message from their elders – and in Japan's era of economic downturn, this filled them with all the more trepidation about the future, a trepidation that young women largely lacked.

Conclusion

What I have aimed to discover in this research is how, against a background of information that relies heavily on problems and misconduct of youths, "unspectacular" youth have perceived themselves to be under the pressures of adult social norms. As I felt it important to draw attention to the less noted aspects of "the generation gap," I stressed the position that "the generation gap" need not imply young people energetically proclaiming different values for themselves or catching the eye of the media; rather, it may be far more subtle.

Looking at the context in which the younger generation grows up, it is essential to take note of covert types of pressure that are continuously present. These pressures are reflected in language usage, in values that brought success in the past but seem out of place in the present (such as those contained in the definition of the individual as subservient to the social network), or that are caused by persons in prestigious positions measuring life's realities against visions of how society should ideally be. Such pressures are often beyond immediate awareness. For these reasons I tried to gain insight into how young people perceive themselves by looking at areas which would not compel them to think directly in terms of "pressure" and "response," and thereby possibly reiterate clichés of youthful misconduct. The information gathered was thus based on questions pertaining to language, the cell phone, the grandparents' generation, and visions of one's future.

In the answers given above, language appeared generally as a cause for tenseness, reflecting strict standards for maintaining distance between elder and younger people. This tenseness pertained not only to inter-generational communication, but also to the relationship between elder and younger pupils themselves.

The use of the cell phone was evaluated along conflicting lines. The cell phone was seen as contributing to a qualitative change of interpersonal relationships, decreasing stress, and relieving fears of isolation on the one hand, while bringing out outspoken comments about wanting to be left alone and undisturbed on the other. The cell phone was also mentioned as leading to increased inter-generational distance by eliminating parents' control and excluding them from knowledge about one's life.

Grandparents appeared to have little impact on the young generation. Feelings towards them, if they existed at all, were positive, and usually included thankfulness for being told about former times of hardship and the war. The grandparents have passed beyond the realm of "adult pressure": the world they grew up in is so far away from the world of youth today that the latter feel almost no moral pressure from the former. This may be one reason why these young people tended to view grandparents in a positive way.

In their visions of their future, males adopted a more troubled attitude than did females, and suggested that their "inner selves" were not up to the pressures they perceived in the outside world. Beyond this, the answers obtained from young men and women in common included no reference to members of the elder generation as having given, or giving, any direct guidance, or of serving as a model for one's own life course. The only emphatic support of any norm expressed in the young people's answers related to preserving "good manners," as we saw in the discussion of cell phone use. A degree of rejection of the elder generation's world could, on the other hand, be detected in the relatively naive, idealistic dreams these youths had of their own future, in which there was a definite "no" to lack of time and leisure, disinterest in nature, and disharmonious family life – the world of many of these youths' parents, and of contemporary Japan as a whole.

None of the answers given by these youths took an aggressive or self-assertive position. At the same time, practically no communicative or argumentative exchange between the different generations could be discerned. The answers I received from the young people themselves about the way they deal with the pressures bearing upon them give the impression that they do not pay much attention to what is being said about them. There appears neither to be open conflict, nor much interaction between the generations. This stands in sharp contrast to the immense amount of material printed or conveyed through the media suggesting a hitherto unheard-of level of misconduct among youth.

Let me conclude by quoting from an interview conducted in October 2001 with a particularly insightful teacher. He believes we should be critical of what is said about young people – a bigger problem, he argues, is the attitude of the older generation, which he holds mainly responsible for creating "the generation gap." In his words:

> "Most teachers are in their thirties. These teachers have enough 'power' to face up to the pupils. But for teachers in their fifties, work at school

is very hard. So these elder teachers fall ill, and sometimes even commit suicide. By and large, while academics in Japan are talking about all kinds of problems of young people, I, for my part, can see a lot of young people who are leading perfectly healthy lives. Unfortunately, many people in their fifties and sixties use the times in which they themselves were educated to measure the present."

Perhaps, therefore, we should pay more attention to what youths themselves make of their lives. Many seem not at all intent on creating a "generation gap," but do appear quite adept at warding off pressure: the pressure of an adult world that perhaps no longer fits the world of today.

Notes

1 It is impossible to list the many titles on this subject that appear month after month, so I shall give only random examples: Kubota 1994; Nakajima 1997; Ogi 1999; *Keishichō shōnen ikusei ka* 2000; Machizawa 2000; Nishiyama 2000; Ogi 2000; Yamaoka *et al.* 2000; Kamata 2001; "Shinkokuka suru bōryoku kōi, ijime, futōkō nado no genjō" [On the present situation, in which violence, bullying, refusal to go to school etc. are becoming ever more serious problems] in *Monbu kagakushō* 2002: 26.

2 Possibilities are always limited: not everyone can be induced to answer questionnaires, and degrees of reflection vary considerably from person to person. Another difficulty that carries particular weight in Japan is the long time usually necessary to reach a stage where a researcher and a young person – in Japan perceived very consciously to belong to different generations – are able to communicate.

3 Such pressure includes *bōryoku* [force, violence], but also the "examination hell," and mothers who demand constant study from their children (*kyōiku mama*) – these are overt forms of pressure that will not be considered here.

4 As long as the young people themselves do not have the opportunity for comparison (for instance, through a period of stay in a foreign country), they would have difficulty translating the emotions they probably feel into intelligible arguments on this point.

5 An analysis of teacher's manuals may be found in Ackermann (1992a: 255–80, and 2002: 56–87).

6 School essays by children and youths are a particularly interesting source for tracing such processes of introspection and the accompanying pressure felt by their authors. Many schools publish their own collections of children's essays. I have discussed children's essays in Ackermann (1992b: 43–56, and 2002: 88–108).

7 There is a strong tradition in Japan of describing social reality in a writing style that is idealistic and/or normative. A reaction against this may be seen in the critical stance taken by the *Seikatsu tsuzurikata kyōiku undō* [Educational movement for spelling out life as it is]. This movement, which began in the Taishō era, trained schoolchildren in the precise observation and description of everyday life in rural and industrial areas. In postwar Japan this movement has played an important role in political opposition as well as in its sharp criticism of normative styles of writing, and it has invested much energy in getting

schoolchildren to learn to express themselves carefully and exactly when describing the lives they and members of their families and their neighbourhoods are leading (see *Nihon sakubun no kai* 1972; *Nara sakubun-kai* 1976; Yamazumi 1987).

8 Unless stated otherwise, the answers were given to me in written form, covering one to two pages. For reasons of space, I can cite only a few answers here, and, from these, only certain passages.

9 Kamata (2001: 82–5) describes how *bukatsu* are often marked by rivalry and in-group pressure, especially when dictatorial relationships between the older and the younger pupils (and not between teachers and pupils) dominate. According to Kamata, older pupils not infrequently put ruthless pressure on younger pupils, for instance, with the aim of pushing the group for which they feel responsible to some victory in sports. Such pressure on weaker pupils may sometimes lead to extreme responses such as suicide, even in calm rural schools.

10 Answers marked with an asterisk * were given by males.

11 This might partly be explained by teachers encouraging pupils to reflect on this subject, and also to directly talk to grandparents about it.

12 Discussions with some of the informants seemed also to suggest that their scope of experience and knowledge of developments in the large cities of Japan was very limited. Moreover, the visions they had of *shūshoku* [finding career-track employment] were based on the expectation that the major decisions affecting their future lives would be made by the company that employs them, and in no way by themselves. Their "naive" perspective of life could therefore be attributed partly to reluctance to making concrete plans for their future, as these would in any case be decided by others, by the company, and by the elder generation that is already part of the corporate hierarchy.

References

Ackermann, P. (1992a) "Menschenformung und Konflikt. Gibt es überhaupt Konflikt an japanischen Schulen?" [Conflict and the formation of personality: does "conflict" exist in Japanese schools?], *Japanstudien. Jahrbuch des Deutschen Instituts für Japanstudien der Philipp-Franz-von-Siebold-Stiftung* 3: 255–80, Munich: Iudicium.

—— (1992b) "Who am I? Testimonies of Silent Controversies in Japanese Schoolchildren's Compositions," in S. Formanek and S. Linhart (eds) *Japanese Biographies: Life Histories, Life Cycles, Life Stages,* Vienna: Verlag der Oesterreichischen Akademie der Wissenschaften.

—— (2002) *"Self" in Japanese Communication/Selbstwahrnehmung in Japanischer Kommunikation,* Universität Erlangen-Nürnberg: Diskussionsbeiträge Erlanger Japanstudien 12.

Foljanty-Jost, G. and Rössner, D. (eds) (1997) *Gewalt unter Jugendlichen in Japan* [Violence among youth in Japan], Baden-Baden: Nomos.

Kamata, S. (2001) *Jiritsu suru kazoku* [The self-reliant family], Kyoto: Tankōsha.

Keishichō shōnen ikusei ka [The police superintendency, department for the education of young people] (2000) *Kodomo kara no SOS – kono koe ga kikoemasuka* [SOS from children – Can you hear these voices?], Tokyo: Shōgakkan.

Kubota, N. (1994) *Yameru gendai shakai to ningen kankei* [Ailing modern society and (the problem of) interpersonal relationships], Tokyo: Sakai Shoten.

Machizawa, S. (2000) *Abunai shōnen* [Dangerous youths], Tokyo: Kōdansha.

Metzler, M.(2000a) "Devianz auf Japanisch – Wissenschaftliche Hintergründe des Verständnisses von Norm und Abweichung" [Deviant behavior in Japanese perspective: scholarly approaches to the understanding of norms and deviancy], Seminar für *Japanologie der Universität Halle-Wittenberg, Occasional Papers* 7.

—— (2000b) "Paradigmen der japanischen Kriminologie – Anmerkungen zur Darstellung devianter Jugendlicher" [Paradigms of Japanese criminology – comments on the portrayal of deviant youths], Seminar für *Japanologie der Universität Halle-Wittenberg, Occasional Papers* 10.

—— (2001) "Abweichendes Schülerverhalten als Auslöser neuer pädagogischer Generationenverhältnisse: Der Fall Japan" [Deviant behavior of pupils triggering new pedagogical relationships between generations: the case of Japan], Seminar für *Japanologie der Universität Halle-Wittenberg, Occasional Papers* 12.

Monbu kagakushō [Ministry of Education, Culture, Sports, Science and Technology, MEXT] (ed.) (2002) *Monbu kagakau hakusho* [MEXT White Paper].

Nakajima, Y. (1997) *Taiwa no nai shakai* [Society without dialogue], Tokyo: PHP Kenkyūjo.

Nara sakubun-kai [Nara circle for (children's) essays] (1976) *Ie no kurashi to seikatsu tsuzurikata* [Home life: spelling out life as it really is], Tokyo: Yuri Shuppan.

Nihon sakubun no kai [The Japanese circle for (children's) essays] (1972) *Kōza seikatsu tsuzurikata* [Lectures on *seikatsu tsuzurikata*], Tokyo: Yuri Shuppan.

Nishiyama, A. (2000) *Shōnen survival kit* [Survival kit for juveniles], Tokyo: Shūeisha.

Nissei Kiso Kenkyūjo (ed.) (1994) *Nihon no kazoku wa dō kawatta no ka?* [How have Japanese families changed?], Tokyo: Nihon Hōsō Shuppan Kyōkai.

Ogi, N. (1999) *Gakkyū hōkai o dō miru ka* [How to look at classroom collapse], Tokyo: Nihon Hōsō Shuppan Kyōkai.

—— (2000) *Kodomo no kiki o dō miru ka* [How to look at children's crises], Tokyo: Iwanami Shoten.

Sofue, T. (1987) *Nihonjin wa dō kawatta no ka – sengo kara gendai e* [How have Japanese people changed from the end of the war to the present?], Tokyo: Nihon Hōsō Shuppan Kyōkai.

Yamaoka, H. *et al.* (2000) *Jūnanasai ni nani ga okotte iru no ka* [What is happening to 17-year-olds?], Tokyo: Junpōsha.

Yamazumi, M. (1987) *Nihon kyōiku shōshi* [A short history of education in Japan], Tokyo: Iwanami Shoten.

5   Youth fashion and changing beautification practices

Laura Miller

A few years ago I was sitting at a table at an outdoor café in Tokyo with a Japanese friend, when an extraordinary looking young woman shuffled by our table wearing platform boots that must have been at least eight inches high. Her skin shone with a dark orangish hue, a sure sign that she got her tan from a tanning salon and not on the beaches of Montego Bay. She was wearing a lime green micro-miniskirt, pink Aloha shirt, and a denim jacket. Her white lipstick and ivory eyeshadow, painted around her eyes penguin style, contrasted with the burnt sienna skin and the swirls of thatchy white hair with pink streaks. She was a perfect example of what the Japanese media had dubbed the kogal (*kogyaru*). I admired her boldness and courage, but my friend, a man in his early forties, said she looked like an "alien" and that she "didn't even look Japanese."

In this chapter I would like to survey some fashions and beauty trends that young people in Japan adopted in the 1990s and into the new millennium, many of them receiving similar censure from older generations. Does this disapproval reflect more than the usual inter-generational disdain found in any society, in which the fashions of youth subcultures are typically seen as depraved or silly? Do Japan's contemporary youth fashions, always in transition, always replaced by yet another fad, represent anything different from style upheavals in past decades, or centuries? This chapter will argue that, in some respects, today's youth are learning to be fashionable in ways quite different from the experience of their mothers and fathers. While new clothing and body styles are not anxiety-provoking in the same way as school refusal (*futōkō*) or shut-in syndrome (*hikikomori*), they nevertheless represent an evident generational shift in ways of thinking.

Some of the themes running through many of the fashions found on the streets of Tokyo are quite distinct in their nature from earlier postwar clothing and body trends. Unlike past generations, today's youth exuberantly combine styles, forms, and beauty ideals from different cultures or historical eras, a process scholars have labeled syncretism, creolization, or hybridity. These syncretic forms represent an undermining of the ethnic homogeneity their parents endorsed and reified as a distinctly Japanese quality. Today's fashions are intertwined with media industries, especially the styles worn by popular music entertainers, which in turn are often driven by the tastes and products of girl-centered subcultures in a convoluted feedback loop. In the past, media and culture industries targeted fewer age-based markets, and held up for emulation narrower models of acceptable appearance. Today, numerous new micro-markets help to establish and maintain more youth subcultures, which in turn contribute to a stronger sense of generational identity. One aspect of this subcultural diversity entails a refusal by both men and women to conform to older mainstream models of masculinity and femininity. These new and diverse fashions and beauty norms are also more egalitarian than in the past, offering a broad range of styles readily available to anyone willing to create or buy them. Finally, while most of the older generations were resigned to living in the bodies they were born with, younger Japanese believe in the possibility of self-transformation through a variety of new cosmetic or surgical means.

Unsettling notions of homogeneity

The appearance of the kogal not only disturbed older Japanese such as my friend, it also confounded foreign observers and media pundits, and kogals surfaced in *Harper's Bazaar* (Hume 2002) and the *New Yorker* magazine (Mead 2002) as objects of fascination. Usually, the unique stylistic sampling of kogal and other Japanese subcultural groups is reduced to a comic or inept effort to copy American or other foreign appearance. One journalist (Mead 2002: 108) wrote that Japanese singer/songwriter Hamasaki Ayumi, at one time considered to have displayed prototypical kogal style, was simply a Britney Spears clone. This overlooks the fact that Hamasaki hit the Japanese pop charts in April 1998, while Britney's debut was not until 1999.

Japanese fashion innovations are not the surface emulation of any specific foreign trend, but are based on a selection of items from different eras, places, and cultures. This practice is sometimes called *mukokuseki* [lacking nationality]. The *mukokuseki* aesthetic of statelessness deliberately invokes images from somewhere or some historical time – Vietnamese peasant trousers, Native American fringe and beads, 1960s paisleys – yet combines or juxtaposes these with Converse running shoes or Japanese geta, baseball caps or Rastafarian knit berets. The end result is a total ensemble that represents no specific place, time, or ethnicity.[1] Merry White (1993: 127–32) noted that Japanese teenagers during the early 1990s were already experimenting with these mixed retro and ethnic styles. Fashion trends in the past were usually characterized by faithful adherence to an overall mode. A lacy pink skirt required a demure blouse, a satin skirt called for the appropriate pumps. The syntax of these older fashion codes left no room for an ensemble, which I spotted once in Roppongi, consisting of a lacy pink skirt, a revealing chartreuse polka-dot tank top, and sneakers.

The suprahistorical and cultural amalgamation found in Japan's youth fashions are not simply evidence of American cultural imperialism. Closer attention reveals that, in many cases, appropriated items are intentionally "misused" or warped. For instance, some kogals playfully incorporated chintzy Hawaiian imagery, using fake plastic leis, orchids, koa seed necklaces, and Polynesian print sarongs, but not in any sincere effort to look authentically Hawaiian. Those who adopted these accoutrements were occasionally labeled "Local Gals" or "Pareo Daughters" (*pareo musume*). Among young men, a practice called *mikkusu shikō* (intended mismatch) combines different apparel, such as a rock-style print T-shirt with baggy surfer shorts, deliberately upsetting coordination with a particular form.

At the same time, mixed fashion is not seamlessly assimilated as "Japanese," but rather retains aspects of ambiguity. Kogals and others play up the artificiality of their appearance. The results straddle sincerity, mockery, and kitsch, making it impossible to tell if or to what degree they are being done tongue-in-cheek. Common or familiar items are inserted into new contexts: a brand-name handbag, with a spineless Tare Panda doll dangling from it, is worn with a cheap plastic skirt and garish barrettes. Some young women recontextualize Japanese summer *yukata* (cotton kimono) by wearing them with punk hairstyles and gaudy make-up. Japanese photographer Aoki (2001) recognized these customized efforts and began photographing young people on the streets of Harajuku wearing a spectrum of mixed forms, such as Cyberpunk, Folklore, and Elegant Gothic Lolita. His published collection later inspired some Americans to copy these Japanese trends.

One of the most controversial strategies for upsetting notions of ethnic homogeneity is by changing the composition of the eyes. For example, the advancement in contact lens technology has enabled anyone to change eye color. Inexpensive, opaque, disposable contact lenses alter eye color completely and allow young people to approximate the unnatural orbs of their favorite *manga* characters.

In addition to color, change may be made to the eye's shape. In the late 1970s I worked in Osaka and developed a strong network of female Japanese friends. I lived in an apartment in the city, and had several sets of spare bedding, so friends would often flop at my place if we were out late and they missed the last train to their distant suburban homes. In this way I came to learn about one of the beauty secrets of ordinary Japanese women: eyelid tapes and eyelid glues. These were temporary techniques to pull the eyelid up just a little, to give the impression of a deep crease. My friends would remove the tapes before going to sleep, but since this was not the sort of thing I had lying around, like Tampons or hair conditioners, they needed to preserve them carefully for application with glue in the morning. The process took a long time and necessitated their getting up earlier than I did. They would clean the eyelid, use tweezers to take up the thin, transparent tape, and place it about 3 millimeters above where the eyelashes grow. Most of my friends refused to skip this regimen, considering it an essential part of their daily beauty routine.

The existence of the eyelid tapes and glues provided an explanation for me as to why so many women at beach resorts refused to go into the water. I also came to understand how, if one became accustomed to seeing one's own face with the eyelids just so, taking the next step and having an eyelid crease made surgically permanent would save time and, over the long run, money. The surgery, colloquially called "double eyelid surgery," is thought to be the most commonly performed cosmetic procedure in Japan (Cullen 2002).

Although accepted by my friends as just one of many beautification practices, outside Japan doing things to the eyelids is the subject of much passionate and scholarly debate. Most often a desire to change the eye shape is seen as obvious evidence of the dominance of a Euro-American beauty ideal, in which the round eyes of the white model are the target of emulation (Kaw 1993). Writers who promote this view often lump all Asians and Asian-Americans together as the recipients of a shared pressure to conform to this ideal. Of course, the situation for Asians and Asian-Americans submerged in the U.S.A. is exactly this case, since they are living in a culture that overwhelmingly denigrates non-European facial features and body types, but for a Japanese person living in Japan, the situation is more complex and multi-determined.

Japanese are not homogeneously derived from one racial ancestry (Katayama 1996). One result is that unlike the populations of China or Korea, a much larger percentage of the Japanese population already has a double-layered eyelid (called *futae mabuta*; a single-layered eyelid is called *hitoe mabuta*). Estimates vary, but according to Mikamo (1896) the double eyelid is the more prevalent variant, found in perhaps 80 percent of Japanese. Other estimates are more modest, but all recognize that a large proportion of Japanese are born with double-lidded eyelids.

One journalist claimed that it was due to "arrested medical skills" in Japan that cosmetic surgery was not formerly as popular as it is now (Cullen 2002), but this is not the case at all. A surgeon named Mikamo pioneered Japan's cosmetic surgery industry in 1896 when he performed the first double-eyelid procedure on a woman who had only one natural double eyelid. Mikamo was trained in Western medicine and was undoubtedly influenced by Western culture, but he made it clear that he was not attempting to reproduce the Caucasian's eye shape in his patients. He strove to maintain a Japanese style double eyelid, one which resembled that portion of the population which already had this feature (Shirakabe 1990). The method for creating the double eyelid pioneered by Mikamo has undergone sophisticated development, and now takes around twenty minutes in an outpatient clinic. A short incision of around 2.3 millimeters is made in the lid, and is then sewn up. These days, aesthetic surgery clinics also offer a non-cutting suture alternative. An extremely thin, non-absorbable thread is sewn in to create a crease. These sometimes disappear over time, and a newer technique will add double stitches with some twisting to make it more permanent. This procedure takes ten minutes and is part of a growing industry in minor cosmetic surgery that is sometimes called "petit surgery" (*puchi seikei*).

News articles suggest that "skyrocketing numbers" of younger women between the ages of 10 and 15 are getting the double eyelid procedure done (*Mainichi Shinbun* 2002). Why is it that only recently larger numbers of younger patients are using a technology that has been around for over a hundred years? One reason is that unlike centuries ago, when double-lidded eyelids were associated with the lower classes of society, it has now become the preferred form. A process of normalization, in which a narrow range of selected images are promoted in media, has created a sense that the double eyelid is the "average" for Japanese people, in the same way that the American media has made it seem that huge, pointed breasts are the average for American women. The normalization of the double eyelid has occurred within the context of Japanese culture, and is not simply a comparison of oneself to Western media. When she gets her surgery, the Japanese girl is not thinking of Britney Spears, but of the large eyes of Hamasaki Ayumi, or the enormous pools of emotion found in her favorite *manga* characters. They are not looking to Hollywood or Madison Avenue, but to Shibuya and the pages of *GirlPop* magazine. An 18-year-old male university student told me he had the double eyelid operation so he would look cute like celebrity Nakai Masahiro. The fact that he also plucked his eyebrows and shaved his chest, something few Americans would consider good attributes of male appearance, makes me think he did in fact have a *mukokuseki* or stateless model of male beauty in mind.

The kogal style began in the early 1990s when high school girls first pioneered an image comprised of "loose socks" (knee-length socks worn hanging around the ankles), bleached hair, distinct make-up, and short school uniform skirts. The etymology of the term is hazy, but most likely it is the clipped form of *kōkōsei gyaru* (high school girls). Driscoll (2002: 283) suggests that "kogal" is derived from English "cool girl," with the "inflection of 'colored girl' as well," but this etymology ignores Japanese phonology. The label *kogal* was never used by the women themselves, who preferred *gyaru* ("girl" or "gal"). Interestingly, the girls' slang concept of *datsu gyaru,* "giving up being a 'girl,'" or "girl-culture dropout," indicates that being a kogal was considered something of a lifestyle or an identity, and not simply "fashion." As the style spread, some kogals increasingly escalated the look, until those with the most extreme saddle-brown tans and white rimmed-eyes were called "mountain ogresses," or *yamanba* by the media. *Yamanba* is the name of the mythical witch featured in numerous Japanese folk-tales. Another term for them was *ganguro*, "black face."[2] A *ganguro* taken to an extreme limit, with even more garish make-up, is called a *gonguro*. Kogals also created styles that verged on the taboo. One was wearing miniskirts so short that underwear would intentionally be displayed, a practice called *misepan*, "showing '*pantsu*' (underwear)." These were actually special underwear, more like bathing suit bottoms, that were worn over one's usual underwear. Kogals began to let their bra straps show under their tops, transforming a colorful or decorated bra strap into a fashion accessory. Kogals also paid attention to the underarm area, drawing hearts or stars, or using temporary tattoos to create underarm art (*waki āto*).

There is some awareness that these styles are a Japanese innovation, and are not simple borrowing. In an issue of a teen magazine, former street model Buriteri, who was one of the pioneers of the look, transforms a blonde Russian girl named "Elena" into a proper *gonguro* with the application of extreme make-up, and by teaching her how to purse her lips or stick out her tongue in the expected expressions (*Egg* 2000). Kogals such as Buriteri deliberately exaggerated features of their looks and behavior in order to set themselves apart from their elders. Therefore, in addition to denoting a *mukokuseki* racial politics, current fashions also function to mark generational and subcultural identities.

Creating generational identity

In a book of essays critiquing contemporary gender issues, the Japanese novelist Murakami Ryū (Murakami 2001), while not celebrating kogal and *ganguro* fashions, nevertheless recognizes them as expressions of an independent girl's culture. Such new "independent" youth subcultures are interconnected with established youth media industries, such as television, magazines, *anime* and *manga*, and are linked to the image-making culture industries, especially the styles adopted by popular music artists.

Until the mid-1960s, most young women read the same magazines as their mothers, and shared in a common beauty ideology. For example, the "Michiko boom" extended from fall 1958 to late spring 1959 in Japanese women's magazines, when the fashions among a wide spectrum of women, regardless of their age or class, were modeled after the Crown Princess Michiko, some of it involving a tennis theme in reference to the tennis court where she met the Crown Prince (Bardsley 2002). Michiko's simple V-necked blouses, easy cardigans, and A-line skirts combined the dash of postwar modernity with an aura of sophistication and privilege. Few young women these days read the same magazines as their mothers or older sisters, nor do they look to the current Crown Princess Masako for fashion inspiration.

Each year there are 3271 different monthly magazines, and eighty-eight weekly magazines published in Japan (*Asahi Shinbun* 1998). Magazines focusing on cooking, hobbies, fashion, lifestyle, travel, gossip, entertainment, music, and other areas are sold according to several different age cohorts.[3] In 1985 alone, 245 new magazines were launched (*Asahi Shinbun* 2003: 245), many of them targeting a female audience. Many more magazines now cater to specialized interests, such as *Hip Hop Style Bible* for young men into hip hop fashion, or *Fine Surf and Street* magazine for the surfer or skateboarder "dudes."

The impact of the body styles, appearance, material objects, and lifestyle preferences of celebrities on fashion trends are also quite evident. For example, although kogals began wearing platform shoes around 1992, it was only when they appeared on the feet of Okinawan-born techno/dance pop music star Amuro Namie in 1994 that the fashion exploded among young women in general. By 1996 platform shoes, boots, and sandals had earned more than $100 million in sales. Although there have been various high rising shoe types throughout history and in different cultures, the modern version of the platform shoe was first introduced in the 1930s by Salvatore Ferragamo. A revival of the style occurred in the 1970s, in both the U.S.A. and Japan. Kogals who re-resurrected the style in the early 1990s were being deliberately "retro," and were not experiencing any fashion "time lag." With their sophisticated knowledge of European haute couture, kogals may well have had the 1930s Ferragamo platform in mind as their model.

Although the full-on *ganguro* or *gonguro* look has almost disappeared, bleached or colored hair is still spectacularly popular. Middle-aged Japanese have long dyed their greying hair black. (One unisex hair-coloring product sold during the Meiji era – 1868 to 1911 – was named The Nice.) However, it was not until the 1960s that some style-conscious people began bleaching their hair. Subdued brown shades were selected by women, while lighter colors were often indicative of semi-delinquent status for young men and women alike. Until the late 1980s, dyed hair was still a minority fashion, but it has gradually become normalized among all members of Japanese society, from young people and entertainers to politicians. Almost all the members of the Japanese soccer team now have dyed hair. Hair colored brown or reddish brown is called *chapatsu*, "brown hair" or "tea hair," and grey, red, pink or white-streaked hair is called *messhu*, "streaked." In a survey of 2420 male and female Japanese high school students in 2000, 38.2 percent had dyed their hair (compared to 24.8 percent of 2109 high school students in the U.S.A.: Shōgakkan 2001). Surveys in fashion magazines give much higher rates. For example, a poll in *Nikkei Trendy* (1997) found that 65 percent of the men had dyed their hair, while a survey of high school girls queried by *Ranking Daisuki* (1999b) says that 65 percent had dyed their hair in a color other than black.

Contemporary hairstyles are often traceable to characters found in *manga*, or to singers and other media stars. A male celebrity who has been a powerful model is Jiro, the lead singer of Glay, one of the top bands in Japan. A history of Jiro's hair was meticulously documented in a semi-biographical book (Caramel Books 1999) in which photographs revealed his hair color transitions. Jiro's hair has been pink, orange, green, blue, black, gold, and white. He has dyed his hair more than ten varieties of brown, and more than five shades of red. To achieve Jiro's hair, young men's magazines such as *Bidan* or *Fine Boys* carry detailed styling and coloring instructions. Young men and women are also adopting a range of styles that includes dreadlocks and hair extensions.

Foreign observers suspect that young Japanese are playing at being Western, but it is truer to say that they are playing at being media characters and Japanese pop stars. An interesting term that points to the contemporary locus for beauty ideals is Cyber Beauty (*saibā bijin*), used to describe women who have the small face and huge eyes of Japanese *anime* and computer game characters, rather than American movie stars. Teenagers dress up as characters from their favorite *manga* and *anime*, a behavior called *kosupure*, from "costume play." One interesting development is the style known as Elegant Gothic Lolita, which combines aspects of a Victorian girl's attire with a dark gothic mood. Although the style developed independently, it is informed by the appearance of Japanese Goth Rock bands such as Dire en Grey and Malice Mizer. Indeed, Elegant Gothic Lolita fashion may be purchased at a Tokyo shop named Moi-meme-moite, which is owned by Mana, the leader of Malice Mizer. Elegant Gothic Lolita features clothing such as front lacing bodices, flounced gowns or bouffant skirts, black lace pinafores, elaborate headgear, and ruffled blouses with leg-of-mutton sleeves, all in monotone black, grey, or white silk brocade or damask. This is not, however, a simple antique reproduction, but is deliberately infused with a Gothic recherché brazenness lacking any Victorian prudishness. There are also hints of the sexual fetish, since the "Lolita complex," or male eroticization of the schoolgirl, is quite widespread (Kinsella 2002). The young women who adopt Elegant Gothic Lolita are not catering to middle-aged men, however, as their primary audience for the fashion are other young people. A sexualized style such as this, popular among high-school aged and younger women, would have been unthinkable thirty years ago.

It could also be said that much youth fashion in Japan derives from female tastes and preoccupations. For example, unlike the American origins of masculine punk or inclusive hippie styles, kogal fashion was an entirely girl-centered product. Female desires and preferences also leak into ostensibly male domains of fashion and popular music. Popular bands and singers such as Lareine, L'Arc-en-Ciel, and Gackt have all stepped out of the pages of *manga* on to the music stage, providing living manifestations of readers' fantasy men. It appears that the genre of comics called *bishōnen manga*, "beautiful young men comics," directed at a female readership, has been a primary source for many contemporary male fashions. I once saw a striking photograph of Camui Gackt, former vocalist for Malice Mizer (he is actually Kamui Gakuto from Okinawa), in which Gackt's androgynous and ethnically indeterminate looks, created with blond hair and blue contact lenses, seemed suspiciously similar to the character Griffith in Miura Kentarō's *manga* series.

Kogal tackiness was egalitarian, and contrasted with the cute and conservative styles that were almost compulsory in the 1980s, and are still prevalent as a style option, although in less saccharine forms. The sweet debutante motif relied on one's having a childlike face and slim body. As one Japanese critic pointed out, the kogal's extreme *yamanba* style was notable in that it could be exhibited by anyone, regardless of their relative attractiveness: "It made cute girls ugly, and ugly girls average" (Hayami 2000: 54). Kogal and *ganguro* looks were based on acquired features – fake tan, fake hair, fake nails, fake eyelashes – that required no pre-existing traits. Unlike the prissy *kawaii* "cute" aesthetic, which demanded features such as a round face, pigeon-toed stance, and undeveloped chest, any young woman could assume the style. In a sense, the kogal look has opened up fashion opportunities to more young women.

This egalitarian access to a fashion sensibility is true for other styles. There are few exclusionary barriers to achieving a *mukokuseki* ["nationless"] appearance. It does not matter who your family is, and you do not have to be beautiful or rich to be fashionable. Despite the media's preoccupation with the craze for brand-name goods, inexpensive yet trendy clothing and make-up is easy to find. Behind the glamorous shops of Harajuku are back lanes (called *ura Harajuku*), where temporary street stalls sell cheap clothing, shoes and accessories, vintage wear and other goods. Some of the terms used to describe *mukokuseki* fashion point to its accessibility. Remake fashion (*rimēku fasshon*) means to add patches, trims, and beads to new clothes, or to restyle used clothing. Girls who wear the folklore, peasant, ethnic, or country styles, often comprised of paisley print skirts and dresses, and peasant blouses, are sometimes called *furugikko*, "old clothes kids," denoting that some of the clothing is recycled. Many young women also create their own unique clothes, despite being made fun of as "handmade queens" (*hando mēdo jō*). The new recycled styles are also termed *enjikei* after a shopping destination for many young people, the Kōenji temple area in Tokyo. Located there is a long shopping arcade housing numerous vintage and used clothing shops, some specializing in 1960s and 1970s fashion. This area has not replaced Harajuku or Shibuya as a locus for congregation and shopping, but has been added to available venues.

A fall-out of the kogal blitz was that it promoted a diluted "gal" style that has become mainstream. "Gal" is still used in teen media such as *Cawaii* magazine, where we find "gal style" used to mean hip, trendy girlhood. The kogal also generated an anti-kogal fashion backlash. New traditional (*nyūtora*), conservative (*konsaba*), and older sister style (*onēkei*) brought back frilly blouses and longer skirts. Instead of a deep tan, some women sought pale skin, resulting in a *bihaku būmu* (beautiful white "boom"). Unlike fashion trends in the past, these new backlash styles have not made other styles obsolete, but are simply offered as more options. They also constitute a form of distancing from trend-setters such as the *ganguro*, who are often from working-class backgrounds and not from the world of trading companies, women's volunteer organizations, and the PTA. The conservative styles adopted by such young people might therefore suggest enduring aspirations for a middle-class adulthood.

New youth fashions offer a wider conception of gendered identity than in the past. Young men are refusing to be channeled into a confining model of masculine appearance, and are using cosmetics and doing other beauty work to improve and diversify their images (Miller 2003b). The extreme kogal-style *yamanba* most blatantly flouted female beauty norms of the past, deliberately rejecting ideas about daintiness and sweetness. They created a type of female campiness usually associated with drag queens, calling into question the presumed naturalness of femininity.

Other new female fashions have allowed increasing expressions of female sexuality (Miller 2000a). There have, of course, been numerous radical fashions in the past that disturbed each era's older generations. But the majority, such as the Taishō (1912–1926) modern girl (*moga*) or modern boy (*mobo*), nevertheless upheld basic ideas of masculinity and femininity. For example, the *moga*'s girlish lack of a voluptuous bustline and her soft, sloped shoulders reflected a non-threatening sexuality. Many scholars have noted that until the early 1990s, the cute girl beauty aesthetic, and not the "sexy woman," was the primary model featured in almost all print media aimed at women (Ochiai 1997). The idea that young women may now select from identities ranging from cute to sexualized is seen in Shiseido's development of two versions of the Tissera shampoo and rinse, "Puchi Sexy" and "Puri Cute." New models of "sexy" beauty have resulted in a focus on the breasts, and there has been a boom in breast-enhancement products and services (Miller 2003c). Because the body itself is now part of the fashion system, the entire body has become a legitimate target for transformation.

Body "possibilisms"[4]

While beauty practices such as eyelid adjustment and bleached hair got their early impetus from the West, a good question to ask is why they became popular only recently. Although technologies for body transformation have been available since the Meiji era, their widespread use is rather new. Perhaps a critical component is a shift in thinking or attitudes about the possibility of changing the body. One of the differences I see between younger Japanese and older generations is the idea that the body is a malleable surface that may be cut, molded, or transformed in new ways. The body was once considered a given, something one had no choice but to live with as inherited. The phrase *shikata ga nai* is commonly used in everyday conversation to mean "it cannot be helped," "it is inevitable," and "nothing can be done," denoting a sense of resignation to aspects of life that cannot be changed. Most features of the body were once considered *shikata ga nai*.

Some writers have interpreted *shikata ga nai* as the reflection of a "dangerous fatalism" (Cortazzi 2001), or a passive apathy (Wolferen 1989). But despite Buddhist philosophical support for such a stance, scholars of the postwar found little evidence of true fatalistic determinism in Japan (Dore 1973; Plath 1966). Instead, it seems that Japanese have pragmatically and aggressively made efforts to manipulate their stations in life. In a brilliant essay which argues against the idea that they are cursed by a "despotism of the mental canals," David Plath (1966: 161) sees expressions such as *shikata ga nai* as an explanatory device available for the allocation of responsibility for unfortunate events, not as ingrained defeatism that cuts off the possibility of change. Susan Long (1999) has found this understanding of *shikata ga nai* among dying patients who make pragmatic decisions to abdicate control.

Historians have also documented the existence of an optimistic philosophy of self-help already present among late Tokugawa (1680–1868) peasantry (Kinmouth 1981). Self-improvement literature of that era aimed at moral and philosophical reformation of the self in order to better serve society (Bellah 1957). Later there were government-sponsored "daily life" campaigns intended to teach people how to improve their hygiene, diet, and consumption patterns, among other things (Garon 1997: 129). An important point is that the self-transformation that these early writers advocated was limited to one's character and health, and rarely meant anything like a cosmetic change in one's inherited body. The goal was never reformation of the self for one's own enjoyment or pleasure.

The pelvic region is one area of the body that is the focus of change for reasons unrelated to either health or character. For men, there are numerous cosmetic surgery clinics which provide specialized procedures in addition to facial surgery. One can get penile implants, silicone injections, or bead insertions. One new fad offered as a technique to upgrade a man's appearance is cosmetic circumcision.

Because the majority of Japanese men are not usually circumcised at birth, many young men are now simply having the foreskin surgically removed at male-only clinics. There are two primary removal methods as well as different penis styles that one may select. A desire to be more appealing to women, who say that the circumcised penis is "cleaner" and "looks better," is often concealed in rhetoric about health concerns. Statistics are not kept on the number of circumcisions performed in Japan. In the rare instances when infant circumcision is performed, the parents must pay for it, since it is not covered by Japan's health insurance system. For adult male circumcision, insurance will only cover it if it is for a medical reason, such as disease or inflammation. Statistics are kept for insurance-covered surgeries, but these do not distinguish between circumcision and other types of penile surgery.

Although no solid numbers are available, the popularity of circumcision among young men is apparent by the number of new clinics opening up with this as a speciality. The average cost of a procedure is US$830 to $1330. The Yamanote Clinic, which has ten branches, places high priority on safeguarding privacy, promising that customers will not run into other clients, that staff members are all male and so "really understand other men's worries," and that "not even one woman" will be found on the premises in order to protect "male pride." Surgery clinics rely on the embarrassment of clients to inflate fees and overcharge them. For example, one clinic claimed that expensive collagen injections were needed before the removal of the foreskin, raising the usual cost of the procedure. According to Schreiber (2002), Japanese newspapers specifically name clinics that are especially unprincipled in this regard.

In advertising for the Shinjuku Clinic, the claim is made that an uncircumcised penis is "not popular" with women, who feel it is "impure" (*fuketsu*). Other ads say that clients will turn into "cool men" (*ikemen*) and have good relations with their girlfriends if they have the operation. Male worries about this aspect of the penis may stem from the role of international pornography, in which the circumcised foreign penis is available for emulation, but more effective is the prevalence of media commentary from young women who openly discuss penile qualities. For instance, an uncircumcised penis is often referred to derogatorily as an "eyeless stick" (*menashibō*) or "mud turtle" (*suppon*). These new views concerning the circumcised penis contrast with historic attitudes towards the practice, in which it was usually seen as quite bizarre. A Tokugawa-era scholar, Hirata Atsutane, wrote that "A Dutchman's penis appears to be cut short at the end, just like a dog. Though this may sound like a joke, it is quite true, not only of Dutchmen but of Russians" (Keene 1969: 170).

A much smaller number of young women are also having cosmetic genital surgery done, ostensibly to boost self-confidence (Connell 2001). The genital surgery sought by these women is usually labia reduction. Those who had the surgery say they want to look like the women they see in adult videos. More common is removal or shaping of pubic hair. One magazine article directed to high school students even demonstrates styling tips for the amount and shape of "V-Line" hair. Each of the six different pubic hairstyles is also associated with a personality type and divination forecast. A poll of favorite "under hair" designs is also included (*Ranking Daisuki* 1999a). According to the high school girls who participated in the survey, the top three styles were the "inverted pyramid type," the "turtle-shaped scrub brush type," and the "downy angel hair type." Personality assessments are given for each of the six styles. For example, the "youthful straight line type" is said to be preferred by someone who is narcissistic: "It doesn't matter who she hooks up with, she's always No. 1." Of course, there are also new, specialized products to buy that will help create the desired effect. An example is Takano Yuri's Etiquette Soap especially for the "delicate" areas of the body.

Young Japanese now believe in the ability of science to refurbish their hair, penises, eyelids, and other aspects of the body, things that were once considered *shikata ga nai* (what "cannot be helped"). Beauty advertising exploits this new belief in the possibility of change. For example, Takano Yuri Beauty Clinic, whose promotional materials include bubbly proclamations such as "I became a new self!," promises that clients will acquire new identities with their treatments. A breast-enhancement product also promises women that they will "discover the new you" once their bodily conversion has occurred. The combination of new clothing opportunities and body restyling means that younger Japanese have more models and strategies available to them for playfully critiquing notions of gender and racial homogeneity. Young Japanese are experimenting with different surface identities not only to upset rigid racial categorization and gender models, but also to underscore severance with the older generation. A smooth young man with plucked eyebrows, long red hair and big, luminous eyes is a powerful form of *oyaji* ("old man") rejection. When a teenager in Harajuku dyes her hair white with pink streaks, she knows she does not look like any teenager hanging around UCLA and Westwood (she knows because she has seen *Beverly Hills 90210*). Japan's own thriving popular culture industries are providing young people with their own models for beauty.

There has long been hesitation in Japan over technologies and surgeries that alter the inherited body. While older generations are still reluctant about such procedures as organ transplants, younger Japanese are happily having their bodies pierced, tattooed, and sculpted in new ways. And, unlike the extreme fashions of the past, the way many young people look today is not something that can quickly be discarded or altered in a public restroom before returning home. Until 1981, I knew no Japanese men or women who had pierced ears, and remember that people often made negative remarks about my own. Now, pierced ears are quite common and unremarkable. A 2001 survey of high school students found that 23.1 percent now have pierced ears (Shōgakkan 2001).

The generation gap as reflected in one's appearance has elements of both history and life course (see the Introduction to this volume). In their attempts to mark themselves in opposition to the parental generation, young people differ little from past generations in their use of fashion as a means for creating and displaying new identities. What is fundamentally new about this generation's play with fashion, however, is the manner in which gender and ethnic identity are no longer essentialized, but are seen rather as malleable aspects of identity open to reconstruction. Finally, the ways in which young people are willing to dye, cut, pierce, mold, and otherwise alter their bodies reflects a new historical attitude about the possibility and desirability of changes to the body.

Acknowledgments

Thanks are extended to Jan Bardsley, Scott Clark, Gordon Mathews, Bruce White, and Gavin Whitelaw for their help.

Notes

1 See Iwabuchi (2003) for more on *mukokuseki* and racial erasure in media images.
2 Very dark tans are also part of a separate "B-Girl" style, which more consciously appropriates African-American fashions, either retro 1970s Afros and bell-bottoms or more recent hip hop styles found in the U.S.A.
3 See Inoue and Josei Zasshi Kenkyūkai (1989) for more on the diversification and fragmentation of magazine readerships.
4 I brazenly pilfer Plath's (1966: 165) idea of "moral possibilism" as inspiration for my subheading.

References

Aoki, S. (2001) *Fruits*, London: Phaidon Press.
Asahi Shinbun (1998) *Japan Almanac 1998*, Tokyo: Asahi Shinbun.
—— (2003) *Japan Almanac 2003*, Tokyo: Asahi Shinbun.
Bardsley, J. (2002) "Fashioning the People's Princess: Women's Magazines, Shōda Michiko, and the Royal Wedding of 1959," *U-S Japan Women's Journal* 23: 57–91.
Bellah, R. (1957) *Tokugawa Religion*, New York: Free Press.
Caramel Books (1999) *Caramel Box Super Edition: Jiro from Glay*, Tokyo: Sony Magazines, Caramel Books.
Connell, R. (2001) "Plastic Surgery Gives Lip Service to Women's Worries," *Mainichi Interactive Wai Wai*. Online: <http://mdn.mainichi.co.jp/waiwai/face/index.html> (accessed 5 May).
Cortazzi, H. (2001) "The Curse of *shikata ga nai*," *Japan Times*, April 16.
Cullen, L. (2002) "Changing Faces," *Time Asia*, 5 August.
Dore, R. (1973) *City Life in Japan: A Study of a Tokyo Ward*, Berkeley: University of California Press.
Driscoll, C. (2002) *Girls: Feminine Adolescence in Popular Culture and Cultural Theory*, New York: Columbia University Press.
Egg (2000) "Buri no depa gonguro" [Buri's gonguro project], August.
Garon, S. (1997) *Molding Japanese Minds: The State in Everyday Life*, Princeton: Princeton University Press.
Hayami, Y. (2000) "Yamanba gyaru ga dekiru made" [The making of *yamanba* girls], in N. Fushimi (ed.) *Queer Japan* Vol. 3. *Miwaku no busu* [Fascinating ugly], Tokyo: Keisōshobo.
Hume, M. (2002) "Tokyo Glamorama," *Harper's Bazaar*, October.
Inoue, T. and Josei Zasshi Kenkyūkai (1989) *Josei zasshi o kaidoku suru* [Deciphering women's magazines], Tokyo: Kakiuchi Shuppan.

Iwabuchi, K. (2003) *Recentering Globalization: Popular Culture and Japanese Transnationalism*, Durham, NC: Duke University Press.

Katayama, K. (1996) "The Japanese as an Asia-Pacific Population," in D. Denoon, M. Hudson, G. McCormack, and T. Morris-Suzuki (eds) *Multicultural Japan: Palaeolithic to Postmodern*, Cambridge: Cambridge University Press.

Kaw, E. (1993) "Medicalization of Racial Features: Asian-American Women and Cosmetic Surgery," *Medical Anthropology Quarterly* 7(1): 74–89.

Keene, D. (1969) *The Japanese Discovery of Europe 1720–1830*, Stanford, CA: Stanford University Press.

Kinmouth, E. H. (1981) *The Self-Made Man in Meiji Japanese Thought: From Samurai to Salary Man*, Berkeley: University of California Press.

Kinsella, S. (2002) "What's Behind the Fetishism of Japanese School Uniforms," *Fashion Theory* 6(1): 1–24.

Long, S. (1999) "*Shikata ga nai*: Resignation, Control, and Self-identity in Japan," in S. Long (ed.) *Lives in Motion: Composing Circles of Self and Community in Japan*, Ithaca, MY: Cornell University Press.

Mainichi Shinbun (2002) "Schoolgirls Swept Up in Cosmetic Surgery Fever," 14 September.

Mead, R. (2002) "Letter from Tokyo: Shopping Rebellion," *New Yorker,* 12 March.

Mikamo, M. (1896) "Plastic Operation of the Eyelid," *Chugaii Jishinpo* 17: 1197.

Miller, L. (2000a) "Media Typifications and Hip *Bijin*," *U.S. Japan Women's Journal* 19: 176–205.

—— (2003b) "Male Beauty Work in Japan," in J. Roberson and N. Suzuki (eds) *Men and Masculinities in Contemporary Japan: Dislocating the Salaryman Doxa*, London and New York: Routledge.

—— (2003c) "Mammary Mania in Japan," in *positions: east asia cultures critique*, 11(2): 271–300.

Murakami, R. (2001) *Dame na onna* [Women who are no good], Tokyo: Kōbunsha.

Nikkei Trendy (1997) "Chapatsu, piasu no tsugi wa mayu no teire" [After *chapatsu* and piercing, eyebrow care].

Ochiai, E. (1997) "Decent Housewives and Sensual White Women: Representations of Women in Postwar Japanese Magazines," *Japan Review* 9, International Research Center for Japanese Studies.

Plath, D. (1966) "Japan and the Ethics of Fatalism," *Anthropological Quarterly* 39 (3): 161–70.

Ranking Daisuki (1999a) "Pantsu no chūshin dō natteruno?" [What's it like inside your undies?], March, vol. 5.

—— (1999b) "Minna no nama dēta no kinkyū wotchingu" [An urgent look at your raw data], March, vol. 5.

Schreiber, M. (2000) "Cosmetic Surgery on Virile Member Comes at Stiff Price," *Mainichi Daily News*, May 5, vol. 5.

Shirakabe, Y. (1990) "The Development of Aesthetic Facial Surgery in Japan," *Aesthetic Plastic Surgery* 14: 215–21.

Shōgakkan (2001) *Dētaparu: saishin jōhō, yōgo jiten* [DataPal: up-to-date information and encyclopedia of terms], Tokyo: Shōgakkan.

White, M. (1993) *The Material Child: Coming of Age in Japan and America*, New York: Free Press.

Wolferen, K. V. (1989) *The Enigma of Japanese Power*, New York: Alfred Knopf.

6 "Guiding" Japan's university students through the generation gap

Brian J. McVeigh

How, in spite of "the generation gap," do youth make the transition from financially dependent students to financially independent workers? From unmarried "children" to married parents? Of course, this transition occurs differently in different places, and we should expect great cross-cultural variation in terms of problems, policies, and programs for integrating youth into the adult workforce. In this chapter I explore how university students in Japan view "the generation gap" – defined as perceived differences between age cohorts – and the ideology that legitimizes the transition.

The above questions cannot be answered unless larger political economic forces that influence decision-making are taken into account. Thus, in order to explore the attitudes of university students, I frame my study within the basic philosophy governing Japan's political economic practices and arrangements: *shidō* ("guidance," "leadership," "supervision," "instruction"). Besides being closely associated with Japan's industrial policy and economic national statism, *shidō* is also associated with other official projects such as schooling, morality, post-secondary advancement, and employment. I argue that the ideology of *shidō* stitches together the rift between youth and elders conventionally described as "the generation gap." In other words, *shidō* legitimizes as well as facilitates entry into the labor force (after "vacationing" at university). The generation gap is, in a certain sense, a paradox: young people challenging older folk because they feel they are ready – indeed, entitled – to jump across the gap to the other side of adulthood, where independence, autonomy, self-confidence, and competence reside. *Shidō* acts as a signpost for navigating through educational institutions and making that leap because it links together education, examinations, employment, and economics, which all concern the laborious climb to a middle-class lifestyle.

After a few words about methodology, I introduce this chapter's issues by asking: Are the changes we are witnessing among Japan's youth due to a fundamental historical shift or to typical life course adjustments? I also briefly delineate Japan's philosophy of *shidō*. Next, I discuss how students described the generation gap, as well as how they perceive those individuals

– i.e. adults – who occupy the other side of the gap. I then explore the meaning of "guidance" among students and how it provides a bridge that non-productive, childless individuals cross to become productive, child-rearing persons.

The focus of this study is on students attending *daigaku* – four-year universities or two-year colleges. Twenty-one interviews with both *daigaku* students and graduates of *daigaku* were conducted. In addition, a questionnaire was sent to 334 students (135 males and 199 females) at five four-year universities and one two-year junior college (only ten students, all female, were from the two-year junior college).[1] It asked who plays a salient role in decision-making among students. I divided the *daigaku* into selective and less selective types: the former includes two highly ranked *daigaku* (one ranks among "Tokyo's six greatest" – i.e. Tokyo, Waseda, Keiō, Hosei, Meiji, and Rikkyō – while the other ranks immediately below these); the latter includes four *daigaku* that are considered mid- or lower-ranked. I might add that my living and working in Japan during the past fifteen years, with most of that time spent teaching university students, also informs my thinking.

Historical shift or life course?[2]

Does the current generation gap in Japan point to a historical shift, or is it just the result of the periodic life course? Are we witnessing major tectonic shifts in Japan's politico-economic landscape that are configuring key values and educatio-employment choices of Japan's youth? Or are we merely seeing a recurrence of the perennial struggle between the young and the not so young? I contend that it is the latter.

Of course, we cannot ignore changes occurring in Japan, but I suggest that a large grain of salt is in order when the media, observers, and other sundry commentators adopt the perspective that "Japan is changing" when the real issue should be "how is Japan changing?" Japan is indeed changing, but such changes, until more evidence appears, seem to reflect adjustments to globalization, demographics, and technological innovations, not radical reworkings of core ideo-institutional arrangements defining Japan's politico-economic and educatio-employment systems. In other words, I contend that the changes we are witnessing are *structural* (the components of a system taken individually) rather than *systemic* (the structural pattern formed by the constellation of components). The state and corporate elite are probably not overly interested in modifications to the structural components (e.g., government, ministries, corporations, educational institutions, individuals). However, they are very much concerned with how the constellation of components work in tandem to form a systemic pattern that "guidance" legitimizes (and interlinks educational bureaucrats, businesses, schools, and students).

Shidō is used frequently by teachers, principals, and the Education Ministry when discussing matters ranging from primary to tertiary-level schooling.[3] This should not be surprising, since Education Ministry officials are charged with the task of guiding, managing, and promoting education, moral development, cultural activities, scientific progress, and religious matters. Their mission, like those of other ministries of Japan, is activist and goal-oriented (McVeigh 2002).

Guidance, then, is a general ideology permeating and configuring the more specific realms of economics and education, but significantly, it also interlinks the complex system of official socio-educational institutions, hiring and employment practices, and corporate culture. Elsewhere I have analyzed the interlinkages between official guidance, moral education, and socialization for Japan's techno-meritocracy and economic national statism (McVeigh 1998). In this chapter I focus on what tertiary-level students have to say about it and how it relates to the generation gap.

The "generation gap" from the students' perspective

Questions about "the generation gap" (*jenerēshon gyappu*) elicited responses that can be roughly categorized into two conceptual domains: "negative associations" and "differences," with the latter receiving the most attention from students.

Differences

Very rarely did students concretely explain what a "generation gap" meant. Mostly, they provided tautological answers with "difference" (*sai*), unsurprisingly, being the operative term: ways of thinking, opinions, topics of conversation, ways of speaking and feeling, knowledge, values, customs, and worldviews (*kachikan*) are different, they stated. Not a few merely reworded the question: "A generation gap is a gap [*gyappu*] emerging between generations" or "A distance [*hedatari*] between generations." *"Sedai no chigai"* (difference in generations) and *"ishiki no chigai"* (difference in consciousness) were also fairly common responses, as was "Discrepancies [*zure*] in thinking." Several students, however, attempted to be more specific: the generation gap concerns differences in the "degree of serious consideration" (*jūshido*) given to academic credentials (*gakureki*); it relates to how adults "make life at the company the most important thing"; it involves differences in *kotoba-zukai* (language use); "when two groups do not have anything to talk about"; and "the difference between young people and older people who have experienced society." Other responses included "Times are changing and adults are not keeping up" and when people "don't understand the *jōshiki* [common sense, which carries a strong moralistic component] of others because of age differences." From one male student came the cheeky response, "You're an adult – why don't you know?" Assuming that such "differences" exist between generations, it is possible to see why it is believed that young people require "guidance."

Negative associations

Not many students portrayed the generation gap negatively. People – i.e. adults – on the other side of the generation gap were described as not listening to young people, confused (*tomadou*), inflexible, and preferring "unfashionable things." One male student said the generation gap comes to mind whenever he hears his aunt say, "These days, kids are 'blah, blah, blah.'"

Students' views of "adults"

Questions about the meaning of "adult" (*otona*) elicited responses that may be roughly categorized into seven conceptual domains. Listed from the most salient to the least as determined by students' comments, these are: (1) abilities; (2) other-oriented; (3) independence; (4) confidence; (5) discernment; (6) practical definitions; and (7) negative associations. Taken together, these categories describe individuals who *do not* require "guidance."

Abilities

Adults can do anything, and they do it *kichin to* (an adverb meaning neatly, accurately, or punctually), students stated. They have the ability to put into effect what they have thought about and have acquired a type of freedom afforded by adulthood: "I'll be able to do anything I want." Adults also "can do their work well," and they "can do the proper thing in the proper way" (*atarimae no koto o atarimae ni dekiru*). Abilities are gained by "maturing socially and as a human" (*ningenteki ni*) and by "accumulating experience." Thus, being an adult means "knowing the pain and joy of life a little more than children do." Adults "have walked across the world and know how things really work." A "person with common sense" (*jōshiki no aru hito*) was a common description of an adult. Thus, someone who "isn't eccentric" (*jōshiki hazure o shinai*; i.e. not contrary to common sense) is also an adult.

"Control" as an ability was another common theme emerging from discussions with students, expressed in such terms as "self-control" (*jiseishin* or *jiritsu*) or "self-management" (*jiko kanri, jibun kanri*). Related to control was emotional coping: they "don't snap over little things." Adults also have "deep thoughts," and, having grown past the turbulence and uncertainties of teenage-hood, are mentally mature (*seishin teki ni seichō suru*), mentally stable (*seishin teki ni antei suru*), and mentally adult-like (*seishin teki ni otona-ppoi*). Being an able adult carries moral implications: adults behave "correctly and know common sense" (*jōshiki*). They have "morals" (*moraru*). They also take responsibility (*sekinin*) for their own actions. "People who have social responsibility, keep order, and can judge things can be called adults."

Other-oriented

Ideally, adults should have a positive impact, especially on younger people. Thus, an older person should become a model (*mohan*) for the younger generation, or a model (*mihon*) for how to live. In short, an adult should be "a person I can respect." An adult is someone who can teach sincerity (*jitsu no aru koto*). Taking others into consideration is also important: "An adult can consider things from another's perspective" and "think about and look at one's self and various things objectively." More specifically, adults do not "bother others," "understand manners," and always "act politely" (*reigi tadashiku*). Thus, they follow society's rules and are able to "put up with things" (*gaman suru*). Knowing about others' concerns and acquiring "worldly knowledge," adults "possess a wide view of things" and understand *seken* (the moral community of others). They also work for the good of the national collective: "An adult is someone who makes Japan's economy the most important thing." More than just a mature individual, a real adult has been accepted into the general collectivity as "a member of society" (*shakaijin*).

Independence

Being "independent," expressed in phrases such as *hitori dachi, jiritsu shite iru* (different Chinese characters than *jiritsu* above), "being independent in the world" (*yo no naka ni jiritsu suru*) were common definitions of adulthood. Adults are economically and mentally (*seishinteki ni*) independent. More concretely, independence means being free from or not relying on one's parents; following one's own path; going out into society and being able to live by oneself; living by one's own power; and making one's own livelihood. Adults are also those who "proceed straight ahead on their own path" and "are not carried away by those around them." Even "if they are not guided, they are able to open their own path."

Confidence

One theme that emerged with discussions of students appears to point to a typically (though not unique) trait visible among Japanese youth: lack of confidence. Adults, by contrast, are said to be self-possessed and to understand themselves. They decidedly have a "self" (*jibun, jibun jishin*) and "understand where they stand and know what they should do." Adults, because they possess their own ideas, have an "established way of thinking" and "firmly possess their own ideas." They are able to act resolutely. Being confident, they are "mentally strong" and "firmly live as a person." Adults can clearly express their opinion and have their own will, and they can convince you of the validity of their ideas.

Discernment

The ability to judge and adopt a fair, moderate stance was associated with adults, who have "correct discretion"(*tadashii funbetsu*); can accurately judge (*kichin to handan dekiru*); calmly judge (*reisei ni handan suru*) a situation; discern the situation (*ba o wakimaeru*). Adults have "gained a heart of appropriate compromise." In short, they "look around at the situation and then can act." Adults "make judgments by themselves and then take responsibility for those judgments." Importantly, they possess "techniques to discern good people from bad people."

Practical definitions

Some students provided "practical definitions" of being an adult, based on what might be termed circular reasoning. For instance, anyone over 20, who has participated in Adult Day, can legally smoke and drink, has a job, votes, has a wife and children, has been "completely formed," is financially secure, takes care of a family, and can do housework on their own, is an adult.[4] Adults can also be characterized as "extremely busy."

Negative associations

A number of students provided uncomplimentary descriptions of adults: they are *kudaranai hito* (stupid or worthless people), *haraguroi* (malicious; literally, "stomach-black"), "cowardly living things" (*hikyō na ikimono*), or people who "get mad." One student explained that adults are "children who are very proud but have forgotten their dreams," while another said they "have lost a sense of adventure." One said adults are "hemmed in by work."

Here it is worth noting what appears to be a changing perception about the meaning of "work": the increase in *furiitaa*, or youth who do not enter career-track employment but rather work part-time or in odd jobs (see Mathews, Chapter 7, this volume). For its part, the "establishment" does not appear to favor developments such as *furiitaa*. For example, the Education Ministry has tasked a panel with developing a system to "teach schoolchildren the meaning of work and help them determine what kind of careers would suit them" in order to "curb the trend among young people of quitting jobs only a short time after landing them or of being reluctant to work at all." Officialdom sees youth "growing increasingly unenthusiastic about working, given the current tough job market and a rising trend to take a casual approach to job-hunting and make a way of life out of being a 'freeter' – a job-hopping, part-time worker" (*Yomiuri Daily* 2002). It is important to keep in mind that becoming a *furiitaa* may not be a choice; it might illustrate adjustment to a forced sort of "freedom" rather than resistance. It is not clear how many have chosen such employment willingly, and *furiitaa*-style work may be thrust upon many young people. Necessity and pragmatism, not choice or option, may be the reasons *furiitaa* are on the rise.

"Guidance" from the students' perspective

Interestingly, questions about the meaning of "*shidō*" elicited many more useful responses than did "generation gap" or "adult." These responses may be roughly categorized into a number of conceptual domains which, listed from the most salient to the least as determined by what the students had to say, include: (1) schooling/education; (2) moral direction; (3) life course; (4) negative associations; (5) independence, self-improvement, and individuality; (6) social verticality; and (7) motivation.

Schooling/education

"Guidance is everything I learned in school," said one student. Not surprisingly, the linkage between schooling and guidance was extremely strong in the minds of students, and sometimes "to teach" and "to guide" are combined in the term "*oshiemichibiku*." It is "education one receives not only from one's parents, but from one's school," said another. "It is what we all learned together while in school." In addition to regular course work, guidance at high school was also apparent within the context of sports and martial arts training and the need to follow the rules of "group activities" (*shūdan kōdō*). It was also related to "feelings of intimacy" (*shinkinkan*) between teachers and students. Some associated *shidō* with self-cultivation, as in "general education" or "cultured learning" (*ippan teki kyōyō*). In this regard, *shidō* should "expand a student's strong points" and "foster good students."

Moral direction

A large number of students explained *shidō* as a type of "morality" (*dōtoku*). Simply put, it involves being told what is bad and what is good. Thus, guidance is "not just about education, but about life in general." As another student put it, "it includes not just studying but behavior as well." Guidance is for one's "way of living" (*ikikata*).

A very common word associated by students with *shidō* is *tadashii* ("correct"). Guidance is "really about teaching the definition and significance of correctness" and "correcting [*tadasu*] our mistakes." Students mentioned *tadashii hōkō* (correct direction); *tadashii michi* (correct path); *tadashii koto* (correct things); *tadashii kotae* (correct answer); *tadashii kōi* (correct behavior); *tadashii kangae* (correct thoughts); and "correct way of doing something" (*tadashii yarikata*). Students need to be taught the reasons for doing "correct things" and the "correct habits of daily life." They occasionally need to be told "do it right!" This is important so "we can go out into society and know what's correct so we can do our work well."

Guidance keeps people on the straight and narrow: "it prevents us from making mistakes"; "it is being warned not to do bad things"; it is "being given a chance to think about one's mistakes (*hansei suru*)." To follow guidance is behaving in such a way that "one becomes a model for others" and "we can teach things to people so as to become a model." It is about "raising people to have a humane heart (*kokoro*)."

A subcategory of moral guidance might be called general social knowledge. For example, students associated *shidō* with knowledge needed for living in society and getting along with others. Thus, it was often associated with *shitsuke* (breeding, discipline, manners), teaching common sense (*jōshiki*), and teaching the "rules of society" (*shakai no rūru*). Guidance involves "giving immature people and those who don't know much a vision for the future" and "teaching the attitude one should take toward life." Such knowledge should be respected because it contains the ways of doing things that are handed down to the next generation. This is why "people who guide [*shidō suru*] have humanity, social status, and dignity." Guidance is given within corporate culture – "New employees at a company have company rules [*shakun*] hammered into them [*tatakikomareru*] and must learn the company's operations" – or it may mean something more intimate, such as to "face someone and have a talk."

Life course

The metaphor of "path, "route," or "direction" is central to guiding pre-adults through the generation gap to adulthood. Thus, guidance is about recommending *yori yoi hōkō* (a better direction); "advising on a better path"; giving a "sense of direction"; giving "a hint of what direction to go in"; "making a path" (*michi-zukuri*); or "clearing the path for someone"; "helping someone go in the direction of their goals"; or "receiving instructions about facing toward a goal." Good guidance is a means to "showing the way" or being "guided toward a goal," especially "when I'm lost." It is "not just teaching, but being led to a goal." Guidance establishes "signposts" (*michishirube*) on the way to becoming an adult and concerns giving advice to people who are lost or upset. It indicates a "path for living in a better way" (*yori yoi ikiru tame no michi*) and for "making someone follow the right path and correcting their mistakes."

Someone who offers the appropriate guidance is a "person who can lead" or is able to "push me in a good direction and really teach me to have a goal." Such people take the lead and "direct others in a responsible way." However, for some, *shidō* should not be about indicating a path already set, but helping younger people to see a path with many possibilities. Therefore, one "should not be forced to take a certain path."

Negative associations

For a number of students, *shidō* had negative meanings. They described it as something formal or stiff (*katagurushii*) or as an inconvenience (*meiwaku*). It was associated with strict or rigid education (*katai kyōiku*), or "being taught things in a strict fashion." To "be strictly guided (*kibishiku shidō sareru*) is no good." One student explained that guidance is teaching in "a one-sided way" (i.e. lack of student participation in class). One student described it as similar to a "sermon" (*sekkyō*). It may also mean "being forced to do something," or "being forced to follow regulations": "I think it has something to do with being coerced. It is important to let everyone have their own opinion." Some students linked *shidō* to scoldings, violations (*ihan*), and admonishments (*chūi*): "In my mind, *shidō* equals a warning of some type." Another student opined that "In the end, because I decide things on my own, *shidō* doesn't have much meaning."

Independence, self-improvement, and individuality

For some, guidance is about being given a choice, about being "led and given advice so one can decide for oneself," or being guided "until one finds the path one should take." Guidance is "becoming a person who can decide one's own future." It is "being guided to what one thinks is the best, but one should be allowed to decide and choose for oneself." It involves being "permitted to act freely within limits defined by responsibility." Guidance is education that makes the most of "an individual's individuality" (*kojin no kosei*). It is about "being given experience, new knowledge, and to have one's possibilities expanded." *Shidō* is "what's necessary to improve oneself" and to "make someone grow up." It is advice to which one can refer for improving oneself, a "program" (*puroguramu*), or "preparations for becoming an adult member of society."

Social verticality

While *shidō* may be about "independence, self-improvement, and individuality," it is also about being socialized to accommodate one's self to political economic realities. In this regard it implicates "hierarchical relations" (*jōge kankei*) and explains "how society itself can be built." Guidance, then, helps construct a *tate shakai* (vertical society) that "is easy to control" (*shihai shiyasui*). Many associated guidance with *kōhai–sempai* (subordinates/juniors–superiors/seniors) relations, particularly in relation to occupational mentoring practices: it is "people on top teaching people on the bottom what they don't know." It is also "what one's superior (*jōshi*; or an older, more senior person – *toshiue*) does when you fail or cannot do something, or do not know how to do something." Guidance is "giving *kōhai* help when they're working."

Motivation

Being guided can have an inspirational aspect. Some students explained that the essence of guidance was to motivate someone or to give advice so as to persuade someone. "People shouldn't be forced, but people should be given a start, an opportunity (*kikkake*)." One should also be granted "enthusiasm" (*netsui*). Students who receive guidance should also "be cared for." After all, *shidō* means to have something conveyed to one "with love" and "to be looked after from the beginning to the end."

Is guidance a matter of caring? Or a subtle form of compulsion? Certainly it is both, and this ambiguous quality makes it difficult to investigate. In any case, it may be said that *shidō* is broad enough to absorb and subsume individual students' hopes for the future and aspirations for independence and individuality (*kosei*). Within Japan's educational system, then, students are

> apt to foster within themselves a "disposition to keep making an effort" on the one hand, and a "subtle sense of being classified" on the other hand. These together make up an attitude towards life commonly held by Japanese people: to try hard in one's own station of life.
>
> (Shimizu 1992: 129)

These two sentiments, namely perseverance and accepting one's socio-economic position, in no small measure assist students in crossing the generation gap and are regarded as key values by the educational authorities. And it is through receiving guidance that many are able to make that crossing.

Who influences students

According to the questionnaire results, the role of school officials in "guiding" students, while not absent, was not very prominent. At least this was the *perception* of students, who attributed a great deal of decision-making power to themselves. To the request "Please rank in order of importance the persons who influenced you in deciding which *daigaku* to attend," at 68.2 percent "myself" far outweighed all other categories, including agents of official educational institutions (high school guidance counselors and other *sensei*). However, to the request "Please rank in order of importance the persons who helped you decide your life goals," "myself" was ranked as number one by only about half the students, while taken together, agents of official educational institutions and "parents/guardians" were ranked as number one by 34.5 percent. To the request "Please rank in order of importance the persons who gave you advice on various matters" students ranked as number one "friends" (34.4 percent), while "parents/guardians" came in second at 23.6 percent; 21.1 percent ranked "myself" as number one (Tables 6.1–6.3).

Above, I reported – based on the results of my questionnaire – how not a small number of students claimed they made important decisions by themselves. The truth is probably that they *think* they have, or at least they feel that it is *expected* of them by current catch-phrases to answer in this way. As elsewhere, authority figures more likely than not exert subtle influences on students, thereby allowing the latter to perceive that they

Table 6.1 Both sexes: "Please rank in order of importance the persons who influenced you in deciding which *daigaku* to attend" (%)

Rank	1	2	3	4	5	6
Myself	68.2	17	9.2	2.9	0	0
High school guidance counselor	7.4	12.5	21.5	24.5	17.9	1.4
Other *sensei*	1.7	5.6	13.4	22.7	29.6	9.5
Parents/guardians	13.1	40.4	21.2	11.6	5.9	1.4
Friends	4.4	14.6	19.4	20.9	23.6	2.3
Other; please specify	3.5	7.1	4.7	1.7	0.9	2.6

Table 6.2 Both sexes: "Please rank in order of importance the persons who helped you decide your life goals" (%)

Rank	1	2	3	4	5	6
Myself	51.4	16.1	13.1	7.7	4.7	0.3
High school guidance counselor	12.2	18.8	20.6	20	13.4	2
Other *sensei*	4.7	9.2	11.6	20.3	31.4	6.2
Parents/guardians	18.5	36.2	20	13.1	5.9	0.9
Friends	6.5	13.7	22.7	23.6	21.8	1.1
Other; please specify	4.4	4.1	4.4	1.7	0.9	2.9

Table 6.3 Both sexes: "Please rank in order of importance the persons who give you advice on various matters" (%)

Rank	1	2	3	4	5	6
Myself	21.1	16.1	19.1	9.5	10.4	2
High school guidance counselor	6.8	7.7	16.7	32.6	15.2	2.6
Other *sensei*	1.7	5.6	8.6	24.2	36.2	3.8
Parents/guardians	23.6	32.6	26.9	6.5	3.5	0.3
Friends	34.4	29	17.6	7.1	5.6	0
Other; please specify	3.5	2.9	2.9	1.7	0.3	0.6

themselves are in control. I have my doubts about what the students themselves reported. The reasons for my suspicions are perhaps misplaced, but readers will forgive my skepticism about recently heard talk of a "third opening" led by Japan's youth on the order of the Meiji Renovation or the occupation era. I feel compelled to say this because such discourse reminds me of the mantras I have heard so many times over the years: "internationalization," "emerging individualism," and how Japan is about to finally open up to global markets. I might add that the latest discourse on "Japan's new type of youth" resonates with talk (and complaints) about *shinjinrui* ("new type of person") of the 1980s.

Although the results of the questionnaire are not very salient, they do reveal certain patterns: for females and for students from less selective schools, authority figures, whether teachers/officials from school or parents/guardians, perform a more significant role in guidance. None of this is surprising: academic/future career guidance means different things depending on one's high school (academic or vocational), gender, and socio-economic background. In this sense, individual choices, and their relation to the generation gap, cannot be appreciated unless macro-level and ideological forces are considered. "Being guided" does not mean individuals lack choice or decision-making abilities; but it does mean that their choices transpire within larger politico-economic dynamics.

Consider gender. When it came to deciding which *daigaku* to attend, 76.2 percent of males as against 62.8 percent of females ranked "myself" as number one (Tables 6.4 and 6.7); 6.5 percent of males ranked "high school guidance counselors and other *sensei*" as number one while 11 percent of females assigned a number one ranking to counselors and other *sensei* in relation to choosing *daigaku*. Almost twice as many females as males ranked "parents/guardians" as number one for choosing *daigaku*. For "rank in order of importance the persons who helped you decide your life goals" males ranked "myself" more than females (10.7 percent higher), and for "rank in order of importance the persons who gave you advice on various matters" males ranked "myself" more than females (9.9 percent higher)

Table 6.4 Male: "Please rank in order of importance the persons who influenced you in deciding which *daigaku* to attend" (%)

Rank	1	2	3	4	5	6
Myself	76.2	7.4	9.6	3.7	0	0
High school guidance counselor	5.1	14.8	22.9	24.4	20.7	0.7
Other *sensei*	1.4	5.9	14.8	25.9	31.8	7.4
Parents/guardians	8.1	45.9	17.7	10.3	8.1	1.4
Friends	5.1	20.7	23.7	14.8	20	0.7
Other; please specify	1.4	2.2	5.1	2.2	0.7	1.4

Table 6.5 Male: "Please rank in order of importance the persons who helped you decide your life goals" (%)

Rank	1	2	3	4	5	6
Myself	57	11.1	13.3	5.1	5.9	0.7
High school guidance counselor	10.3	21.4	20	17.7	14	2.2
Other *sensei*	5.9	9.6	13.3	21.4	32.5	3.7
Parents/guardians	13.3	38.5	22.2	13.3	7.4	0.7
Friends	9.6	17	19.2	25.1	20	0.7
Other; please specify	2.2	3.7	3.7	2.2	1.4	3.7

Table 6.6 Male: "Please rank in order of importance the persons who gave you advice on various matters" (%)

Rank	1	2	3	4	5	6
Myself	27.4	14	17.7	11.8	11.8	1.4
High school guidance counselor	6.6	10.3	18.5	27.4	17.7	1.4
Other *sensei*	0	6.6	10.3	30.3	36.2	3.7
Parents/guardians	19.2	34	27.4	6.6	5.1	0
Friends	43.7	22.9	13.3	6.6	6.6	0
Other; please specify	1.4	3.7	3.7	1.4	0	0

(Tables 6.5 and 6.8, 6.6 and 6.9). To the latter, females ranked as number one "parents/guardians" somewhat more than males.

A comparison of students from selective and less selective schools also revealed differences. In regards to choosing *daigaku*, about 20 percent more students from selective schools chose "myself" as the most important decision-making influence. Moreover, agents of official educational institutions (11.4 percent more) and "parents/guardians" (11.1 percent more) played a larger role for students from less selective schools in deciding which

Table 6.7 Female: "Please rank in order of importance the persons who influenced you in deciding which *daigaku* to attend" (%)

Rank	1	2	3	4	5	6
Myself	62.8	23.6	9	2.5	0	0
High school guidance counselor	9	11	20.6	24.6	16	2
Other *sensei*	2	5.5	12.5	20.6	28.1	11
Parents/guardians	16.5	36.6	23.6	12.5	4.5	1.5
Friends	4	10.5	16.5	25.1	26.1	3.5
Other; please specify	5	10.5	4.5	1.5	1	3.5

Table 6.8 Female: "Please rank in order of importance the persons who helped you decide your life goals" (%)

Rank	1	2	3	4	5	6
Myself	47.7	19.5	13	9.5	4	0
High school guidance counselor	13.5	17	21.1	21.6	13	2
Other *sensei*	4	9	10.5	19.5	13.6	8
Parents/guardians	22.1	24.6	18.5	13	5	1
Friends	4.5	11.5	25.1	22.6	23.1	1.5
Other; please specify	6	4.5	5	1.5	5	2.5

Table 6.9 Female: "Please rank in order of importance the persons who gave you advice on various matters" (%)

Rank	1	2	3	4	5	6
Myself	17.5	17.5	20	8	9.5	2.5
High school guidance counselor	7	6	15.5	36.1	13.5	3.5
Other *sensei*	3	5	7.5	20	36.1	4
Parents/guardians	26.6	31.6	26.6	6.5	2.5	0.5
Friends	28.1	33.1	20.6	7.5	5	0
Other; please specify	5	2.5	2.5	2	0.5	1

daigaku to attend. For deciding life goals, about 20 percent more students from selective schools chose "myself" as the most important person. Students from less selective schools chose as number one agents of official educational institutions (22.3 percent) and "parents/guardians" (20.2 percent), while students from selective schools ranked as number one the same persons at 10.8 percent and 16.6 percent, respectively. Again, schools appear to play a bigger role for students from less selective schools. This pattern repeated itself for the request "rank in order of importance the persons who gave you advice on various matters": students from less selective *daigaku* chose agents of official educational institutions (11.7 percent) and "parents/guardians" (26.9 percent) as the most important influence, while students from selective schools chose the same persons at 5 percent and 19.8 percent, respectively.

As for "Other," "instructors from *juku*" was a common answer for Tables 6.1, 6.4, 6.7, 6.10, and 6.13. Other specified answers included: *sensei* at preparatory school; "someone I respect"; boyfriend; seniors (*sempai*); girlfriend; people at my part-time job; older brother, lover, "members of my

Table 6.10 Less selective *daigaku*: "Please rank in order of importance the persons who influenced you in deciding which *daigaku* to attend" (%)

Rank	1	2	3	4	5	6
Myself	58.9	23.5	11.2	2.8	0.6	0
High school guidance counselor	11.7	12.9	27.5	21.9	14.6	1.1
Other *sensei*	2.8	4.4	13.4	22.4	28	8.9
Parents/guardians	17.4	38.7	17.9	14.6	5	1.6
Friends	3.3	12.3	17.9	23	26.4	2.8
Other; please specify	5	7.8	4.4	1.1	1.1	3.3

Table 6.11 Less selective *daigaku*: "Please rank in order of importance the persons who helped you decide your life goals" (%)

Rank	1	2	3	4	5	6
Myself	42.1	19.6	16.8	10.1	3.3	0.6
High school guidance counselor	16.2	21.9	18.5	17.9	10.6	1.6
Other *sensei*	6.1	7.8	11.7	18.5	30.8	4.4
Parents/guardians	20.2	30.3	20.7	14.6	5.6	1.1
Friends	6.1	14	19.6	21.3	23	1.6
Other; please specify	6.7	5	3.3	0.6	0.6	1.6

Table 6.12 Less selective *daigaku*: "Please rank in order of importance the persons who gave you advice on various matters" (%)

Rank	1	2	3	4	5	6
Myself	27.5	20.2	19.6	9.5	5	1.6
High school guidance counselor	8.9	6.7	16.2	34.2	13.4	2.2
Other *sensei*	2.8	7.3	9.5	20.7	32	3.9
Parents/guardians	26.9	31.4	26.4	6.1	3.9	0
Friends	30.8	30.3	19.1	7.8	6.1	0
Other; please specify	2.8	2.2	2.2	1.6	0.6	1.1

school club"; *sensei* at *juku*; books, grandmother; public opinion (*seron*); older sister; *fuzoku dakara* ("because the school is affiliated"; i.e. guidance was unnecessary because, being from an affiliated high school, the *daigaku* accepted her automatically). Specified answers for Tables 6.2, 6.5, 6.8, 6.11, and 6.14 included: "I give priority to what I have in my own heart"; people at my part-time job; nearby adults; society/others (*seken*); lover; members of my school club; "a place at which I volunteered"; university guide (*jukenkō gaido*); *sensei* at *juku*; grandmother; "I listen to what's going on around me";

Table 6.13 Selective *daigaku*: "Please rank in order of importance the persons who influenced you in deciding which *daigaku* to attend" (%)

Rank	1	2	3	4	5	6
Myself	78.8	26.9	7	1.9	0.6	0
High school guidance counselor	2.5	12.1	20.5	28.2	21.7	1.9
Other *sensei*	0.6	7	13.4	23	31.4	10.2
Parents/guardians	8.3	42.3	25	8.3	7	1.2
Friends	5.7	17.3	21.1	18.5	14.1	1.9
Other; please specify	1.9	7	5.1	2.5	0.6	1.9

Table 6.14 Selective *daigaku*: "Please rank in order of importance the persons who helped you decide your life goals" (%)

Rank	1	2	3	4	5	6
Myself	62.1	12.1	8.3	5.1	5.7	0
High school guidance counselor	7.6	15.3	23	22.4	16.6	2.5
Other *sensei*	3.2	10.2	11.5	22.4	32	8.3
Parents/guardians	16.6	42.9	19.2	11.5	6.4	0.6
Friends	7	13.4	26.2	26.2	20.5	0.6
Other; please specify	1.9	3.2	5.7	3.2	1.2	4.4

Table 6.15 Selective *daigaku*: "Please rank in order of importance the persons who gave you advice on various matters" (%)

Rank	1	2	3	4	5	6
Myself	27.5	11.5	18.5	9.6	10.2	2.5
High school guidance counselor	4.4	8.9	17.9	30.7	17.3	3.2
Other *sensei*	0.6	4.4	7.6	28.2	34.6	3.8
Parents/guardians	19.8	33.9	27.5	7	3.2	0.6
Friends	38.4	27.5	16	6.4	5.1	0
Other; please specify	4.4	3.8	3.8	1.2	0	0

books; girlfriend; seniors (*sempai*). Specified answers for Tables 6.3, 6.6, 6.9, 6.12, and 6.15 included: "someone I respect"; "I decide my own life"; girlfriend; experts; people at my part-time job; "I listen to what's going on around me"; boyfriend; "I decide myself – *I* am someone I respect."

Conclusion

The Japanese media are filled with reports on how the latest crop of Japanese youth is challenging the status quo.[5] Some view this challenge as positive, while others see it as negative. Indeed, for every upbeat report about how independent, self-assured, and pioneering Japanese youth are (reports usually penned by non-Japanese), as if ready to transform Japan, there is a report that they are selfish, hedonistic, and darkly introspective. Fashion-savvy, well traveled, and uninhibited is not the same as tolerant, cosmopolitan, and communicative. To be sure, some Japanese students are keenly conscious of Japan's social problems and eager to take out the old and bring in the new. From my experience, such students, usually products of the elite education system, are often well heeled, well informed, and articulate, but not "typical" university students. In other words, there seems to be a degree of elitism in popular portrayals of Japanese youth.

This said, the youth of Japan are certainly materially richer but arguably more alienated than their parents ever were. Compared to their parents, Japanese youth, in the words of one Japanese professor, "are more worldly but not necessarily more mature." However, increased alienation among one sector of society does not necessarily lead to significant changes. It leads to grumbling, minor adjustments, and perhaps, to reiterating the latest rhetoric in order to appear fashionable. Indeed, to this observer, both officialdom and youth seem, for lack of a better term, "conservative," i.e., preserving state-guided capitalist corporatism (not pursing neo-liberalism underpinned by Anglo–American style individualism).

Acknowledgments

I am grateful to the students who took the time to answer my queries and complete the questionnaire. I would like to express my gratitude to Akiko Sugawa, Haruko Toyama, and Lana Yuen for their assistance in collecting data. I would also like to thank David Slater, Amy Borovoy, Dawn Grimes-MacLellan, Philip MacLellan, Rebecca Fukuzawa, Diane Musselwhite, Robert Yoder, and Laurie Wesselhoff for useful comments.

Notes

1 The questionnaire makes no pretense to statistical sophistication, but merely provides an impressionistic outline of student thinking.

2 For treatments of Japanese scholarship on "life course" in English, see Long (1984). In connection to this and works on generational differences, see Plath (1980, 1988), and White (1993). For additional information on youth in Japan, see *White Paper on Youth* (Cabinet Office 2001a) and *Lifestyle and Thinking of Japan's Youth* (Cabinet Office 2001b). In addition, refer to Part 3 of *White Paper on Citizens' Lifestyle* (Cabinet Office 2001c).

3 See LeTendre (1994) and Yoneyama (1999) for treatments of "guidance" within the educational context.

4 "Adult Day," held in mid-January for 20-year-olds by local governments, is Japan's coming-of-age rite of passage.

5 Increasingly, media reports about youth sound more like reportage from American society. There is a perception that youth crime is on the rise (though depending on which statistics one refers to, youth crime is not necessarily increasing). Teachers talk more about students who *kireru* ("snap") – suddenly exploding into a violent rage for no apparent reason. A sex education expert "is alarmed by the increasingly decadent life-style of youth that has made them more susceptible than ever to sexually transmitted infections" (Wijers-Hasegawa 2002) while *enjo kōsai* is no longer a neologism but a mainstream expression ("compensated dating"; a term describing high school female students engaging in prostitution). One observer describes "scenes of inter-generational fury" such as *oyaji-gari* (loosely glossed as "old-man hunting"): "Most attackers hail from the nation's massive middle class" and the most commonly reported motive is "boredom" (Kelts 2002: 75): "While outrageous youth fashions are nothing new in Japan, openly outrageous behavior is new.... Younger Japanese sprawl on the floor, devouring fast food and gabbing on their cell phones. On the sidewalks, the high-fashion young race past their elders, riding bikes, skateboards, or scooters, or clomping on foot, often knocking into their elders and sneering in open annoyance. Late into the night, school-age loiterers sit on curbstones outside convenience stores, smoking cigarettes, playing boom boxes, and uttering threatening epithets as they snicker at the mostly single male customers, many of whom fear oyagi-gari-style attacks" (Kelts 2002: 78).

References

Cabinet Office (2001a) *Seishōnen hakusho* [White paper on youth], Tokyo: Ministry of Finance.

—— (2001b) *Nihon no seishōnen no seikatsu to ishiki* [Lifestyle and thinking of Japanese youth], Tokyo: Ministry of Finance.

—— (2001c) *Kokumin seikatsu hakusho* [White paper on citizens' lifestyle], Tokyo: Ministry of Finance.

Kelts, R. (2002) "Witch Women and Father Hunters: Japan's New Generation Gap," *Doubletake* (spring): 75–79.

LeTendre, G. (1994) "Guiding Them On: Teaching, Hierarchy, and Social Organization in Japanese Middle Schools," *Journal of Japanese Studies* 20(1): 37–59.

Long, S. O. (1984) *Family Change and the Life Course in Japan*, East Asia Papers No. 44, Ithaca, Cornell University-China-Japan Program.

McVeigh, B. J. (1998) *The Nature of the Japanese State: Rationality and Rituality,* London: Routledge.

—— (2002) *Japanese Higher Education as Myth,* Armonk, NY: M.E. Sharpe.

Plath, D. W. (1980) *Long Engagements: Maturity in Modern Japan*, Stanford, CA: Stanford University Press.

—— (1988) "The Eighty-year System: Japan's Debate over Lifetime Employment in an Aging Society," *The World & I*, May.

Shimizu, K. (1992) "*Shido:* Education and Selection in a Japanese Middle School," *Comparative Education* 28(2): 109–29.

White, M. (1993) *The Material Child: Coming of Age in Japan and America*, Berkeley: University of California Press.

Wijers-Hasegawa, Y. (2002) "Youth Sex on Rise, as are Serious Infections," *Japan Times*, June 19.

Yomiuri Daily (2002) "Ministry Panel to Develop Job Guidance for School Kids," October 29.

Yoneyama, S. (1999) *The Japanese High School: Silence and Resistance*, London: Routledge.

Part III

How young adults challenge the social order

7 Seeking a career, finding a job

How young people enter and resist the Japanese world of work

Gordon Mathews

Shūshoku katsudō and "lifetime employment"

A pivotal time in Japanese young people's lives is when they leave school and start to work. This process is by its nature filled with uncertainty – "What shall I do with my life?" is for young people throughout the world a question not easily answered – but this is particularly the case in Japan, when the employment system that was once taken for granted can be taken for granted no longer.

In 1999 to 2000 and in 2002, my research assistants and I interviewed 105 university students, new company employees, and temporary and freelance workers in their twenties in Tokyo and Sapporo, as well as fifty-two older employees, parents, teachers, and career counselors about the Japanese "generation gap."[1] Of these young people, 61 were women and 44 were men; they were either graduates working at career-track, freelance, or temporary jobs (58) or students soon to graduate (47). A topic that came up again and again in our interviews with students was *shūshoku katsudō*: "seeking career-track employment." This takes place for university students in the second half of their third year,[2] and involves perusing the announcements of companies, attending company information meetings, sending out one's resumé, taking the written examinations of companies, going through interviews with different levels of management, and eventually receiving, with luck, an offer of employment. The process is exhausting, requiring many months of effort, but may be decisive for one's life.[3] Some of the students whom we interviewed dove wholeheartedly into this process in pursuit of their corporate futures; some participated only reluctantly, seeing *shūshoku katsudō* as the entry to a constraining adulthood; and a few forsook *shūshoku katsudō* completely, to follow their own dreams and perhaps permanently leave the middle-class paths of their parents.

Shūshoku katsudō is so crucial in Japan because it may take place only once, at an early point in one's adult life. In societies such as the United States, there is considerable variability as to when a person enters career-track employment; a young person can travel, or study, or follow alternative paths before "getting serious" and pursuing a career. In Japan, on the other hand, formal age limitations have made the employment system more rigid. As Genda has written, "The labor market in Japan is primarily open for fresh graduates.... If a young person lets this one best chance slip away, then it may be very difficult ever to find meaningful work...a situation that will affect the shape of one's career for one's entire life" (2001: 82).

Shūshoku katsudō has been a matter of grave import more for young men than for young women, many of whom have seen the company as a temporary workplace before marriage and children (see Sasagawa, Chapter 10, this volume). Although young women today are, at least in theory, able to pursue career-track jobs on an equal footing with men, many of the women we interviewed who engaged in *shūshoku katsudō* did not see their future jobs as determining their life chances, since they did not feel that they would remain in those jobs for life. They had a more flexible outlook towards *shūshoku katsudō* than did the men we interviewed. *Shūshoku katsudō* is a process experienced quite differently by secondary school graduates as opposed to university graduates. For the former, the job market has greatly shrunk, leading many more secondary school graduates to pursue further education, whereas for the latter, the focus of this chapter, there may still be an expectation of finding regular employment.[4] But for all these groups in common, *shūshoku katsudō* represents one's single best chance at entry into a career.

Shūshoku katsudō is closely tied to "lifetime employment." If changing jobs were the norm rather than the exception in the Japanese employment structure, then *shūshoku katsudō* would lose its power, since one might choose jobs and careers at intervals throughout one's working life. However, if "lifetime employment" is indeed practiced, then *shūshoku katsudō* takes on extraordinary importance. The prevalence of "lifetime employment" in Japan has often been exaggerated. In fact, "lifetime employment" has never been the primary mode of employment among Japanese workers – "only about 20% of all employees work for one company from immediately after graduation from school until reaching retirement age" (Takanashi *et al.* 1999: 7); white-collar workers more than blue-collar workers and men far more than women have been so employed. Young people have long had a high rate of leaving their companies within their first three years of employment, during which they were still deemed employable by other companies (Clark 1987 [1979]: 167–79); this trend has become even more prevalent in recent years (*Asahi Shinbun* 1999). Nonetheless, among university-educated males working for large companies, "lifetime employment," at least between the ages of 30 and 60, has been the general practice. Beyond this, it has served as a Japanese cultural ideal, as what Japanese parents most want for their sons, if not necessarily for their daughters. This has been "the Japanese dream."

The cost of this practice is apparent in its effect on individuals: by being obliged to choose one's career course at a young age, generations of Japanese young people have lost the chance to discover their own potential talents. This is one reason for the stereotypical unhappiness of so many Japanese salarymen (see, e.g., Mathews 1996: 82–7). This cost has also been apparent in its effects upon tertiary education; because of "lifetime employment" and resulting corporate recruitment policies, the function of universities in Japan, especially private universities, has been largely that of channeling students to companies, with education itself very much diminished. However, the merits of this practice should also be appreciated. "Lifetime employment" was often able to create a sense of common purpose between the individual employee and the company (see, e.g., Mathews 1996: 57–62), a sense of commonality that has been acclaimed as the root of the extraordinary Japanese economic success in the fifty years after World War II (see Vogel 1980: 131–57; Arai 1997).

That economic success is today no more. "Lifetime employment" worked well as long as the Japanese economy was growing, but has been eroding as the Japanese economic malaise of the 1990s continues into the twenty-first century. The first wave of corporate restructurings took place in 1997 to 1999, signifying "the collapse of the policy that 'whatever happens, corporations will maintain their employees' jobs'" (Yamada 2002: 128). Companies such as Matsushita began to offer "voluntary" early retirement in 2001, leading to a new wave of outpouring in the Japanese press about "the death of lifetime employment": "Matsushita Kōnosuke, the founder of the lifetime employment system in Japan in 1929…must be turning in his grave" (Sekine 2002: 75).

In fact older employees are not getting laid off nearly as much as the mass media imply; the Japanese unemployment rate is at its lowest among people in their forties and fifties, and is far higher among those in their twenties (Genda 2001: 27; Japan Information Network 2002; Ōkubo 2002: 173), who have yet to gain entry into "lifetime employment."[5] Nonetheless, faith in "the lifetime employment system" has vanished in Japan. Most of the white-collar employees we interviewed, both young and old, expressed a lack of trust in the companies they worked for: in one older employee's words, "In the past, you could completely depend upon the company, but increasingly, it's as if the employee and the company are just using each other." As the business consultant Ohmae has said, "We have no loyal army of company men in Japan anymore.… Those who know how to swim are trying to jump off the boat" (*Economist* 1999: 16). A recent survey showed that among employees in the world's ten largest economies, Japanese workers express the least loyalty to their companies (*Japan Times* 2002b). The university students I interviewed reflected this loss of faith; one said, "Yes, I'll do *shūshoku katsudō*, but I don't have much hope. Even if I do find a regular job, who knows if it will last?"

In this environment, various new types of companies and workers have emerged. Some employers, often foreign or high-tech companies, hire their employees on a contractual basis; personnel dispatch companies (*haken gaisha*) send employees skilled at translating, bookkeeping, or computers from company to company; there are also increasing numbers of freelance specialists. But one particular new breed of employee has garnered extraordinary attention. *Furiitaa* are young people who do not take regular career-track employment (those who either fail at or refuse to engage in *shūshoku katsudō*) and who become unskilled part-time workers: clerks at convenience stores and fast-food outlets, waitresses, and so on. "The number of young Japanese who take part-time work rather than full-time jobs has tripled in fifteen years ... 23 percent of university graduates [now fall] ... into the [*furiitaa*] category" (*Asahi Evening News* 2000). It is estimated that there were two million *furiitaa* in 2000 (Yamada 2001b: 52), and perhaps over three million today (Majima 2002: 16).[6]

Why have *furiitaa* attracted so much attention? One explanation is based in gender. Men, culturally, have been expected to be breadwinners in Japan, as women have not, and this has meant career-track employment; but increasingly, men cannot find such employment. Somewhat more women than men engage in all the categories of "non-lifetime employment" listed in the preceding paragraph, including *furiitaa* (Kaneko 2002: 16); but male *furiitaa* seem, in particular, to excite Japanese popular indignation, because to their fathers' generation their path in life is unthinkable. By the standard wisdom, young people who do not engage in *shūshoku katsudō* but become *furiitaa* are doomed to be losers in life. But then, why do many young people apparently choose that path? One way to explore this question is to compare the outlooks of those who have succeeded in *shūshoku katsudō* and entered career-track employment, and those who have not.

Young employees and their discontent

Those young people who have entered career-track employment are distinctive in that they were able to find such employment in a time of economic contraction. They thus represent an elite of sorts; but nonetheless, these new employees were vehemently criticized by the corporate elders whom we interviewed. As one middle-aged executive told us, "Young people in this company are asleep. They have no initiative, no guts; they really don't know how to think! ... They've received training from the company. But it's too late: they've been asleep for twenty-some years, and so a few months of training won't help!" Such a view is echoed by a range of corporate personnel managers queried about the students seeking employment (Kugisaki 2002: 75–7): today's job-seekers are described as lacking in common sense.

Criticism of young employees has been a staple of Japanese corporate life for many decades; young workers have born the brunt of their elders' criticisms, only to become elders themselves, criticizing later generations. This implies that young workers today will, in due course, become like their elders in their dedication to their work, just as have earlier generations (see Rohlen [1974: 209] for a succinct expression of this view). However, this may not be the case: the current situation in which young employees find themselves may be so different from the past that young employees today may never become like their elders.

Consider two young company employees whom I interviewed at an interval of ten years. In 1990, at the height of the Japanese boom, a new bank employee said:

> "I feel that I made a terrible mistake entering this bank – I hate to think I'll be working for this bank all my life. But since I can't escape it, I guess I'll have to master this work, somehow.... Who knows, maybe I will eventually come to live for the bank."

This young man assumed that his "mistake" was a mistake for life. A new employee at a large telecommunications company told me in 2000:

> "I didn't have any particular interest in this company when I entered it. I just wanted to use it: while getting paid, I'm learning all I can about Internet technology; then I'll go somewhere else.... The employment system here has changed, to accommodate young people; now we don't lose our benefits when we quit, but can transfer them to other companies. This is what this company has to do if it's going to survive."

Young telecommunications employees have more market value than bank workers in Japan today. Yet this employee's attitude was widely shared among the young employees we interviewed, most of whom seemed detached from their companies, and quite willing to leave.

This attitude is reflected in the growing rate at which young employees quit career-track jobs: some 30 percent of university graduates now quit within their first three years of employment (*Asahi Shinbun* 1999). Some have skills that can lead them to better jobs, but the great majority of job-hopping young employees we interviewed experienced not financial gain but loss from their leap. If they switched companies within the same industry, they joined smaller, less prestigious companies; if they switched industries, they faced an even more precipitous decline in salary and status. Given the prevalence of seniority-based pay, those who quit their companies tend to suffer financially because of this choice. Why, then, do so many young employees quit?

The simple answer is that these young people's discontents with their companies outweighed the financial loss they may experience in leaving their companies. We were told consistently by young employees about how conservative and unchanging their companies were. In the economic downturn, companies such as Nissan have been transformed, and companies such as Sony have long been innovative. But almost all the companies of the employees we interviewed have preserved lifetime employment and seniority-based pay;[7] this has meant that, structurally, elders continue to wield power. Japan, as one analyst put it, "is a country run by old men for old men" (Lehmann 2002), and this certainly seems to be the case with companies.

As one young employee told us, "Despite what you've read...not much has changed in how companies operate in Japan, because people continue to act the same way as before, following the same hierarchy that can't be overcome." In another's words,

> "Even now, companies don't recognize the need for change. Older employees seem to be so involved in the company that they can't recognize how bad the present situation is. Maybe new employees see this; but there's a hierarchy, so the top people don't listen to the young people. I've heard that some companies now have meetings so that the top executives can listen to the views of young people. But they do this only because it's popular now.... Younger staff have experienced this kind of false communication a lot, and they can't believe it anymore."

Most of the young employees whom we interviewed felt discontent, but believed that there was no way they could express their discontent within the company. As opposed to the older executive we heard from earlier, criticizing young employees for their lack of initiative and ideas, these young employees felt that they had plenty of ideas, but no way to express them meaningfully within the corporate hierarchy.

Beyond this, there is the apparent fact that working conditions for new employees have worsened. Genda writes that "young employees today do not sufficiently recognize that, as compared to young employees in past generations, they have meager opportunities to develop their abilities through corporate training.... The work environment for young people has definitely taken a turn for the worse" (2001: 57–8). This has happened, he argues, not simply because of the economic downturn, but also because companies devote their budgets to sustaining the jobs and high salaries of older employees, skimping on their training of young employees, who, they believe, might not remain with the company. Because companies are not hiring many new employees, the working conditions of those who are hired have become more stressful (2001: 225, 16).

The gap between younger and older employees in Japanese companies today may be interpreted partly as a gap between Japanese cultural discourses and corporate structure. Bookstores feature shelf after shelf of books advocating that one ought to "live for yourself and not for your company" (Y. Yamada 1999); mass media emphasize individual expression and "finding your own path in life." Despite this, however, companies generally continue to be structured to emphasize the individual employee's total long-term immersion in the organization: the sacrifice of self to company. In one young employee's words, "Lifetime employment remains, as does seniority-based pay – but those are remnants of an earlier age. The way people think now is different. The current reality is one way, but the way people have come to think is another." The young employees whom we interviewed have internalized these cultural discourses, and assume that the corporate structure is an anachronism. If the Japanese economic downturn continues, most felt that their companies' policies of lifetime employment and seniority-based pay could not possibly continue. In one young employee's words, "the Japanese corporate system is like communism because it pays employees not on the basis of ability but of need – paying men in their fifties more because their children have to go to college.... Just as communism collapsed in Russia, this system will collapse." However, the system is not changing yet, and this contributes to the discouragement felt by many young employees.

There is a distinct gender difference in corporate loyalty among those whom we interviewed. We have seen how women opt for new forms of employment more than men; within the old corporate structures, the women we interviewed felt particularly detached from their companies. Even those women on career-track paths equivalent to their male co-workers expressed a desire to quit, or had already quit; statistics (Japan Information Network 2002) show a higher rate of female job-changing than male job-changing in Japan.[8] One reason for this is that women, whatever their formal position, may feel they are corporate outsiders as compared to men. As one young female employee explained,

> "There is a 30-year-old man in my company who has completely internalized its values; it's like he's an old man. Women are outside the hierarchy; they don't believe in it as much. But men, once they enter, are automatically part of the hierarchy, so they have to follow it."

Men, expected to be breadwinners, may be more conservative in their lives and values, as women, not so bound to conventional work careers, are not.

But generational difference seems finally more pivotal than gender difference in explaining why young people fail to stay in their career-track jobs: most young people whom we interviewed, men and women in common, felt a distinct discontentment: the corporate world they now worked within was not where they wanted to spend their lives. This attitude may have been more or less present in past decades too, but young employees then were more likely to stay in their companies. Today, because of the multiplicity of conditions discussed above, they are not – although what this means for their future remains to be seen.

Furiitaa and other outsiders

The foregoing makes it clear why many young people are discontented within the Japanese corporate world: because it is no longer seen as a secure path, its pressures may seem no longer worth bearing. But the consequences of not entering a career-track job may be even greater – one may risk becoming shut out of the vaunted middle class, or from the ability to support a family, for one's entire life. Why are many young people willing to take this risk?

First, however, we must consider to what extent young people *choose* not to enter a career track, and to what extent they have tried and failed to enter a career track. It is often difficult to tell whether a young person becomes *furiitaa* from choice or necessity – a university student who does not yet have a clear idea of what she wants to do submits only a few resumés to companies, and becomes a *furiitaa*: did she choose, or was she forced into that path? Several people we interviewed could not say whether it was choice or necessity that led them to become *furiitaa*: it was a combination of both: "I went through *shūshoku katsudō* without really looking for a job. It was basically just 'something to do.'" One survey (reported in Yamada 2001b) has shown that 27 percent of *furiitaa* saw their ideal future ten years hence as being a regular company employee, as opposed to 32 percent who dreamed of becoming a freelance professional and 16 percent who dreamed of being supported by a spouse. This survey indicates that the desire to become a regular employee is rivaled by the desire to be independent. Gender difference is important here: while more than twice as many men as women dreamed of becoming regular employees, only women dreamed of being supported by a spouse. As with being a corporate employee, being a *furiitaa* may have different meanings for men and women. Nonetheless, the ideal for a plurality of men and women in common was to become neither salaryman nor spouse, but an independent professional.

Again, why do so many young people spurn regular employment? There are opposing interpretations offered by Japanese social critics. One interpretation is that young people lack the work ethic of their elders. They can lead an affluent life with their parents as "parasite singles" in M. Yamada's celebrated term (1999); and indeed, some 60 percent of *furiitaa* live with their parents (*Furiitaa kenkyūkai* 2001: 83). Temporary work may pay as much as regular employment in the short term,[9] and *furiitaa* often need not work as hard as regular employees, since their working hours are fixed. A store clerk in his mid-twenties told us, "When my shift ends, I can do whatever I want to; I'm completely free. That would be impossible if

I were a salaryman" – *furiitaa*, unlike salarymen, can have their own time and lives apart from their company. This attitude arouses scorn in the Japanese mass media. "The unemployment rate is increasing among young people because they don't want [career-track] jobs.... Japan is spoiling its young people!" one popular guide to the Japanese economy maintains (Yamada 2002: 127, 219). A sociologist writes that Japanese young people, living off their parents at home and thus living affluently off their low-paying jobs, "hinder the nation's economy and sap the society's vitality" (Yamada 2001a: 10).

Another, contrasting interpretation, as we have seen, is that the problem is not spoiled young people but the employment system created by their elders: lifetime employment serves those already within that system, and shuns those outside. Genda writes: "In order to support the wages of middle-aged and older workers in the company, young workers' employment prospects are reduced" (2001: 225); he wonders if young people might not eventually explode in anger at this situation (2001: 90). This is not yet happening, he argues, only because young people do not realize how they are being exploited. Yamada writes (considering young people from a different angle than in his 2001a article cited above) that *furiitaa* are "dreamers who provide a source of cheap, disposable labor.... It appears almost as though the dreams these people hold for the future serve the purpose of getting them to accept their status as manual laborers" (2001b: 54). Almost all the *furiitaa* we interviewed expressed such dreams, whether grandiose ("I want my band to become well-known ... all over the world") or more mundane, if still, perhaps, improbable ("I want to design web-pages and computer games.... I want to become an events promoter, putting on performances and concerts"). These *furiitaa* were in their twenties, and had not yet faced the failure of their dreams; they may, as Yamada argues, be the unwitting victims of an economic system that duplicitously sacrifices their futures.

Both the above explanations have validity: clearly many young people have a cushion of affluence provided by their parents; just as clearly, these young people are victimized by an employment system that cannot furnish them with the opportunities it provided for their fathers. There is also, however, a third explanation: *furiitaa* are not only spoiled "parasite singles" nor are they only unwitting dreamers. Some young people may fully understand the economic odds against them, but may feel such repugnance at the lives their fathers have led that they are willing to abandon the pursuit of regular employment in order not to have to live such a life themselves. Over and over again in our interviews, male *furiitaa* spoke as did a young deliveryman: "I don't know what I want to do, but I don't want to be a salaryman working for a big company.... That's like being dead." In some cases this attitude may stem from "sour grapes" – the fact that a young person failed to find a job in a company, and thus disparages that path – but more often it seemed to reflect genuine abhorrence.

Japanese salaried workers have long paid a high personal price for their corporate belonging; they have been wedded to their companies, putting their families a distinct second in their lives;[10] even now, death from overwork is hardly uncommon (Efron 2000). Such sacrifice could be justified as long as it contributed to Japan and its growth; but today that appears a delusion. As a university student explained,

> "The *oyaji* [middle-aged salaried worker] has no attractiveness now – books and movies depict him as a miserable figure, just following his boss's orders and then getting thrown away by the company, and having no place to go, certainly not home. Children see their fathers and think, 'Why should I study hard and become like that?'"

As a *Japan Times* editorial stated (2002a),

> The young generation has a negative perception of the lifetime employment system, and with good reason. Company allegiance is no longer synonymous with lifetime service.... Even career-track workers ... may be suddenly forced to take early retirement.... At home, jobless fathers are often regarded as "nuisances."

These different factors in conjunction form a powerful argument against becoming a career-track employee, despite the economic uncertainty that this refusal entails; this is why many young people will not enter career-track employment.

As we have seen, there are a number of alternative paths of employment in Japan today, but most of these paths, such as becoming a freelancer, require specialized skills, as becoming a salaryman or a *furiitaa* does not. For a fresh graduate unable or unwilling to engage in *shūshoku katsudō*, becoming a *furiitaa* may seem the only available option. It is difficult to overestimate the shock *furiitaa* have represented for their elders in Japan. As an older employee said,

> "Now, young people are emerging who are unimaginable in past Japan; the word *furiitaa* has emerged to describe them.... This is a problem of the social structure of Japan; they can't be fit into existing organizations. People in the mainstream are frightened of these people."

The puzzlement and abhorrence aroused by *furiitaa* can easily be seen in the mass media. A book discussing *furiitaa* (*Gakken* 2001) is entitled "*Furiitaa*: Why? What should we do?"; an advertisement for a university in a widely read magazine (*Aera* 2002) tells its readers (prospective students' parents) that its motto for students is, "We won't let you become a *furiitaa*."

Furiitaa violate the cardinal social expectation of Japanese middle-class adult society that young people – particularly men – should embark on a stable career in a large organization; *furiitaa* threaten the postwar Japanese social order, since they belong to neither company nor family (having no families of their own). They are seen as throwing away their futures: much anti-*furiitaa* rhetoric is class-based, as if to say, "Why are these young people disdaining the middle-class status that we, their parents, have struggled for so many years to attain?" They are also seen as throwing away the future of Japan. Unlike regular employees, they are not paying into the pension schemes that will support their elders once they retire – and in a society as rapidly aging as Japan, this is a serious problem. In fact, as Ōkubo notes, "Japanese daily life could not function without *furiitaa*" (2002: 128), and these *furiitaa* support, through their cheap labor, the lifetime employment enjoyed by their fathers. But amidst the negative popular perception of *furiitaa*, this fact is not often noted.

It is remarkable that despite the negative views society at large holds of *furiitaa*, surveys (Satō 2001), as well as our own interviews, show that *furiitaa* are in virtually all respects happier with their working lives than are regular workers – an extraordinary situation given the fact that *furiitaa* make so little money and have such limited prospects compared to their career-track counterparts.[11] That *furiitaa* seem happier in the workplace than their regularly employed fellows says much about the pressures of the Japanese workplace. However, if *furiitaa* seem happier in the present, what of the future? What will happen to these *furiitaa* as they become older? Yamada (2001b: 55) offers this dark view:

> The day will come when [*furiitaa*] ... wake up from their dreams. The parents who have supported their affluent lifestyles will grow frail, and [*furiitaa*] ... themselves will grow older and reach the point where they will be discarded as a source of unskilled labor.... There is no guarantee that in the future the streets will not be overflowing with no-longer young people who have lost their hopes and dreams, possess no job skills, and have played no part in raising the next generation.

However, most of the *furiitaa* we interviewed were optimistic about their lives, and, to a degree, about Japan. No longer was the Japanese societal lockstep – of husband at work, married to his company, wife at home to raise children to become future workers and mothers – necessary to follow. These young people believed they could live following their own paths.

I interviewed a freelance interpreter in her early thirties, who had been a *furiitaa* but had developed her language skills, and was now able to live as a respected professional; she contracted out to companies but remained free of their constraints. She said, "We're in a very lucky age now, because you can leave the Japanese mainstream; you can live your own life." This woman enjoyed speaking with university students, to tell them, "There are people like me in Japan, too. You too can live this way, if you choose, and if you really work at it." Perhaps they can, if they have the pluck and the skill that this woman has had – certainly a small but very real percentage of *furiitaa* may be able, eventually, to follow their own lives' dreams. This, however, will depend not just on themselves, but on the future structure of Japanese society.

Conclusion: the future of the Japanese employment system

In this chapter we have examined two groups of young people: those who have succeeded at *shūshoku katsudō* and become regular employees, and those who cannot or will not follow that path. The standard view is that those who fail to become regular employees may be doomed to a bleak future. On the other hand, however, the regular employees we interviewed seemed less happy with their lives than the *furiitaa*, a finding paralleled by survey data. In an era in which "lifetime employment" can no longer be relied upon, regular employees wonder why they should have to tolerate the long working hours and rigid hierarchy of their companies, something from which the *furiitaa* are free. Today, *furiitaa* may indeed have it better. But what, again, of the future?

If the Japanese employment system continues as it is today, then those young people who become regular employees will be the winners. They may face more uncertainty than in the past, but most will probably continue in their careers; at the same time, while some *furiitaa* may succeed in becoming freelance specialists, most will probably continue indefinitely as *furiitaa*. At least economically, the former group will be winners and the latter group losers – especially if, as they age, their pool of temporary jobs becomes taken up by new generations of young people. If, however, the Japanese economy transforms – if the current indebted state of Japanese companies becomes untenable, and widespread corporate collapses follow – then some of the *furiitaa*, and, even more, those who have had the skills to become freelancers, may turn out to be not losers but winners, for they will have more flexibility to survive than those who have spent their working lives within a single organizational confine.

It is possible that both of these processes will take place – the Japanese economy will continue its ongoing decline with both whimpers and bangs, until finally a new employment system is devised allowing for both types of employment. It must be emphasized, however, that the structure of Japanese institutions is profoundly interlinked: "lifetime employment" is directly related to *shūshoku katsudō,* which in turn is linked to the examination system, which is linked to the gendered division of men at work, women at home, all of which are linked to the cultural value of sacrifice of self to one's primary group. These are stereotypes, but they have been largely the case in the institutions of postwar Japan. Now, however, that system is being eroded, not least by the young people we have discussed who no longer engage in *shūshoku katsudō*. They are, in effect, helping to destroy the Japan that their parents and grandparents built.

They are certainly not challenging the adult order in any organized, collective sense. Indeed, if anything, seen as a group, *furiitaa* are unwitting victims of the decline of the postwar Japanese economic order rather than conscious agents of its transformation. Yet by their individual choices and fates – to fail at *shūshoku katsudō*, to not engage in *shūshoku katsudō*, or to succeed and then quit one's company, perhaps to follow one's own uncharted path – they are collectively serving to undermine the structure of postwar Japan. What remains to be seen is the effect of this undermining. Will these young people who have remained outside *shūshoku katsudō* turn out to have been unwitting revolutionaries thirty years from now? Or will they simply be sad losers? Only the future will tell.

Notes

1 I thank Shimomura Yumiko, Shingai Motoko, and especially Takamura Kazue for their great help in locating interviewees and transcribing interviews in the 1999 to 2000 research, which was funded through the Tokyo University of Foreign Studies. I thank Takamura Kazue and Shitakubo Minako for their help in locating interviewees in the 2002 research, which was funded through a Summer Grant from the Faculty of Social Science, the Chinese University of Hong Kong. This chapter has benefited from the critical readings given it by S. Kotani and L. Nakano.

2 This timing has been regulated by government bureaucrats, in consultation with company personnel departments and educators, to ensure that companies do not "jump the gun" and hire too early, thus obtaining unfair advantage. However, this system has had problems, since it is not in companies' best interests to adhere to it (see Ōkubo 2002: 42–5).

3 Japanese bookstores offer dozens of volumes guiding their young readers through the perils of *shūshoku katsudō*. See, for example, Shūshoku sōgō kenkyūjo (2002), a manual advising its readers down to the exact details of "how to present yourself in the photograph you include in your CV" and "how to answer interview questions such as 'what's your favorite word?'"

4 Between 1990 and 2000, the number of secondary school graduates newly employed in regular jobs has declined from 622,000 to 242,000. During the same period, the number of newly employed university graduates has declined only slightly, from 324,000 to 301,000 (*Asahi Shinbun* 2002: 104). Rates of university enrolment have greatly increased in this period, from about 25 percent of the relevant age cohort in 1990 to almost 40 percent in 2000, with another 12 to 14 percent in junior colleges or technical schools (*Asahi Shinbun* 2002: 248), as both effect and cause of the loss of regular employment opportunities for secondary school graduates. See Ōkubo (2002: 24–41) on the collapse of the labor market for secondary school graduates.

5 Although the unemployment rate in Japan is highest for those in their twenties, Japanese mass media attention is overwhelmingly focused on men in their forties and fifties who lose their jobs. This is because (1) these older men tend to have

families to support, as young people, who often still live with their parents, do not, and (2) young people can readily find temporary work, as their elders generally cannot. Thus the problem of the latter is of immediate societal concern.

6 *Furiitaa* is a term combining the English word "free" and the German word "*arbeit*," "part-time work"; it was coined in 1987. *Furiitaa* have been defined by the Ministry of Health and Welfare's 2000 White Paper on Labor as "those aged 15–34 who are engaged in part-time or non-regular employment. For those who are now employed, it includes men who have been continuously working for less than five years, and for women, those who are not yet married. For those who are not now employed, *furiita* are those who are not in school, or who are not taking care of housework, and who are looking for part-time or non-regular employment" (Majima 2002: 13). This definition is bound by categories of gender and age: when a person becomes 34, when a man has been working for five years, or when a woman gets married, these people are no longer considered *furiitaa*, but simply part-time workers. A more inclusive conception of *furiitaa* puts their number at four or even six million (Majima 2002: 16).

7 Assessing how much Japanese employment practices are in transformation, Holzhausen writes that "although the seniority rule is further losing its influence on promotion and wage decisions … the core of the Japanese employment system, i.e., the long-term development of human capital *inside* the firm, is not yet subject to change" (2000: 221).

8 There are two tracks of employment for women in Japanese companies: *ippanshoku*, or "general work," the clerical duties of the "office lady," and *sōgōshoku*, career-track work indistinguishable in theory from that of men. The women we interviewed in the latter group seemed as disillusioned as women in the former group. To some extent, this was because even though these women were formally in the same position as men, they often continued to be treated differently from men in the company.

9 The largely seniority-based pay of "lifetime employment" is structured so that new employees are paid comparatively little, but their salary climbs as they become older, reaching a peak in their fifties. Thus, in the short term, working as a *furiitaa* may sometimes be as lucrative as being a regular employee. However, after a few years *furiitaa* earn only a fraction of their regularly employed counterparts' salaries.

10 A 1991 survey asked a range of company workers "To which do you give first priority when home needs and company needs conflict?"; over 80 percent indicated "the company" (Takanashi *et al.* 1999: 103).

11 Kotani (personal communication) has provided an interesting explanation for why *furiitaa* are happier than regular company workers: "*furiitaa* are beggars, but *seishain* [regular company employees] are slaves." *Furiitaa* snap up any temporary jobs that are available for minimal wages, but they are free, unlike regular company employees, who must wholly surrender themselves to their companies.

References

Aera (2002) "Shinai, sasenai, furiitaa" ["I won't become a *furiitaa*/we won't let you become a *furiitaa*"], Advertisement for Hannan University, November 18.

Arai, K. (1997) *Shūshin koyōsei to nihon bunka: gēmuronteki apurōchi* [Lifetime employment and Japanese culture: an approach from game theory], Tokyo: Chūō Kōronsha.

Asahi Evening News (2000) "Report Details Job Crisis," June 28.

Asahi Shinbun (1999) "Rishokuritsu: 'sannen inai' ga fueru" ["The rate at which young people quit their work within three years is increasing"], November 6.

—— (2002) *Asahi Shinbun Japan Almanac 2002*, Tokyo: Asahi Shinbun.

Clark, R. (1987) *The Japanese Company*, Tokyo: Charles E. Tuttle. Reprint of (1979) New Haven: Yale University Press.

Economist, The (1999) "Survey: Business in Japan," November 27.

Efron, S. (2000) "Stress Exacting Harsh Toll on Corporate Warriors," *Japan Times,* May 30.

Furiitaa kenkyūkai [Temporary Workers' Research Group] (ed.) (2001) *Furiitaa ga wakaru hon!* [A book for understanding temporary workers], Tokyo: Sūken Shūppansha.

Gakken (ed.) (2001) *Furiitaa: naze? dō suru? [Furiitaa*: Why? What should we do?], Tokyo: Gakushū Kenkyūsha.

Genda, Y. (2001) *Shigoto no naka no aimai na fuan* [The vague uneasiness of work], Tokyo: Chūō Kōron Shinsha.

Holzhausen, A. (2000) "Japanese Employment Practices in Transition: Promotion Policy and Compensation Systems in the 1990s," *Social Science Japan Journal* 3(2): 221–35.

Japan Information Network (2002). Online, <http://www.jinjapan.org/stat/stats/09LAB33.html>.

Japan Times (2002a) "Narrow the Wage Gap," editorial. Online, <http://www.japantimes. co.jp> (accessed July 12).

—— (2002b) "Japanese Workers Least Loyal To Firms, Survey Discovers." Online, <http://www.japantimes.co.jp> (accessed September 5).

Kaneko, M. (2002) *Shitte toku suru furiitaa dokuhon* [A *furiitaa* reader], Tokyo: Akashi Shoten.

Kugisaki, K. (2002) *Shūshoku: kimi wa dekiru ka?* [Can you succeed in finding a career-track job?], Tokyo: Saizusha.

Lehmann, J. P. (2002) "Gerontocracy and Its Perks Sap Resources," *Japan Times.* Online, <http://www.japantimes.co.jp> (accessed April 22).

Majima, S. (2002) *Hataraku furiitaa otasuke gaido* [A guide for working *furiitaa*], Tokyo: Nihon Jitsugyō Shuppansha.

Mathews, G. (1996) *What Makes Life Worth Living? How Japanese and Americans Make Sense of Their Worlds,* Berkeley: University of California Press.

Ōkubo, Y. (ed.) (2002) *Shinsotsu mugyō* [New graduates, no work], Tokyo: Tōyō Keizai Shinpōsha.

Rohlen, T. (1974) *For Harmony and Strength: Japanese White-Collar Organization in Anthropological Perspective*, Berkeley: University of California Press.

Satō, H. (2001) "Atypical Employment: A Source of Flexible Work Opportunities?," *Social Science Japan Journal* 4(2): 161–82.

Sekine, S. (2002) *Sarariiman daidassō no susume* [A recommendation for escaping the salaryman's life], Tokyo: Nikkei BPsha.

Shūshoku sōgō kenkyūjo (2002) *Shūshoku no akahon* [A manual for finding career-track employment], Tokyo: Goma Books.

Takanashi, A. *et al.* (1999) *Japanese Employment Practices*, Japanese Economy & Labor Series, no. 4, Tokyo: Japan Institute of Labour.

Vogel, E. F. (1980) *Japan As Number One: Lessons for America*, Tokyo: Charles Tuttle.

Yamada, M. (1999) *Parasaito shinguru no jidai* [The age of "parasite singles"], Tokyo: Chikuma Shobō.

—— (2001a) "Parasite Singles Feed on Family System," *Japan Quarterly*, January–March.

—— (2001b) "No Future for Freeters," *Japan Echo*, October.

Yamada, S. (2002) *Nihon keizai nyūmon* [An introduction to the Japanese economy], Tokyo: Tōyō Keizai Shinpōsha.

Yamada, Y. (1999) *"Kaisha" yori mo "jibun" ga katsu ikikata* [How to live so that you win out over your company], Tokyo: KK Besutoserā.

8 Mothers and their unmarried daughters

An intimate look at generational change[1]

Lynne Nakano and Moeko Wagatsuma

Introduction

The rising age of marriage has inspired widespread public commentary about the generation of women in their twenties and thirties who are said to be free, selfish, and reluctant to marry. Media representations paint a generation gap between these women and their family-oriented, responsible mothers in their fifties and sixties. This view of generational difference is widespread, although surveys show that the shift to later marriages has been gradual – the average age of first marriage for women has risen from 24.7 in 1975 to 27.0 in 2000 (Ministry of Health and Welfare 2000) – and the overwhelming majority of women (89.1 percent according to a 1997 survey) want to marry (National Institute of Population and Social Security Research 1999).

In this chapter, we consider generational change from the perspectives of unmarried women in their twenties and thirties and their mothers in their fifties and sixties. Drawing upon developments in feminist studies that have explored social life – particularly the reproduction of class inequalities – through the intimate relationships of family life (see Stacey 1990; Ortner 1998), we suggest that a close reading of family relationships reveals some of the ways in which people experience generational differences in Japan today. What generational conflicts separate mothers and daughters? What do mothers and daughters have in common? How do changing social contexts play out in the intimate spaces of mother-daughter relationships? We first examine how the media has discussed young, unmarried women and their transition to marriage. In Japan, as in other places, the media powerfully shape ideas and opinions. Generational differences experienced in everyday life cannot be understood apart from the ways in which such differences are articulated in public debates – although they also, of course, transcend such debates.

Public images: young women as free and selfish

Delayed marriage emerged as a social problem in the early 1990s when it became linked, in state-sponsored research, to the declining birth rate. The Economic Planning Agency chose low fertility (*shōshika*) as the theme of its 1992 White Paper on People's Lifestyles, and identified delayed marriage (*bankonka*) and non-marriage (*hikonka*) as the main causes of the trend. By the mid-1990s, social commentators warned that fewer children combined with the rapid aging of society could trigger a crisis in the social welfare system. State planners have thus viewed delayed marriage as a negative development that threatens the future of society.

Social anxiety about whether young, middle-class women will eventually submit to the nuclear family as wives and mothers is not new. In the 1980s, the media coined the term "*dokushin kizoku*," or the aristocracy of the unmarried, to describe urban, unmarried people who purchased luxury goods, traveled, and preferred to rent apartments rather than invest in condominiums. In the 1990s, media attention continues to focus on unmarried women's wealth, consumer power, and freedoms – to date and have sex, travel, live where they please, and choose not to marry.

The media and an expanding consumer sector have meanwhile celebrated women's life choices and self-oriented consumption. The women's magazine industry that has emerged since the 1970s urges young women to exercise fully their choices at work, in romantic relationships and in consumption. Magazines articulate the choices available and provide examples of women who have benefited from career and consumer opportunities in Japan and overseas. ALC, a company known for its language learning-related businesses, publishes *Chance*, a magazine that provides information for women interested in studying or working abroad. The magazine encourages women to pursue their dreams, as in the following captions showing attractive unmarried women in glamorous overseas locations such as Paris and Los Angeles:

> "I have the courage to do what I want because I don't want to look upon myself with regret later on."

> "To attain a more authentic self, I'll keep pursuing what I want."
>
> (*Chance* 2001)

Women's magazines encourage women to "live for themselves" (*jibun rashiku ikiru*) rather than follow convention. State policies since the 1980s have also encouraged the trend toward self-realization (*jiko jitsugen*) and diverse lifestyles (*raifusutairu no tayōka*). The White Paper on People's Lifestyles, known for articulating recent trends, urged in 1995 that society move toward "diverse lifestyles that allow us to live fully" (*yutakasa o jikkan dekiruyō na tayōna ikikata*) (Economic Planning Agency 1995). The idea that one may marry at one's own pace or decide not to marry occurs within this larger context.

As marriage is expressed increasingly in public discussion as a woman's choice rather than a social obligation, conservative commentators have attached moral weight to the decision to marry, with marriage and reproduction being the "morally correct" option. Conservative commentators have used sociologist Yamada's popular book, *Parasaito shinguru no jidai* [The age of parasite singles] (1999), for example, to argue that unmarried people are endangering Japan's future by refusing to accept the adult responsibilities of marriage and family while engaging in a culture of dependence on their parents, conspicuous consumption, and selfish materialism. In contrast to the 1970s and 1980s when moral anxiety coalesced in women's sexual behavior (with conservative observers criticizing married women for having affairs and unmarried women for reportedly having sex freely, particularly with foreigners), since the mid-1990s morality has been tied to the decision to enter into the marital relationship itself.

Magazines have published stories suggesting that unmarried women's mothers also bear responsibility for the delayed marriage trend because they support their daughters' single lifestyle. Recent reports accuse mothers of wanting vicariously to enjoy their daughters' career successes and glamorous lives. An article in the national magazine *Aera* entitled *"Haha wa gūtara musume o suterarenai"* (mothers can't let go of their lazy daughters) featured stories of mothers who pamper their unmarried daughters by cooking their meals, cleaning their rooms, and washing their clothes (Ono 1999).

The moral tone of recent debates has evoked moral counter-arguments. Unmarried women writers have deflected accusations of selfishness by arguing that they are working at their careers and caring for their parents. Sarada (1998) notes that unmarried daughters can become a source of security for their parents as they age. Haruka (2002) argues that unmarried women's lives are not necessarily full of enjoyment and freedom. She describes her experiences of caring for her ailing father while managing her career and trying unsuccessfully to maintain a romantic relationship. Some mainstream mass media have argued that women are living as best they can at their own pace. An *Aera* special issue entitled *"Onna wa watashi de ikiru"* (Women live for themselves) (*Aera tokubetsu henshū for women* 1999) introduces unmarried women's stories sympathetically, explaining that the women are trying to live meaningfully according to their own principles rather than merely "enjoying freedoms."

The themes outlined above, of a woman's right to personal choice combined with criticisms of selfishness, reappear in the mothers' and daughters' narratives we collected from our interviews. These themes formed the discursive context in which mothers and daughters negotiated generational and personal differences. Central to these inter-generational negotiations is the institution of marriage.

Changing meanings of marriage

National surveys show that women want to marry but a growing majority do not believe that marriage is necessary.[2] Tsuya argues that the institution of marriage does not adequately meet women's needs, as it forces women to carry out domestic chores in addition to paid work. Marriage delay, she suggests, reflects young women's growing ability to control their own lives (2000: 319).

The decline of marriage as a central feature of women's life strategies is also a product of larger social and economic changes. From the 1950s through the mid-1970s, when the mothers in this study were starting families, women achieved middle-class status by making a "good marriage," understood to mean marrying a man with a stable income and salaried job. In the economic recession of the 1990s, however, corporations have been less able to support such families. Ochiai (1994) states that women who married between 1950 and the mid-1970s created the "postwar family system" (*kazoku no sengo taisei*) consisting of families with full-time housewives and few children. She argues that this system is a product of peculiar demographic and economic conditions; namely a large population of young people and a rapidly growing economy. She suggests that in the period of low economic growth beginning in the mid-1970s, young people cannot hope to imitate the marital choices of their parents (1994: 86–7, 202–4). In explaining why young women are delaying marriage, Yamada (1996) argues that because of the difficulties of finding a man capable of providing a lifestyle equivalent to that enjoyed by their mothers due to Japan's economic straits, and with rising expectations of finding love and sexual attractiveness in partners due to the growth of a dating culture, many women are unable to find a man who meets their demands.

As women have gained greater occupational, educational, and marital choices, marriage is no longer the only route to middle-class status and some question whether "middle class" has any meaning for young people at all (see Sato 2000). Marriage has become less important for women's social mobility and economic viability but currently there is no consensus on what constitutes a good life for women.[3] Consequently mothers and daughters were interested in talking about competing approaches to living well.

Mothers and daughters

We interviewed fifty-nine women between the ages of 20 and 65 in 2000 to 2002 and have selected three mother–daughter pairs to feature here.[4] We do not claim that these women represent their generation; we believe that every person represents only herself. However, we have selected six women with diverse experiences and whose narratives nonetheless resonate with those of other women we met. All three pairs would be considered "middle class" by most people and all lived in the Tokyo metropolitan area. Selecting women from Tokyo is appropriate because the city is the center of a vibrant singles' popular culture. The daughters have a variety of educational qualifications: one is a high school graduate, one has a degree from a technical school, and one is a university graduate. Of the mothers, two have qualifications beyond high school and one has a university degree. One mother grew up in Tokyo and two moved to the city as adults. One mother considers herself a businesswoman while the other two see themselves as housewives even as all three have both work and domestic experience.

We introduce their stories in detail because we believe that analyses of lived experience serve as a corrective to studies that rely entirely on statistics and surveys. In-depth interviews that explore discursive interpretations of generational difference provide an alternative means of understanding how generations experience conflict and change.

Aiko and Keiko

> *A pastor's wife*: "I've never regretted this marriage."
> *Daughter*: "If my mom's okay with [her marriage], then I can't say anything, but I don't think it's fair."
>
> Kodama Aiko (65), Kodama Keiko (28)[5]

Aiko has been a professional housewife for forty years. As a young woman, she wanted to have a career but gave it up to marry a pastor. Keiko, her youngest daughter, became a social worker after graduating from university; she lives with her parents. Mother and daughter are on good terms, yet Keiko is anxious to become independent of her parents. She would like to marry but does not want a marriage like that of her parents.

Aiko obtained the qualification needed to teach kindergarten, but gave up her career to support her husband upon the request of her future father-in-law. Aiko explains, "Without thinking of economic stability, I married him without giving it serious thought." She has not regretted marrying, yet admits she has made sacrifices:

> "When I was young, women's happiness was in marriage, but today, I think only part of our happiness comes from marriage. In marriage, women have given up many things including their individual dreams."

Aiko has contradictory hopes for her daughter. She wants Keiko to be economically independent, yet not so self-reliant that she would lose interest in spending time with her mother. Aiko has encouraged Keiko to acquire some sort of professional qualification that would insure she could make ends meet, yet Aiko also enjoys seeing Keiko pursue her less practical interests. She financed Keiko's foray into art school, for example, in spite of her husband's opposition.

Keiko admires her parents' closeness but views their relationship critically. When Keiko's paternal grandmother fell ill, Keiko's father announced that as the eldest son, he would look after her. In practice, however, the caregiving duties fell entirely upon Aiko. Although seeing her mother care for her grandmother inspired Keiko to study social welfare, she felt that her mother unfairly ended up doing all the work. Keiko explains:

> "My dad says, 'You should do things in your own way,' but my mom ends up doing the work. And when my dad says, 'No,' it's 'No,' and 'Yes,' it's 'Yes.' He makes the decisions and my mom has to follow.... This is what I don't like about my parents' generation – their gender relationship (*danjokan*). If my mom's okay with it, I can't say anything, but I don't think it's fair."

Just as Aiko gave up her career to marry, Keiko was convinced by her parents to give up her plans to study art. She described how her father persuaded her to study social welfare instead:

> "My dad said, 'I don't know whether you're really serious about art, but it would be hard to make a living and you wouldn't be able to enjoy your life. If you want to draw as a hobby, that's fine, but it would be better to have some sort of [professional] qualification.' That persuaded me to change my plans."

After working at a social welfare center and living away from home for four years, Keiko decided to quit and enroll in a vocational school of illustration: "I told my parents, 'Before getting married, I'm going to do what I want.'" After studying at the school, however, Keiko realized that she was not suited to such work. She returned to social work after completing the art course. Now living with her parents again, she wants greater distance from them, explaining that she has become overly dependent upon them.

Keiko has decided to move out of her parents' home and rent an apartment. She has a new boyfriend whom she would like to marry although he earns less than she does. Keiko wants to marry to please her parents: "In getting married, I'll be taking my parents' feelings into consideration. Just living together as a couple would be fine, but I think that understanding my parents' feelings is also a part of happiness."

Analysis

Aiko's and Keiko's choices as young women were shaped by the social and economic contexts of their times. Keiko, for example, could delay making a commitment to marriage or to a specific career knowing that she could return to her parents' home if she ran low on funds. She was able to change careers with her mother's financial support. Such an option was not available to Aiko. In other words, a smaller family, wealthier parents, and greater educational and work opportunities for women gave Keiko more choices than her mother had had at the same age. Keiko seems to fit the profile of the "parasite single" described by Yamada (1999), yet living with her parents was not a lifestyle of pampering as his book suggests. Rather, it made Keiko aware of her differences with her parents and reaffirmed her determination to become independent of them.

Keiko's conflict with her parents was based on their different life course perspectives, with the older generation encouraging the younger to make prudent choices. Changing historical circumstances, however, created different kinds of choices for mother and daughter. Aiko chose between having a career and supporting her husband's career. Keiko chose between different kinds of careers measured according to conflicting standards of job security and personal interest. Keiko's main concerns involved work rather than marriage. This perspective is reflected in surveys indicating that the number of women who want to become full-time housewives has fallen to 20 percent, with the majority wanting to work regardless of whether they marry.[6] This conflict also shows that Keiko is not the sole agent of social change. Her parents, even more than Keiko, want her to pursue a career.

Keiko expressed her desires through public discourses ("I'm going to do what I want") that were not available to her mother's generation. She had access to these forms of expression because she saw herself as part of a generation for whom choice and assertion of personal will are allowed and perhaps expected. Her mother may feel equally inclined to "do what she wants," but such talk is seen as inappropriate for women of her generation. We suspect that these discourses of individual choice will remain with women of Keiko's generation as they proceed through their life course.

Hiroko and Mio

> *A working mother*: "I thought, 'That's the way things are.'"
> *Daughter*: "I enjoy having time to myself."
>
> Fukuda Hiroko (57), Fukuda Mio (23)

Hiroko works at a small printing company and looks after her mother at home. Her daughter, Mio, a high school graduate and the youngest of her four children, works as a "contract staff"[7] for a computer customer service firm. Mio says she feels little pressure from her parents. They approve of her relationship with her boyfriend whom she is thinking of marrying. Hiroko's husband is uninterested in family matters, but Hiroko hopes that her daughter will marry a man who will participate in family life.

Hiroko met her husband while working as an "office lady." At the time of her marriage, she said she had not fully considered a woman's choices in life.

> "When I was in my twenties ... if you worked at one place for a few years, people asked, 'When are you getting married?' or 'Do you have a boyfriend?' I'm not sure whether by that time I'd already given up [other plans], but there was [an understanding] that that's the way things were."

Hiroko's husband told her before they married that family is of "least importance" to him. Hiroko accepted this at the time, but in thirty years of marriage she has come to understand what he meant:

> "We had four children but he wasn't interested in family at all. He cared about his work, his male buddies and his brothers more than his own family. It was true even with money. He gave his brother money when we hardly had enough [for ourselves].... [In our family] I realized that I'd become an intermediary between my husband and my children. [Finally, I] told them they'd better talk to one another directly."

Hiroko now wonders whether she may be to blame for her husband's emotional distance, because she had never demanded that he give more to his family. She says she would not recommend a person like her husband to her daughters: "A man who's only interested in work is no longer desirable [as a marriage partner]." Mio is accepting of her father, explaining:

> "My father likes to work. That's what interests him and he feels happy when he gets results.... When I was little, I liked him a lot, but when I grew up, he still came home only once a month [due to his business trips].... I've eaten with him only twice so far [with just two of us] in my life! I feel it's too bad [*sugoku zannen desu*]."

Hiroko worries about Mio's job security because Mio did not attend university. She suspects that Mio, aware that her parents were experiencing financial difficulties, decided to start working so her parents would not have to pay for her university education. Mio sees the matter differently, emphasizing her desire to work:

"I'd always dreamed of working at a bakery. At first I thought I'd work there for ten or twenty years but after I started, I felt that four years was enough. I wanted to do ceramic art or computers and I wanted time and money [for myself]."

She recently completed a computer course and has started working at a computer firm. Between jobs and wanting to get away after a breakup with a boyfriend, Mio went to England, her first trip overseas. In England, Mio met her current boyfriend, whom she would like to marry. Mio wants him to be a part of her family. She says:

"I don't think women's happiness is necessarily in marriage. I feel happy meeting people or having my own time.... [After getting married] I definitely want to continue having meals with my husband. If possible, I'd like to do things together on weekends, although we'd still have our own schedules."

In Hiroko's view, the idea of following one's dream prevalent among young women is double-edged:

"I feel envious on the one hand and insecure for them on the other. Young women go after what they want. If they're not satisfied with work, they'll look for something else and I think that it's basically a good attitude. But I worry because a woman should have children if she can, and as she gets older it becomes more difficult."

Hiroko wants her daughters to take advantage of opportunities available to young women and has encouraged all her daughters to move out because she does not want them to share the burden of caring for her mother. She also worries that with too many choices, her daughters may miss the opportunity to marry and have children.

Analysis

Like many women of her generation, Hiroko married without considering other options. She was not bothered that her husband seemed intent on leaving domestic matters to her. Mio's primary concern, however, is the willingness of her future husband to participate in family life. This generational difference is reflected in opinion polls showing that increasing numbers of women want a companion rather than a wage-earner for a husband.[8] These different expectations at marriage, however, did not inspire conflict, as Mio and her mother now agree that a husband today should be a companion. Hiroko's critical reflection upon her marriage is not unusual, as national surveys show that older women feel more dissatisfied with their spouse than those who are younger.[9] Mio's father's lack of interest in family created an inter-generational alliance between mother and daughter, and Hiroko has appropriated some of her daughter's ideals for herself.

Mio's disagreements with her mother emerged from their different positions in the life course. In urging Mio to receive an education, Hiroko took a long-term view of Mio's future based on her greater life experience. As a young person, Mio talked of pursuing her interests. Both women addressed Mio's choices based on their interpretations of young women today. Hiroko wanted Mio to take advantage of opportunities available to young women to receive an education and pursue a career. Mio resisted by explaining that she wanted to realize her dreams. Public discussions of Mio's generation provided the discursive framework that allowed mother and daughter to agree (in their assessment of spousal choices), and differ (in their opinions of how Mio should prepare for her future). These same narratives of generation allowed social change to occur. Based on her understanding of "young women today," for example, Hiroko urged choices in love, work, and education for her daughter that she had not chosen for herself. Public discussion of generation did not determine action for any individual, but made new forms of action thinkable, and therefore possible.

Satoko and Naoko

> *A career woman*: "Being married means being more trustworthy."
> *Daughter*: "I want to be independent from my parents."
> Takagi Satoko (59), Takagi Naoko (31)

Satoko runs her family's pharmacy, passed down to her from her parents, and is married to a retired salaryman. She has made it clear that she wants her daughter to marry a financially stable man. Naoko, the eldest of three daughters, is a vocational school graduate and works as a dietitian at a hospital near her parents' house. After her parents' persistent objection to a former boyfriend whom she had been seeing for ten years, Naoko moved out of their house and says she is satisfied with living alone.

Satoko had been told as a child that she would take over the family business. She had not liked the idea but accepted her fate, and attended university to become a pharmacist. At age 27, through her mother's introduction, Satoko married a salaryman trained as a pharmacist who agreed to move into her family home so that Satoko could run the business. She explained that she married relatively late for the time and said she understood the current trend toward delayed marriage:

> "In high school [I thought] that I'd marry at 24 but when I graduated from university I was 22. In the next two years I was busy with work and didn't have time to think about marriage. So I'd say that a university

graduate wouldn't feel ready to settle down until at least 25. I thought 30 would be about right for me, but by then, most of my friends had married so I guess that's why I did too."

The family's business has declined over the years. The shop that supported two full-time pharmacists when Satoko was a child can no longer support the whole family. Still, Satoko feels satisfied with her life. She explains that although she did not marry for love, it turned out to be good match:

> "Whenever he does something for me, I feel grateful. He's such a nice person. Maybe [I feel this way] because I haven't expected anything from him."

Satoko encouraged her daughters to obtain some sort of professional qualification beyond high school: "When we were young, few women attended university, so my husband didn't think our daughters' education was important. But I thought that from now on, this will be an asset [for women] and we argued about it." Satoko had her way, and all her daughters obtained degrees beyond high school.

Naoko has struggled with her mother's attempts to control her life. She describes her mother as "overprotective" (*kahogo*), recalling that when she was a student, her parents would not allow her to take a part-time job and disapproved of her friends. Naoko sees differences between her own marital ideals and those of her mother:

> "I like a person who has his own views and who can reasonably make ends meet. But my mom likes a man who's ambitious in his work and, for example, wants to have his own shop."

This difference became apparent when Naoko introduced her former boyfriend to her parents:

> "My parents thought he wasn't good enough in terms of his educational level and his work. Also, he didn't make a good first impression.... They didn't like him and I felt that they would never let me marry him."

Naoko explained that despite their efforts, she and her boyfriend could not maintain the relationship and they broke up:

> "My boyfriend's mother knew very well that my mom didn't like him.... I thought it would be hard for us to get married. Also, our financial situations weren't stable and then we just couldn't make up our minds [about marriage]."

Perhaps in the belief that a pharmacist husband able to take over the family business would be an appropriate match for Naoko, Satoko suggested several arranged meetings (*omiai*), but Naoko refused. For the past year, Naoko has been living alone in a rented apartment. She is dating a new boyfriend and is relieved that her parents are not opposed to him.

Analysis

Naoko and Satoko both made life choices according to their parents' expectations. Satoko agreed to take over the family pharmacy and marry a man chosen by her parents, and Naoko became a dietitian and broke up with her boyfriend according to her parents' wishes. In retrospect, Satoko appreciates the guidance she received from her parents and similarly attempts to influence her daughter's life. Their conflict was based on their different positions in the life course, since both complained about parental interference as young women. Yet Naoko has had more room to maneuver than her mother had when she was young. Unlike her mother, Naoko refuses to meet men introduced by her parents and has insisted on choosing boyfriends for herself. In addition, Naoko was able to move out of her parents' home to escape their influence. Greater work opportunities and acceptance of diverse living situations for women have allowed Naoko a measure of freedom beyond that experienced by her mother.

Mother and daughter disagreed over the meaning of marriage. Satoko wanted her daughter to marry a man who could provide a financially secure life. Naoko, however, wants to marry a man whom she can respect as a person. Unlike current discourses that see young women as free from constraints, however, Naoko has compromised on her marital choices according to her parents' wishes. Naoko's marriage has been delayed, not because of her personal agenda, but due to parental pressure.

This conflict may be read in several ways. It is grounded in the family's particular socio-economic class standing. Naoko's wish to live as she chooses conflicts with her mother's upper-middle-class aspirations and hopes that one of her children will carry on the family business. Naoko's refusal to follow her parents' wishes may result in a class downgrading and the loss of the family business. Their views of class reproduction emerge from their positions in the life course. As young women, neither was interested in reproducing their family's class position. As a mature woman, however, Satoko has invested much of her life into maintaining the family business, and feels that she would be letting down her parents if the business ends with her generation.

The family's declining class status reflects historical changes such as the erosion of a class of small shopkeepers in the 1970s and 1980s and of salaryman positions in the 1990s. The conflict is also rooted in competing interpretations of what constitutes young womanhood. Satoko explains that marriage can be delayed to allow young women to establish a career and achieve financial stability. Naoko argues that ambition and security are no longer appropriate standards in choosing spouses. Even in their disagreement, both generations speak in a common public language about what it means to be a young woman today.

Discussion

This study of the discursive conflicts between mothers and daughters in the intimate arena of family life reveals that one generation did not impose its will so easily on another in the interest of either stasis or change. Rather, social changes occurred in complex ways through negotiations between generations. Mothers and daughters both had a stake in reproducing past values and in investing in strategies to face the future. These stories show that the young should not simply be cast as representatives of the future with their parents assigned the role of vestiges of the past. In negotiations between generations, young people made decisions that generated social changes even as they reproduced their parents' values. Their parents tried to impress their values upon their children, even as they too grappled with the historical changes that were shaping society in the present.

Our study shows that young women had many more choices than their mothers had had at the same age. Unlike their mothers, the daughters had had more than one serious boyfriend, and a variety of educational and career options; they could rely on their parents for financial assistance and a place to live. In this sense, young women are the beneficiaries of social and economic changes that have occurred in the thirty years since their mothers married. The increased wealth of society, as well as smaller households, allows families to provide economic and psychological protection for their daughters. The changing job market and rising educational standards have encouraged women's labor force participation and have increased women's power to decide for themselves where and how to live. The rise of a consumer sector targeting women encourages women to view these choices positively.

Young women also faced greater insecurities than did their mothers. Their mothers married with expectations that their lives would improve materially over time. Their daughters faced greater risks, as full-time positions for women are becoming scarce, and as marriage too is less able to guarantee an improved material life. Sato (2000) argues that until the mid-1980s, people believed that if they worked hard enough they could become "middle class," but says that young today people feel that there are no guarantees of success.

As both mothers and daughters believe that marriage is no longer the only means to achieve social status and security for women, generational conflict emerged over how daughters should secure their futures. Mothers and daughters debated and disagreed over daughters' choices regarding education, jobs, potential marriage partners, and housing. Generational conflicts did not involve daughters wanting to devote themselves to leisure and career while mothers pushed them to marry. Rather, the conflicts involved, more abstractly, different interpretations of what was necessary for women to live well in a changing society.

This said, mothers and daughters often had different interpretations of how to live well. Regarding potential marriage partners, daughters said nearly unanimously that they wanted a man who would make a good companion while their mothers had mixed views. Some talked about emotional compatibility, but many whom we interviewed said that the ideal spouse should provide a financially secure life for their daughters. A similar conflict arose over educational and career choices. Daughters talked about "self-improvement" and "doing what I want," while their mothers urged more economically and socially secure choices. Are these conflicts a result of life-course positions or historical changes in society? We suggest that it is both. Young women fighting with their parents over the lover of their choice is certainly nothing new. Yet generational conflict is also a site of social change in Japan because it occurs through current discourses urging women to marry for love, to take risks, to improve themselves, and to choose jobs that will allow them to develop their potential. It is only through these recent public discourses that the women's actions become intelligible to themselves and to those around them. These emergent narratives celebrating choice were not available to the mothers in their youth. We suspect that young women today will continue to expect to have choices as they proceed through the life course.

A close look at family relationships shows that social change occurs in unpredictable ways. Change does not arise only from young people making decisions different from those of their parents. Change may also occur because young people make the same decisions as did their parents, but in different historical circumstances. Mother and daughter, for example, Aiko and Keiko, both followed the advice of the older generation. Being an obedient young woman for Aiko meant that she became a full-time housewife. For Keiko, obeying her parents meant that she was an unmarried 28-year-old who lived with her parents and had a career. Change may occur even when the older generation acts to reproduce the past. Satoko, in an effort to reproduce her upper-middle-class position, encouraged her daughter to delay marriage until she found a man capable of providing her with this status. This move to preserve social status ironically contributes to the trends toward delayed marriage, fewer children, and greater career prospects for young women. Change may also arise because the older generation, rather than the young, embrace new values. Hiroko encouraged her daughter to attend university, pursue a career, and choose a man committed to family, choices she had not made for herself.

Having grown up in relative comfort, the daughters we interviewed were not worried about maintaining and improving their social status. Their mothers, on the other hand, were members of a generation that expected and experienced continued material improvement. Parents were willing to provide financial support to ensure that their daughters would enjoy a similar life (see Miyamoto *et al.* 1997; Tsuya 2000), a willingness to help which was grounded in their desire to secure their daughters' futures in an insecure society. Ortner (1998) makes a similar argument in explaining why "Generation X" parents in the United States are willing to support their "slacker" children in an economy that no longer guarantees the class reproduction of all middle-class children.

Although changing class, economic, and demographic structures in Japan are important in understanding mothers' perspectives, these structural factors do not explain young women's hesitance to embrace the middle-class lifestyles of their parents. Here it is useful to consider the ways in which public media, in an active relationship with the women themselves, define young women as part of a generational cohort. As we have seen, public discussion constructs the generation of women in their twenties and thirties as free to explore a wealth of choices. Young women are urged in public discourse to choose a lover and a job that meets their expectations. The idea that young women should rightfully have choices profoundly influenced both mothers and daughters. In practice, young women may have more limited and modest choices than the media declared; yet mothers and daughters believed strongly that the younger generation is entitled to a range of choices. This belief made new choices imaginable, possible, and desirable.

Conflicts between mothers and daughters were shaped by personalities, changing socio-economic class status, experience, relationships within the family, and the ambitions and educational levels of family members. Nonetheless, mothers and daughters expressed conflict in terms of currently popular discussions of generational differences. Mothers expressed their concerns over young women's selfishness, freedom, and casual view of marriage even as they wanted their daughters to have choices in work, leisure, and marriage. Daughters emphasized the importance of making independent choices even as they were concerned to respect their parents' wishes. Mothers and daughters negotiated choices within a discursive framework that emphasized women's freedom of choice and familial responsibility. In this sense, public discussion of the generation gap did appear in women's lives. It provided the discursive material through which mothers and daughters made sense of their relationship and their place in the world.

Notes

1 The research was made possible by a 2001 Summer Grant for Research and a 2001 to 2002 Direct Grant awarded to Lynne Nakano by the Chinese University

of Hong Kong. We thank the Department of Japanese Studies and the Cultural Relations and Identities in East Asia Programme of the Hong Kong Institute of Asia-Pacific Studies, both of the Chinese University of Hong Kong, for their support.

2 According to a 1998 survey, 65 percent of women chose "people need not marry" over "people should marry." Over 80 percent of women and about 70 percent of men under age 40 believe that "people need not marry" (NHK hōsō bunka kenkyūjo 2000: 32–3).

3 A 1997 survey of unmarried women found that 20.6 percent wish to become full-time housewives, 34.3 percent want to stop work temporarily and return later and, 27.2 percent wish to work throughout their married life (National Institute of Population and Social Security Research 1999: 70).

4 We interviewed mothers and daughters separately to elicit their views of one another.

5 All names given are pseudonyms and some details of the informants' biographies have been slightly altered to preserve their anonymity.

6 A 1997 National Institute of Population and Social Security Research found that over 60 percent of unmarried women intend to work after marriage (1999: 70).

7 "Contract staff" are generally not provided with substantial benefits.

8 In the past two decades, social reasons for marrying such as "to fulfill my parents' expectations" and "to gain the respect of society" have fallen in surveys, while emotional reasons have risen. In a 1997 survey, the most common reason women gave for wanting to marry was "to have a place of spiritual comfort" (National Institute of Population and Social Security Research 1999).

9 An Economic Planning Agency survey found that at age 40, 56 percent of women say their spouse is the person with whom they feel most comfortable and who understands them best. Only 35 percent of married 70-year-old women make this claim (Group Rim 1994: 203).

References

Aera tokubetsu henshū for women (1999) *Onna wa watashi de ikiru* [Women live for themselves], March 20.

Chance: *Kaigai de manabu, hataraku, kurasu tame no yume jitsugen magajin* (2001) [*Chance*: the magazine for actualizing dreams of studying, working and living overseas], June.

Economic Planning Agency (1992) *Heisei 4-nen kokumin seikatsu hakusho* [1992 White Paper on People's Lifestyles], Tokyo: Keizai Kikakuchō.

—— (1995) *Heisei 7-nen kokumin seikatsu hakusho* [1995 White Paper on People's Lifestyles], Tokyo: Keizai Kikakuchō.

Group Rim (1994) *Kekkon shimasu, kekkon shimasen* [I will marry, I won't marry], Tokyo: NTT Publishing Company.

Haruka, Y. (2002) *Kaigo to ren'ai* [Elder care and romantic love], Tokyo: Chikuma Shobō.

Ministry of Health and Welfare (2000) "Heisei 12-nen jinkō dōtai tōkei geppō nenkei (gaisū): kon'in" ["2000 Population statistics: marriage"]. Online, <http://www.mhlw.go.jp/toukei/saikin/hw/jinkou/geppo/nengai00/marr.html> (accessed December 18 2002).

Miyamoto, M., Iwakami, M. and Yamada, M. (1997) *Mikonka shakai no oyako kankei – okane to aijō ni miru kazoku no yukue* [Parent-child relationships in a late-marrying society – future of family with reference to money and love], Tokyo: Yūhikaku.

National Institute of Population and Social Security Research (ed.) (1999) *Dokushin seinensō no kekkonkan to kodomokan: heisei 9-nen: dai 11-kai shussei dōkō kihon chōsa, dai II hōkokusho* [Basic survey on birth 1997, second report, "Views on marriage and children of unmarried youth"], Tokyo: Kōsei Tōkei Kyōkai.

NHK hōsō bunka kenkyūjo (ed.) (2000) *Gendai nihonjin no ishiki kōzō dai 5-han* [Surveys on views of contemporary Japanese, 5th edn], Tokyo: NHK Shuppan.

Ochiai, E. (1994) *21-seiki kazoku e* [Toward a twenty-first century family], Tokyo: Yūhikaku.

Ono, S. (1999) "Haha wa gūtara musume o suterarenai" ["Mothers can't let go of their lazy daughters"], *Aera*, May 24.

Ortner, S. B. (1998) "Generation X: Anthropology in a Media-Saturated World," *Cultural Anthropology* 13(3): 414–40.

Sarada, T. (1998) *Parasaito shinguru* [Parasite single], Tokyo: Wave Shuppan.

Sato, T. (2000) *Fubyōdō shakai nihon: sayonara sōchūryū* [Unequal society Japan: goodbye to all middle classes], Tokyo: Chūō Kōronsha.

Stacey, J. (1990) *Brave New Families: Stories of Domestic Upheaval in Late Twentieth Century America*, New York: Basic Books.

Tsuya, N. (2000) "Women's Empowerment, Marriage Postponement, and Gender Relations in Japan: An Intergenerational Perspective," in H. Presser and G. Sen (eds) *Women's Empowerment and Demographic Processes: Moving Beyond Cairo*, New York: Oxford University Press, pp. 318–48.

Yamada, M. (1996) *Kekkon no shakaigaku* [Sociology of marriage], Tokyo: Maruzen.

—— (1999) *Parasaito shinguru no jidai* [The age of parasite singles], Tokyo: Chikuma Shobō.

9 What happens when they come back

How Japanese young people with foreign university degrees experience the Japanese workplace

Shunta Mori

In recent decades, Japanese returnees with undergraduate degrees from foreign universities have often been scorned as drop-outs from a Japanese career ladder connecting educational and occupational institutions. They have been said to lack proper Japanese socialization. This includes the ability to cooperate with others and to conform to the group, an ability believed to be very important in working for companies and government offices. Returnees were even characterized as a source of contamination of Japanese culture, having acquired the virus of "unJapaneseness" through their educational sojourn overseas. Over the past two decades, however, from the mid-1980s up until now, this situation has been changing. From the mid-1980s up to the early 1990s, returnees were proclaimed to have the abilities necessary for "the internationalization of Japan," the ideological goal of the nation. These abilities, however, were not enough; returnees also had to be able to adapt to Japanese organizational culture, and were rejected if seen as unable to fit in. From the early 1990s on, as economic growth in Japan slowed, the "the internationalization of Japan" faded as an ideological goal. However, the globalization of the Japanese economy has continued, as has the recruitment of returnees. At the same time, younger Japanese have come to feel increasingly ambivalent about maintaining the old Japanese social system, as it has ceased to represent fairly their generational interests. They have come to feel that the system is run by the older generations for the sake of the older generations. In this socio-economic context, returnees from abroad and young Japanese who have not been educated abroad have begun to share similar antagonism toward unchanging Japanese organizational culture and social institutions. Both groups have come to feel disenfranchised and alienated from traditional Japanese management practices such as long-term seniority-based employment.

In this chapter, I describe changes in the social images of returnees in Japan and their relation to the Japanese younger generation.[1] "Returnee" in this study is defined as a Japanese who spent his or her school years (K-12) in the Japanese school system in Japan, and then, having gone overseas and graduated from university, returned to Japan.[2] I will use the Japanese term *ryūgakusei*, meaning "one who studies/studied abroad," almost interchangeably with *returnee*. First, then, let me briefly review the history of study abroad in Japan in order to put the theme of this chapter in a broader context.

The history of studying abroad and returning to Japan up until the mid-1980s

In the Nara period (710–794), studying abroad was a national mission and *ryūgakusei* were elite emissaries to foreign lands, namely China. After that time, until the end of the Tokugawa period (1615–1868), few Japanese left Japan to go overseas. The Tokugawa Shogunate officially banned any contact with foreigners, not to mention going overseas to study. In the final years of the Tokugawa period, despite the official ban, many Japanese went overseas on fact-finding missions sponsored by their clans, during a period in which Japan was undergoing great social transformation. Finally the ban on overseas travel became meaningless, given the changing social circumstances both in and out of Japan. In this context, those who went on fact-finding missions were not perceived as violators of the ban but rather as courageous leaders of the coming new era.

In the Meiji period (1868–1912), *ryūgakusei* were deployed by the national government as elite travelers to seek and learn about Western institutions and technology. The West became the model for modernizing Japan, as is clear from the national slogan of *datsua nyūō*, meaning "Out of Asia, Be a Member of the West." *Ryūgakusei* were at first selected from the established elites, sponsored by the government, and upon their return to Japan, assumed or resumed important jobs. However, as the system of higher education and organizational career paths was established and overseas study become possible for youths of wealthy families on private sponsorship, returnees without powerful contacts in the established system in Japan began to lose their influence. Japanese who used overseas study as an alternative to a Japanese academic career began to be viewed as "drop-outs" from the Japanese system, and from the "proper" path of elite education. These returnees were seen as deviants, regardless of their educational achievement overseas. Bennett, Passin and McKnight, whose work was the first and still one of the most comprehensive studies of Japanese returnees, refer to Japanese students bound for the U.S.A. from the middle Meiji to the early Showa era:

> These "self-sponsored" students had a different outlook from that of the early Meiji overseas students, or that of government-scholarship holders of any period. The early students who had gone to America were in a

sense emissaries of Japan, assigned to learn as much as possible and put it to work on their return. . . . The grantees had every reason to feel that their foreign education would bring them respect and reward from their society. On the other hand, the students without official sponsorship simply took their chances; their foreign study was outside the elite educational channel, which was becoming more and more important as the road to success in public life and career.

(Bennett et al. 1958: 34)

The number of *ryūgakusei*, both officially and privately sponsored, decreased dramatically from around 1940 until 1970 due to war, restriction on overseas travel, and the high cost of overseas study. In the postwar reconstruction era, overseas study was possible only for a limited number of Japanese. Returnees were mostly grantees of foreign, especially American, fellowships such as the Fulbright Scholarship. Recipients of such grants were usually perceived as elite modernizers. But on return to Japan these recipients, unless they were rooted firmly in Japanese society before their sojourn abroad, found employment only on the fringes of society, outside the main channel of elite careers in Japan (Saitō 1984, 1989).[3]

In the late 1970s, overseas study became accessible to Japanese people from ordinary backgrounds. However, the negative image of *ryūgakusei* persisted. Consulting businesses in Japan encouraging overseas study were blamed for creating and taking advantage of "the overseas study boom," and the media claimed this boom to be a "social problem" (*Asahi Shinbun* 1979; Saitō 1979). The study abroad boom was created by drop-outs from Japanese entrance examinations, who sought educational alternatives overseas, as well as by those who wanted to travel overseas under the guise of English-language training programs. At the same time, prestigious scholarships continued to offer study-abroad opportunities to a few selected Japanese, and large companies had begun to send their elite employees to study at graduate schools overseas, especially MBA programs. In short, despite the increase in their numbers, the dichotomy between the elite and the drop-out continued to characterize Japanese *ryūgakusei*.

In explaining the continuing marginality of returnees in contemporary Japan up to the 1980s, I seek to expand on the discussion of Bennet *et al.* (1958), to argue that two institutions are crucial in explaining their marginality: university education and the employment system. Education in Japan has been viewed as a basic mechanism to facilitate meritocratic social mobility and to produce leaders for the nation. This attitude has persisted from the Meiji era throughout the twentieth century. Kitsuse *et al.* (1984: 164) state that "the Japanese educational system. . .is highly standardized and universally perceived as *the* instrument for gaining access to prestigious occupational positions in government and business organizations." Universities in Japan are very finely hierarchically differentiated; scores from achievement tests conducted nationwide are used to rank all institutions of higher education. Entrance into quality schools is possible only by passing a series of examinations throughout schooling, which require memorization of encyclopedic knowledge. Yet, despite this severe competition to enter Japanese universities, the quality of their graduates, including those at the top level, is not considered high by international standards.[4] Given this situation, why did Japanese companies devalue Japanese high school graduates who had foreign university degrees? What was so important about Japanese higher education? What kind of "forbidden fruit" did the *ryūgakusei* eat overseas that made them somehow appear corrupted in Japanese eyes?

Let me present several explanations for this (see Mori 1994: 84–93), explanations particularly valid for the 1980s, but that continue to have a certain, though diminishing, validity today. One explanation is that passing the competitive examination has been seen as evidence of perseverance and effort (*doryoku*), a highly regarded personal trait in Japan. The more competitive an examination, the more respect one would attract for passing it. This notion has been based on the fundamental egalitarian view that anybody can succeed through hard work. Although by its very nature an examination is a win-or-lose competition among individuals, examination-takers were seen as "spiritually" united because they shared a stressful and critical time. In fact, the examination system has been severely criticized in Japan, but nonetheless has been accepted as a relatively fair mechanism by which social opportunity is allocated on the basis of academic effort. I argue that the examination has been a sacred ritual for legitimate social differentiation in Japan. It has been used as a socially accepted criterion of stratification. It has not mattered what and how hard one studied at university. What has mattered most is what school one entered via the sacred ritual of examinations.

A second explanation is that the social experience gained during university years has been regarded as crucial for molding these young people. Through interacting with friends on campus, participating in extra-curricular activities, and working as part-timers at various jobs, students have received a "liberal arts education" outside the classroom. During their secondary school years, they were too busy to have such diverse experiences because they had to concentrate on university entrance examinations; but after entrance to university they were open to such socialization. By joining clubs during their university years, for example, students could develop social skills that formed a basis for human relational skills important at work. In fact, personnel managers of companies favored members of university sport clubs because they were seen as knowing how to work with others in a hierarchical team setting. One personnel manager of a bank said to me in an interview in 1984 that "sports club members are physically tough and spirited. They work well in groups and are easy to use at work."

A third explanation relates to the importance of personal networks based on university affiliations. Although being a graduate of a quality university did not automatically guarantee a prestigious job in a large company, it has provided easier access to such jobs. Up until the 1970s, it was a common practice of large companies to accept applications at the earlier stages of recruitment from a limited number of universities. For personnel managers, graduates of established elite universities were safe and familiar, in that they knew what to expect from them. After all, managers themselves were often alumni of such universities.

Along with different patterns of university education, employment practices have also served to bar returnees from working in large Japanese companies. Many of the personnel managers in large companies I interviewed openly admitted that they expected university graduates to use their alumni network as resources for their business. A manager at a trading company said this in an interview conducted in 1984:

> "Graduates from famous universities have the 'old boy network,' a very important asset to companies. A diploma from an elite university is a passport to a privileged circle of that university's alumni. The bigger a company becomes, the more important its relationship with government bureaucrats. In this context, employees with a powerful university alumni network help companies a lot in doing business."

Beyond this, there was the perceived "individualism" of returnees, for which they were shunned by Japanese personnel managers. Japanese companies, as noted earlier, have educated their employees to be flexible team members who can maintain good relationships with their colleagues. But returnees have been viewed as having individualistic traits that prevented them from being good team members; thus returnees were not seen as able to become part of the "corporate warrior" culture.

Another reason that personnel managers did not want to hire returnees is that companies usually recruit their new employees from fresh university graduates each spring.[5] Each new cohort of employees has gone through corporate training lasting a few weeks or months; those outside this schedule, such as foreign university graduates, would miss such training, which was seen as essential for preserving corporate coherence and harmony. There has also been the salary scale, based largely on age and length of employment; returnees, who were often older, would disrupt this system. A corporate manager spoke to me as follows in 1984:

> "In general, we at Japanese companies would not want to hire overseas returnees and foreigners on a regular basis. This is because we would have to restructure our employment/management system and practices in order to hire them. Restructuring the system costs too much and

generates many problems. If graduates of Japanese universities suffice, we would not actively seek returnees."

For all the above reasons, the employment of returnees from overseas universities was quite restricted in Japanese companies through to the mid-1980s.

The changing images of returnees: the mid-1980s to the 1990s

In the mid-1980s, the so-called bubble economy era, the view of overseas study changed. Overseas study became quite popular as an option for pursuing a university education. Changing circumstances such as the appreciation of the yen in the foreign exchange market and the development of internationalization facilitated this change.[6] Overseas study became an alternative means of gaining educational opportunities. It was more adventurous than going to school in Japan, but was not necessarily stigmatized as much as in the past. The rhetoric of internationalization served to legitimize overseas study by emphasizing the idea that Japan needed to become more linked to the world beyond Japan; returnees, it was said, would play a vital role in this.

In this new situation, many returnees began to secure jobs in Japan, not only with foreign but also with Japanese companies. Quite a few personnel managers whom I interviewed told me that during these years they had employed returnees with good academic backgrounds and serious motivations. In addition, many Japanese companies rushed to expand their business activities overseas, and often such expansion was made possible by returnees. Thus, Japanese companies had begun to recognize that returnees had many useful assets. The advent of returnee recruitment by Japanese companies had a significant impact on the public image of returnees, because the main reason for returnees' rejection in Japan was the negative sanction put in place by Japanese companies. Returnees now had a new label – they were catalysts of internationalization – and this new label replaced their previous labels, as either dropouts or elites. To illustrate the change in media reportage, let me list some headlines of newspaper articles on the employment of returnees:

1987
- March 5   "Mitsui Bank Starts Mid-Career Recruitment: Their Real Target is Returnees" (*Nihon Keizai Shinbun*)
- June 26   "Fukutake Bookstore Corporation Hires U.S. Returnees to Promote Its International Strategies" (*Nihon Keizai Shinbun & Nikkei Sangyō Shinbun*)
- July 14   "Employment Strategies in Japanese Companies Drastically Change: Internationalization Needed – Returnees and Foreigners Targeted" (*Nihon Keizai Shinbun*)

- July 20   "Becoming Global Companies: Internationalization of Human Resources Through Recruiting Returnees" (*Nikkei Sangyō Shinbun*)
- August 15   "Interview with NEC's Personnel Manager ('We have hired 130 *kikokushijo* [see n. 2] and returnees, about 10% of university graduates hired this year. They are needed for internationalizing our operations')" (*Nikkei Sangyō Shinbun*)
- October 8   "Daiwa Bank Actively Begins Hiring Returnees" (*Nikkei Sangyō Shinbun*)

1988
- February 17   "Matsushita Electronics Begins Annual Recruitment of Returnees: Starting with Returnees from the U.S., 10 to 20 to be Recruited Every Year" (*Nihon Keizai Shinbun*)
- March 13   "Nippon Telegraph and Telephone Hires Returnees..." (*Nihon Keizai Shinbun*)
- March 29   "Assisting the Employment of *Ryūgakusei*: A New World in the Field of Employment Expands. Placement Information Magazines are Popular and Other Publishers Follow" (*Nikkei Sangyō Shinbun*)
- April 15   "Motorola-Japan Hires Returnees from the U.S. for Their Language Abilities and Negotiation Skills" (*Nikkei Sangyō Shinbun*)
- April 21   "Shimizu Construction Hires Returnees to Promote its Internationalization" (*Nikkei Sangyō Shinbun*)
- May 4   "Japanese Industries Begin Employing Returnees. Internationalization: The Overseas Experience of Returnees Needed..." (*Nikkei Sangyō Shinbun*)
- May 12   "Returnees can Help Alleviate Trade Conflict with the U.S." (*Nihon Keizai Shinbun*)

This change in attitude toward returnees was apparent in my interviews with personnel managers. A personnel manager of a major city bank spoke in 1986 as follows:

"Given the internationalization of the financial market, we are not sure what will happen in the future. So we want to invest in returnees who have a challenging spirit. Many of them lived alone in a foreign country and have worked hard to graduate, so we think they have potential abilities and strengths to overcome future difficulties."

Despite this shift in attitude, however, internationalization as a national ideological goal did not change the deep-rooted social mores and institutional practices of Japanese companies and organizations. It is true that these had started to crumble, so that returnees were able to enter mainstream workplaces in Japan; but the processes of change were slow and complicated. The most notable new development in the mid-1980s facilitating the employment of returnees was that employment information companies started to distribute journals with job placement advertisements and to organize job fairs outside as well as within Japan. Given the booming Japanese economy and its expansion overseas, there was a labor shortage, making returnees a target for employment. A senior research analyst of a major federation of private industries spoke to me in 1986 as follows:

> "The main reason for hiring returnees has been the lack of skilled labor in Japan. The economy is now booming and more workers are needed, especially in new fields like computer systems engineering and foreign exchange. People who were traditionally excluded from the elite career salaryman market have become eligible, provided that they have the abilities and characteristics needed in these booming fields. These include returnees, those who voluntarily changed their jobs or were pulled out by headhunters, and women who have graduated from four-year Japanese universities."

He continued by saying that when the labor shortage ends, this new demand for returnees would stop because returnees were not the best pick for Japanese companies. He emphasized that "returnees have to have a Japanese identity, Japanese morals, and the ability to work with others in the organization." In other words, while the returnees' image had been transformed from being outcasts to catalysts of internationalization, this "internationalization" did not signify a transformation of Japanese organizational culture, or more broadly, a transformation in Japanese society. Japanese companies still demanded that returnees retain what they saw as a Japanese identity, i.e. possessing the willingness and ability to conform to Japanese organizational culture.

What Japanese companies wanted most from returnees was their "international skills": the ability to speak foreign languages (especially English), familiarity with foreign (especially Western) business customs, and the ability to interact with foreigners without feeling timid or inferior. However, Japanese companies rejected returnees with "individualistic" attitudes and behavior, characteristics often equated with having been "Westernized." What Japanese companies expected from returnees was "*wakon yōsai*," "Japanese spirit/Western knowledge," a slogan used in the mid-Meiji period to emphasize Japanese identity as the base upon which Western ideas would be added. Although returnees were no longer considered elites except in special cases, they still retained two contrasting images: catalysts of internationalization and social deviants. In sum, for Japanese companies, returnees were functionally useful and yet at the same time morally objectionable.

In the 1980s, the term *shinjinrui*, the "new breed," became popular in the Japanese mass media, referring to the younger generation in their twenties and thirties. The term signified that the younger generation were so different in their attitudes and behavior that they seemed like a totally new breed of Japanese. However, several corporate managers stated to me in the mid-1980s that "returnees are worse than *shinjinrui* in terms of their adaptability to Japanese organizational culture." As one manager said in 1986, "While *shinjinrui* are not conscious of their differences from older generations, returnees are conscious. So the new generation is made up just of 'benign delinquents,' whereas returnees are true believers, like conscientious objectors, so to speak." Thus, while both returnees and *shinjinrui* were perceived negatively, returnees were apparently considered a more malignant type within Japanese organizations.

New generations and returnees: the mid-1990s to the present

In the 1990s, the bursting of the bubble economy and the continuing economic downturn resulted in the gradual erosion of the Japanese social system. Many companies have gone bankrupt and the unemployment rate has soared.[7] Foreign firms have begun buying out Japanese companies, and drastic reorganization such as the merger of major banks has been sweeping through Japanese industries. However, in the continuing economic downturn throughout the 1990s and into the millennium, Japanese companies have not stopped recruiting returnees. Furthermore, the number of Japanese studying abroad has been steadily increasing. To consider only the United States, there were 13,360 Japanese studying in the U.S.A. in 1985–86, 43,770 in 1993–94, and 46,810 in 2001-02 (Institute of International Education 1985–86, 2002; Mori 1994: 209; Nakai 2002: 79).[8] The increases in the number of returnees working in Japan and Japanese studying abroad are of course related. The fact that more and more returnees are working in Japan has been sending a message to Japanese high school students that studying and graduating from a university overseas is a realistic alternative to graduating from a university in Japan. Because tertiary education and entrance examinations form a pivotal institutional mechanism in reproducing the Japanese social order, as described above, the steady increase in the number of returnees who bypass the Japanese higher educational system may have a serious impact on the Japanese social order (Nakai 2002: 94–111).

The fact that returnees have been continuously recruited by Japanese companies seems to refute the research analyst whom I previously quoted; he stated that Japanese companies are recruiting returnees because of a shortage in particular sectors of the labor market, but that this recruitment would cease once the Japanese labor shortage ended. Today, in an era of high unemployment, the labor shortage has ended, yet returnees are still sought after by companies. There are two reasons for this, one having to do with the economy and the other with the state of management in Japan. First, from the 1990s on, many Japanese companies, regardless of size, have expanded their global operations as economic activities have become increasingly borderless. Internationalization is not a national ideology or rhetoric anymore, as it was in the 1980s, but has turned out to be the hard economic reality of globalization, despite the overall downturn in the Japanese economy. These global developments in the economy have been generating demand for returnees. Second, due to factors such as continuing overall economic stagnation, rapid changes in work environments because of advancing information technology, and the aging population, management practices of Japanese companies have been shifting to more merit-based salary and promotion structures, as opposed to the more traditional structures based largely on seniority. This shift has worked favorably for returnees in finding and staying in jobs in Japanese companies.

While returnees are becoming absorbed into Japanese companies due to changing corporate management systems, younger Japanese have been feeling progressively more alienated from the traditional Japanese management system in recent years. Increasingly, younger Japanese have begun to see themselves as sacrificed to the old social system (*Yomiuri Shinbun* 1998, 2002). As the economy has stopped growing and the unproductive aged population has increased, the real income of the younger generation of workers has decreased, and younger people's share of social security payments in supporting the aged has increased. Under these circumstances, younger Japanese have begun to realize that the seniority-based hierarchy and lifetime employment system do not benefit them at all in a state of economic downturn (see Mathews, Chapter 7, this volume). The old system worked remarkably well while the economy continued to expand, from the end of World War II up until the bubble economy era; but then, as the economy stopped growing, its problems have become overwhelming and have started to backfire against the younger generation.

To compare returnees and the Japanese younger generation as a whole in terms of their perceptions of Japanese organizational culture and social institutions, let me quote from my interviews with both returnees and non-returnees. The first quote is from a 1994 interview with a 27-year-old man who graduated from a state university in the U.S., and who now works as an assistant managing director at a broadcasting company:

> "Japanese are not good at delegating tasks in a systemic way. Everybody just does the same thing at the same time, one thing after another. I wonder why they don't examine projects carefully, divide them into smaller sets of tasks and assign staff members to those tasks, decide leaders for each set of tasks, and then let each leader decide how the work gets done. But Japanese don't like to have or to become leaders. They would rather do their work based on group consensus, even though it takes time to reach such a consensus.... So when I get involved in a project, I tell members to select a leader and delegate

tasks according to individual skills and abilities. Often people select me as a leader, just because I was the one who made the suggestion. I know how it happens, so I accept it. We analyze the project, delegate tasks, and do it according to each member's schedule. We get things done much more quickly than other groups.... I think people in the company have begun to appreciate how I manage projects, and that's why I became an assistant managing director."

The following quotation is from a 2002 interview conducted with a 28-year-old man working for a bank, a graduate of a public university in Tokyo with no experience studying abroad:

"What Japan needs now is strong leadership. This is true for the national government, local governments, private companies, and universities and schools. A Japanese automobile maker [Nissan] was revived from a troubled situation because of its new foreign president. The company's top executives were not able to make difficult decisions because they were too afraid of breaking the norms of the past. They knew what to do, but they couldn't do it because they were too stuck in Japanese social norms. The company I work for has the same problem. It's too top heavy. There are too many executives waiting for their retirement and their large retirement payments, so they can't initiate drastic reforms. I see a gap in interest between their generation and my generation. I may stay in this bank or move to a foreign bank.... Their salary system is mostly based on merit. More and more Japanese companies are adopting this type of salary; I prefer it to salary based on seniority. Why do we need to get paid less than older workers, who work less than we do?... This isn't fair!"

There were many Japanese women among returnees who were dissatisfied with their work environment, especially in terms of discrimination against women.[9] Let me quote from a 1994 interview with a 27-year-old woman, who graduated from a U.S. university. She works for an American cosmetic maker/distributor in Japan, and described her previous employment experience in a Japanese company:

"I just can't stand the way Japanese men in Japanese organizations treat women at work. I worked for a large Japanese chemical company for three years. All I was asked to do was to type and duplicate documents, answer the telephone, make tea, clean tables, and so forth. No men were doing these kinds of work. Two incidents made me decide to quit the company. First, I found out that the salary of an older woman in the office, in her early forties, was almost the same as my salary. She had worked there for over twenty years, and some of the male employees of her age were managers. She said that was not unusual in the company. Second, a man who entered the company at the same time I did became my boss. He wasn't smart at all. Only because he was a male did he become my boss. At that company, and this is true for most Japanese organizations, women only get dead-end staff positions. It's true that some companies now hire a small number of women as career-track manager candidates (*sōgōshoku*) but these cases are exceptional. Women who don't mind being treated as inferiors can stay with Japanese firms. Women who can't accept that move out, if they can."

The following is a quote from a 2001 interview with a 32-year-old woman working for a telecommunications company. She graduated from a university in Kyoto, and has no experience studying abroad.

"I think that Japanese companies are not really utilizing women's abilities, and this is why many able women quit Japanese companies and move to foreign companies. Of course not every Japanese company is gender-biased and not every foreign firm practices gender equality. But generally speaking, the work environment in Japan is male-oriented and it's hard for aspiring women to succeed. This is especially so for older women and those with children. . . . I really think that working conditions and the employment system in Japanese companies have to change in order for women to be able to fully participate in the workforce. And men have to change their attitudes and consciousness about not only women but about themselves, and about gender in general."

These interviews indicate that returnees and younger Japanese share similar frustrations with the organizational culture in Japan in terms of its leadership, its seniority system, and its treatment of women. A nationwide survey conducted by Nomura Research Institute supports this. The survey points out that younger Japanese are dissatisfied with social institutions that are unable to respond to their needs and facilitate what they see as social progress. They also have a strong sense of distrust toward political and administrative systems, which have failed to present and openly discuss national objectives and to clarify the process for achieving such objectives (Nomura Research Institute 1998: 233–4). In general, returnees and younger Japanese have come to share dissatisfaction with the established Japanese social system, for it has not been changing quickly enough to respond to the new world in which Japanese now live.

Conclusion

In this chapter, I have delineated the changing perceptions in Japan toward Japanese returnees, and then discussed relations between returnees and younger Japanese in the context of the recent economic downturn. Returnees have often been said to lack proper Japanese socialization, and have thus been perceived as unemployable by Japanese companies. However, from the mid-1980s until now, as the Japanese economy has continued to globalize regardless of its ups and downs, returnees have become not only employable but often sought after because of their "international" experiences and skills. Despite their functional usefulness for international business dealings, however, returnees have often been expected to adapt to Japanese organizational culture and the Japanese management system based on seniority.

As returnees have begun to join Japanese companies, younger Japanese have come to feel increasingly ambivalent about maintaining that management system, for it has ceased to represent their interests. That system worked well while the Japanese economy was developing and the aged population was not large; but as development has halted and the aged population swelled, the system has begun to place greater burdens on the young than on their elders. Changes in socio-economic context have created a situation in which the younger generation receives smaller returns from the Japanese social system. From this situation, generational conflict may develop.

Returnees and younger Japanese as a whole were on different sides in the past; but today this is not the case, and a generation gap has emerged. While the Japanese economy was growing, both younger and older generations enjoyed its benefits, and the problems of "the generation gap" were attributable to their being at different stages of the life course. Dissatisfied youth became conformist as they became older. Returnees, however, posed a serious threat to both younger and older generations, because returnees had the potential to challenge the foundations of the system upon which young and old alike depended. Returnees were treated as unemployable, or otherwise made to conform to the Japanese way of work if they wished to work for Japanese companies. But the situation has recently changed; returnees and younger Japanese have found each other on the same side, with older generations on the other side. The two groups have begun to recognize in common that Japan's management system and social system at large is for them a problem that must be solved.

In this social and economic situation, both returnees and young Japanese have begun quiet but firm resistance to protect their own interests. As they make decisions in various stages in the life course, such as choosing a university, a company to work for, or a partner in their private lives, they transform the society from within. When a high school senior chooses to attend a university abroad instead of a Japanese university, he or she is contributing to the structural change in higher education in Japan, however small that contribution may be. If a college graduate decides to work for a company because it has adopted merit-based payment instead of seniority-based payment, he or she is contributing to the erosion of the old management system. It is the decisions and actions of people in everyday life that, cumulatively, bring about large-scale social change. In this sense, returnees have become part of a wider generational awareness in Japan, in which returnees and younger Japanese, consciously or unconsciously, have begun to ally against older generations.

Notes

1 This chapter is partly based on my Ph.D. dissertation (Mori 1994) at the University of California Santa Cruz, and follow-up research in the years since. Follow-up research has been partly funded by the Special Research Fund of the Dean of Cultural Policy Division, Shizuoka University of Arts and Culture during 2002.

2 I conducted 100 interviews with returnees and about fifty interviews with non-returnees and with corporate personnel managers from 1984 to 2002, but concentrated on the period 1988 to 1993. The returnees I interviewed were in their twenties and thirties, and all were graduates of American universities. Japanese with foreign graduate degrees but with Japanese undergraduate degrees are not included. *Kikokushijo*, who spent several years during their K-12 years due to their parents' (usually father's) work assignment are not included. For discussion of *kikokushijo*, see Kitsuse *et al.* (1984) and Goodman (1993).

3 Saitō (1984) uses a metaphor to capture the re-entry experiences of the first cohort of Fulbright grantees: the American university degree compared to the U.S. dollar. An American degree has a clear value in the U.S., but in Japan it has to be exchanged for Japanese educational value at a certain exchange rate. He also refers to Japanese sayings in explaining returnees' experiences. In Japan, "A smart hawk hides its talons" and "A nail that stands out gets struck down": thus *ryūgakusei* should not boast about but hide their foreign experience to avoid social disapproval. Those eager to show off their foreign experience would be scorned and shunned. Those who behaved as though they had never studied abroad but used their international skills unobtrusively to help their Japanese colleagues would be successful.

4 In the past decade, Japanese universities have been exposed to international competition and have faced a decreasing number of high school graduates. The Ministry of Education and Science has been implementing reforms to improve universities' research and educational quality. Generally speaking, the American university system – such as the semester system, teaching evaluations, and clearer differentiation of research and education-oriented universities – is considered as the model for Japanese university reforms. The results of these reforms are not yet clear, except that universities unsuccessful in recruiting students are facing financial problems. For the international comparison of universities, *The Gorman Report* (Gorman 1993) ranked Tokyo University, assumed to be the best university in Japan, forty-eighth in the world. This low ranking has often been cited in describing the bad state of higher education in Japan.

5 The Japanese school year begins in April and ends in March.

6 The "internationalization" of Japan was used as a national goal in the 1980s and 1990s, as I describe in terms of returnees employment in this chapter. For discussion of "internationalization" as a national goal, see Befu (1983) and Goodman (1993).

7 The annual rate of unemployment for 2002 was 5.4 percent, the worst in recent history (*Asahi Shinbun* 2003). The rates were 2.0 percent in 1980, 2.6 in 1985, 2.1 in 1990, 3.2 in 1995, 4.1 in 1998, and 4.7 in 1999 (Management and Coordination Agency, 2000).

8 The figures are from the Institute of International Education, *Open Doors: Report on International Educational Exchange (2002)*. Of 46,810 students from Japan in the U.S.A. in the 2001–2002 academic year, 20.7 percent were graduate students, 67.5 percent were undergraduate students, and 11.8 percent were students enrolled in other educational institutions. According to Nakai, about half of undergraduate students are enrolled in junior and community colleges. In 2001 to 2002 there were 31,596 undergraduate students, of whom approximately 15,800 were enrolled in four-year courses. The number attending an annual job forum in Boston organized for Japanese students who are scheduled to graduate from four-year courses is 5,000 to 6,000 (Nakai 2002: 79).

9 The Equal Employment Opportunity Law for Men and Women was implemented in 1986 and revised in 1999. Progress has been made throughout these years regarding working conditions for women. However, employment opportunities for women continue to be restricted in actuality. For example, the largest number of women in the labor force are part-timers, whose payment is approximately two-thirds that of full-timers for the same jobs. Part-timers usually have neither employment security nor benefits. Women in management positions are still rare in both the private and public sectors.

References

Asahi Shinbun (1979) "Medatsu nyūshi shippai gumi, mokuteki o motsu mono wa sukunai" ["Mostly failures of university entrance examinations, few with clear objectives"], October 25.

—— (2003) "Nenkan shitsugyōritu saiaku 5.4%" ["The annual unemployment rate at its worst: 5.4%"], January 31.

Befu, H. (1983) "Internationalization of Japan and Nihon Bunkaron," in H. Mannari and H. Befu (eds) *The Challenge of Japan's Internationalization: Organization and Culture*, Tokyo: Kwansei Gakuin College and Kodansha International.

Bennett, J. (1962–63) "The Innovative Potential of American-Educated Japanese," *Human Organization* 21 (winter): 246–51.

Bennett, J., Passin, H. and McKnight, R. (1958) *In Search of Identity: The Japanese Scholars in America and Japan*, Minneapolis: University of Minnesota Press.

Goodman, R. (1993) *Japan's "International Youth": The Emergence of a New Class of Schoolchildren*, Oxford: Clarendon Press.

Gorman, J. (ed.) (1993) *The Gorman Report: A Rating of Graduate and Professional Programs in America & International Colleges* (6th edn), Los Angeles, CA: National Education Standard.

Institute of International Education (2002) *Open Doors: Report on International Educational Exchange*, New York: Institute of International Education.

Ishikawa, Y. (1988) "The 1988 Job Market for Recent Graduates," *Japan Quarterly*, April to June.

Kitsuse, J. I. (1980) "Coming Out All Over: Deviants and the Politics of Social Problems," *Social Problems* 28(1): 1–13.

Kitsuse, J. I., Murase, A. and Yamamura, Y. (1984) *"Kikokushijo*: The Emergence and Institutionalization of an Educational Problem in Japan," in J. Schneider and J. I. Kitsuse (eds) *Studies in the Sociology of Social Problems*, Norwood: Ablex.

McCornick, A. J. (1988) "Japanese Students Abroad as Agents of Internationalization," Doctoral Dissertation, Stanford University.

Management and Coordination Agency (2002) *Employment Research*, Tokyo: Management and Coordination Agency.

Mannari, H. and Befu, H. (eds) (1983) *The Challenge of Japan's Internationalization: Organization and Culture*, Tokyo: Kwansei Gakuin College and Kodansha International.

Mori, S. (1992) "Nihon kigyō ni yoru gaikoku daigaku-sotsu nihonjin koyō no henka: itsudatsusha kara kokusaijin e? – amerika yonensei daigaku sotsugyōsha no baai" ["Changing employment of Japanese graduates of foreign colleges by Japanese enterprises: from drop-outs to internationalists? In the case of U.S. four-year college graduates"], in R. Iwauchi *et al.* (eds) *Kaigai nikkei kigyō to jinteki shigen* [Overseas Japanese enterprises and human resources], Tokyo: Dōbunkan.

—— (1994) "The Social Problems of Students Returning to Japan from Sojourns Overseas: A Social Constructionist Study," Doctoral Dissertation, University of California, Santa Cruz.

—— (2001a) "Gendai nihon no shakai henka" ["Social change in contemporary Japan"], *Iwaki meisei daigaku jinbungakubu kenkyū kiyō* [Research Bulletin of Iwaki Meisei College-Humanities and Social Sciences], vol. 14.

—— (2001b) "Cambiamenti Sociali Nel Giappone Contemporaneo" ["Social Change in Contemporary Japan"], *Il Giappone Verso Il Terzo Millennio: Radici e Prospettive, Atti del XXIII Convegno di Studi sul Giappone, Associazione Italiana per gli Studi Giapponesi* (AISTUGIA), Republica di San Marino, September 23–25, 1999, Rimini (Italy): Il Cerchio.

Nakai, K. (2002) *Kōsotsu kaigai itchokusen* [Studying overseas directly from high school graduation], Tokyo: Chūō Kōronsha.

Nomura Research Institute (1998) *Kawariyuku nihonjin* [Japanese in transition], Tokyo: Nomura Sōgō Kenkyūsho.

Saitō, G. (1979) "Ryūgaku, yūgaku soshite ryūgaku" ["Study abroad, play abroad and wander abroad"], *Asahi Jaanaru*, December 28.

—— (1984) *Furuburaito ryūgaku ikkisei* [The first cohort of Fulbrighters], Tokyo: Bungei Shunjū.

—— (1989) *Kaigai ryūgaku: kōkōsei kara shakaijin made* [Overseas study: from high school students to adults], Tokyo: Asahi Shinbunsha.

White, M. (1988) *Overseas Japanese: Can They Go Home Again?* New York: Free Press.

Yomiuri Shinbun (1998) "21 seiki e no nenkin kaikaku: wakai sedai ni tsuyoi fushinkan – yomiuri shinbun zenkoku seron chōsa" ["Reforming the pension system towards the 21st century: strong feeling of distrust among the younger generations – Yomiuri Shinbun's national survey"], January 21.

—— (2002) "Kawaru nenkin (1) sedaikan no fukōhei: wakamono hodo hokenryō omoku" ["Changing pension system (1) inequality among generations: the younger the heavier the burden becomes"], January 8.

10 Centered selves and life choices

Changing attitudes of young educated mothers

Ayumi Sasagawa

Introduction

A gap between the generations may be seen in many areas of Japanese life today. Not least, the ways in which young mothers order their lives and raise their children seem to have changed in important ways over the last generation. In this chapter I explore the views of university-educated mothers from two generations, examining their changing attitudes about their lives.[1]

It has often been said that Japanese women have been changing in various ways since the end of World War II, and that increased access to higher education has played a significant role in this. In Japan, women were for the first time allowed to enter university on an equal basis with men immediately after the end of the war. Since then, the number of women entering university has dramatically increased. In 1955, 2.4 percent of girls (and 13.1 percent of boys) of the relevant age cohort entered university. By 2001 this had grown to 32.7 percent of girls (and 46.9 percent of boys) who entered university (MOHLW 2002: 51). It seems inevitable that such a great expansion of university education for women has altered young women's senses of their lives.

This phenomenon of growing numbers of women becoming university graduates is often identified as a positive symbol of postwar social change, indicating greater gender equality. But it is also sometimes depicted negatively, as the cause of late marriage and the sharply declining birth rate in Japan. In the early 1990s, some Japanese political leaders attacked higher education for women, for encouraging women to enjoy their lives "too much" and desert their "primary" role as mothers (Jolivet 1997: 1; Uno 1993: 321).

However, this connection becomes tenuous when we realize that the relationship between university-graduate women and employment was not strong in Japan up until the late 1990s. The rate of female university graduates entering the workforce immediately following graduation has been high. However, if they leave the workplace in order to bear and raise children, as is commonly practiced, the rate of re-entry into the labor market is low in comparison with women from a lower educational background (see Figure 10.1). The 1997 National Lifestyle White Paper reveals that the labor

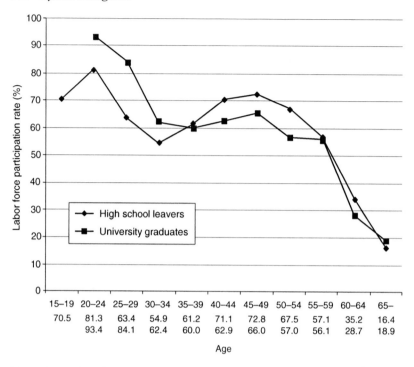

Figure 10.1 Labor-force participation of Japanese women through the life course.

Source: Ministry of Labor (2000)

force participation rate of university-graduate women aged 25 to 64 in Japan was lower than that of some Western countries: 60 percent in Japan in 1990, but 82 percent in the United States, and 81 percent in both Germany and France in 1996 (EPA 1997: 122).

Why do many Japanese university-educated women not seek long-term employment? Both Japanese and overseas researchers cite multiple cultural and institutional factors for why university-graduate women in Japan have such a low rate of employment participation. These include companies' strong preference for hiring male employees with a university degree (Brinton 1993; Lam 1992), the social attitude that the achievement of academic excellence is not feminine (Okano and Tsuchiya 1999: 77–8), and female university students' lack of interest in pursuing long-term plans for career progress (Fujimura-Fanselow 1995; Tanaka and Nishimura 1986).

Researchers tend to agree that for university-graduate women, their domestic role has taken precedence over the use of their higher educational attainments. Several researchers have found that university-graduate women have often needed neither to earn their living nor to support their household finances; marriage to a university-graduate man with a well-paid secure job gave them no strong need to engage in paid work (Mifune 1996; Tanaka and Nishimura 1986). They suggested that university education often functioned to enable women to stay in a privileged position at home.

Another important factor keeping university-graduate women in their domestic role is the "myth of motherhood" in Japan. The "Japanese mother" has traditionally been praised for her self-sacrifice, and Japanese women were taught that they should devote themselves to their children; by and large, society has held to the notion that hardship in the demanding role of child caretaker should be a source of maternal pleasure. There have been changes in some mothers' attitudes, in their resistance to this idealized maternal figure, but motherhood still often signifies self-denial in Japanese society (Sasagawa 1996).

Is this situation changing, with the changing of the generations? At first glance, the fact that many university-educated women still leave the workplace while in their thirties may be thought to signify an unchanging aspect of Japanese women's lives. However, we need to pay attention to the views that motivate these women to behave as they do, in order to see whether younger mothers follow their mothers' generation's principles with the same set of values that their mothers followed. The generation gap may be seen not only in contrasting roles and behaviors, but also, more subtly, in different approaches and attitudes toward the same roles by people in different age groups.

Using an ethnographic approach, this chapter shows the changing attitudes of young university-educated mothers at an individual level. Data were gathered through fieldwork carried out in a suburban city near Tokyo in 1998 to 2000. Fieldwork included interviews with university-educated mothers as well as participant observation in mothers' groups in the community. In this suburban residential area, mothers established social relationships through their association with other mothers in mother-child groups and PTA (Parent Teacher Association) activities, while their husbands were engaged in white-collar jobs and commuted to Tokyo, spending little time in the community. I divided the mothers whom I interviewed into two groups to compare their views. One group consisted of older mothers who entered university in the 1950s or 1960s, and who were in their late forties to early sixties when interviewed. The other group consisted of younger mothers, from their late twenties to their mid-thirties, most of whom went to university in the 1980s. This comparison seeks to demonstrate how these different generations of women in Japan are changing in their attitudes toward motherhood.

Work outside the home

Becoming a full-time mother as a matter of course

In the 1950s and 1960s, from all that I was told, the views of female graduates reflected the views of wider society: that women should leave the workplace once they married. Regardless of academic credentials, companies did not expect female employers to work for more than a few years. Female employees in general were offered jobs without responsibility or promotion opportunities. After her graduation, Yoshioka-san[2] (52) found a clerical job "that anybody can do"; four years later, she left the workplace upon marriage, something wholly taken for granted in Japanese society at that time. Koike-san (58) did not have an opportunity to get a job because her marriage had already been arranged while she was in university.

Although some of these mothers thought about finding a job again while their children were small, this idea was not realistic. They had few people to ask for help in childrearing, except for their own mothers or mothers-in-law. Horii-san (49) once looked for a day nursery in order to be able to go back to work, but she could not gain the right to send her children to a day nursery because all the nurseries she visited were full and her husband was well paid.[3] At that time, day nurseries were considered to be institutions for children from poorer families whose mothers had no choice but to work. The option of leaving a child with a day nursery was not positively accepted by most better-off families. Horii-san said, "To be honest, I didn't try to find a day nursery seriously. In fact I didn't need to work for money, and my desire to work wasn't so strong." Even though some young mothers in those days wanted to have a job, they did not strongly oppose the social agreement that mothers with small children should stay at home.

Working for independence

Mothers of this generation continued, however, to want to have a paid job, planning to return to work after their children had grown up. Some twenty years after quitting their first jobs, Miyagi-san (62) and Nakai-san (60) started to work again on a part-time basis, as a social worker and as an instructor to train people with speech defects, because, in Nakai-san's words, "financial independence is indispensable to obtain my liberty."

Paid work was often identified by older mothers as a means for women to have equal status with their husbands. Kotani-san (51) had an especially strong career aspiration. She married soon after graduation from university, and has worked hard as a self-employed technical translator at home ever since. This was despite the fact that her husband earned more than enough money to support the family. She told me, "I have never thought of quitting my job. I hate to be a man's subordinate. I don't want to be financially supported. I know I am indispensable at home, but I can't be satisfied with family responsibility only."

Koike-san, who had no work experience in her life, was interested in working outside the home. She had no specific idea of what kind of job would suit her and be available to her, nor in fact did she take any action to find a job. However, she had the impression that working outside is something good for self-development and for establishing a more equal relationship with her husband, who felt that a housewife should be completely satisfied with her role at home. For many older mothers, financial independence signified a necessary step for mental independence; hence they had the feeling that a wife's giving up full-time paid work may solidify her subordinate position to her husband.

Full-time workers' strong career aspirations

In the 1990s, by contrast, more young university-educated women continued their work even after childbirth. After the 1986 Equal Employment Opportunity Law, which aimed at ending discrimination against women, some companies started to treat female workers more seriously, accepting more female university graduates and assigning them to jobs with more responsibilities and promotion opportunities.

Matsuda-san (36) was a full-time worker on the managerial track at a middle-sized electronics company. She had worked for the same firm for thirteen years since her graduation:

> "In theory, my firm treats male and female university graduates equally. I started as an assistant in the European division of the sales department, but was given a specialized job, which included writing business letters and translating documents. Finally, I had an assistant for my work. I like working hard and getting money as the reward for my efforts and labor. I feel very comfortable with that kind of lifestyle. Financial reward makes me feel a sense of liberation. I feel that staying at home is a waste of energy."

Matsuda-san was a chief employee (*shunin*) when she was interviewed, and would take a promotion examination for section manager (*kachō*) within a few years. Other informants, such as Eto-san (31) and Nakatani-san (31), were working as specialists – systems engineers – in their workplaces, and also had opportunities for promotion. The younger generation of women had developed their careers by continuing their full-time jobs rather than quitting, and accumulating professional knowledge and skills. They showed a reluctance to stay at home because they wanted to make use of their professional abilities. Paid work was a source of satisfaction for them, rather than a matter of financial necessity. As their examples show, marriage and having children no longer necessarily blocks young mothers' career aspirations.

Changing social and corporate attitudes

Companies' arrangements for employees with small children have been steadily improving. When she was 34, Matsuda-san took a year's maternity leave, and then held a part-time shift for six months. She then returned to a full-time position, but kept overtime work and overseas business trips to a minimum with the permission of her boss. Nakatani-san, who had a 1-year-old daughter, also had at her own request been reduced temporarily to a part-time position at the time she was interviewed. Since historically the company she was working for had employed many women, her union had demanded improvements in their working conditions. If she wished, she would have the option to continue at reduced working hours until her child reaches the age of 6.

Even if a support system for mothers is well established, however, many female workers leave the workplace after childbirth. It is still quite common for full-time working mothers to have no female colleagues with children. When Matsuda-san entered her firm, six female graduates were accepted, but when interviewed, she was the only one of those six still with the firm. Nakatani-san told me that she always felt a sense of guilt when she went home, leaving her colleagues behind. Her boss understood her situation well, but other colleagues, especially those who did not do any housework, could not understand how busy she was. In addition, she was dissatisfied with the fact that there would be a delay in her eligibility for promotion due to the period she spent at part-time.

Despite the lack of understanding displayed by Nakatani-san's colleagues, it is notable that the social stigma attached to working mothers leaving their children in the care of other people has weakened. Younger mothers appear to be much less hesitant in sending their children to day nursery than were their older counterparts. The Ministry of Health, Labor and Welfare, which has jurisdiction over day nurseries, has changed its policies over the past few decades: from policies in the 1960s emphasizing that a child should be raised by his or her mother at home, to policies in the 1990s emphasizing the importance of both maternal and paternal participation in bringing up children and the necessity of child-rearing support by society[4] (Maeda 1997: 223–35). Under the direction of the Ministry of Health, Labor and Welfare, the local government of the city where I carried out research set up the "Family Support Center" in 1999. In this system, a mother who is registered as a "requesting member" can ask a "supporting member" to collect her child from day nursery, and look after the child until she comes home. The main beneficiaries of the system are working mothers; but full-time mothers can also use the system.[5] A similar service is provided by non-profit organizations. For instance, "*esuku*" is a well-known nationwide organization that has established networks for mothers to help each other without charging the expensive fees of privately run agencies. Baby-sitter services provided by private companies are also available, although their expensive rates makes mothers reluctant to use them.[6] Thus, private and public services to support working mothers have become much more accessible, and this both reflects and contributes to changes in societal attitudes towards working mothers.

Leaving the workplace to enjoy mothering

Some mothers of the younger group still left the workplace upon childbirth, as older mothers did a few decades ago. However, this no longer seemed to be a matter of course, but of individual choice. Maeda-san (29) left her computer firm after she got married in order to become a full-time mother:

> "I quit work because I had no confidence in managing the double burden of child-rearing and professional work, and I didn't like my former boss. Working at a computer firm is quite tough, but I enjoyed the job itself. I feel comfortable staying at home now, and enjoy playing with my two sons. A mother living downstairs leaves her 1-year-old baby at a day nursery. But I don't like that option, since the day nursery frequently rings her up even when her child has only a slight fever. Finally, her family moved to be near the day nursery."

Orita-san (30) also used to work as a systems engineer, and left the workplace after she became pregnant:

> "I liked my job. I was so busy that I got to the office at 9 a.m. and left around midnight; and I frequently went to work even on Sunday. My husband was working in the same section as me, but one of us had to transfer to another section after announcing that we would get married. That's a custom that many Japanese companies still have: they always transfer the wife. I was transferred to a section with a completely different type of work, and I lost interest in my job. But this isn't the main reason why I quit. I had already made up my mind that I would leave when I was pregnant. I want to raise my children by myself, and want to be at home when my children come home from school."

In Orita-san's workplace, male and female employees worked under the same conditions – women also had to do overtime work. Both Maeda-san and Orita-san were able to work if they wanted, but they were well aware that working mothers have to cope with many obstacles. They did not want to struggle with the double burden of work and childcare every day. Rather, they wanted to feel comfortable, enjoying time spent with their small children, and did not want to make their children feel isolated from their mothers. These young women thus came to choose a lifestyle which suited their preference and interest, rather than simply leaving the workplace upon marriage as a matter of course.

Housework and who does it

The emergence of the idea of sharing housework

The full-time housewife used to be the object of admiration for many Japanese women; a full-time housewife was the symbol of a family that was sufficiently wealthy to enable the wife not to have to engage in paid labor. The main duty of the housewife was that of "an all-around caretaker" (Lebra 1984: 302), and housewives engaged in the task with a sense of obligation, as if it were a "profession" (Imamura 1987: 18).

Despite the fact that the older mothers whom I interviewed said that being a full-time housewife used to be regarded as a woman's ideal status, no mother told me that she herself held this dream when she was young. Rather, for these women, marriage automatically meant becoming the manager of a household. In Koike-san's words:

> "Becoming a full-time housewife was a matter of course for me. I didn't have any other choice. I was always busy because I put up our relatives when they came to Tokyo, and my husband often brought his acquaintances to our home. I had visitors all year around, so I didn't have time to think of myself."

Miyagi-san told me that although she had little desire to be a full-time housewife, she spent twenty years in this status, since she accepted the idea that housework and childrearing are women's work. Despite spending many hours working at home as a translator, Kotani-san had never asked her husband to share in the housework. Women such as these had no idea of sharing housework with their husbands, who spent little time at home; they took charge of household affairs with a sense of obligation. Moreover, they fulfilled themselves by carrying out their domestic responsibilities and serving their family.

Recently, however, the increasing number of young mothers who continue to work outside the home seems to have changed attitudes towards domestic work and those who perform it. The younger working mothers whom I interviewed did not hesitate to ask their husbands to share the tasks of housework and child-rearing. Some husbands favored the idea of sharing, but few husbands had enough time and/or ability to do so, and their wives accepted the larger share of this burden. Matsuda-san's husband did not hesitate to do housework, but he was extremely busy with work and came home at almost midnight every night. Nakatani-san's husband could not cook, but they shared other domestic work. They took days off from work in turn when their 1-year-old daughter could not go to day nursery because of a fever, but her husband often went on business trips overseas for months, which forced her to manage everything herself. It cannot yet be said that husbands' participation in housework and child-rearing is enough to significantly reduce their wives' double burden; but working mothers no longer believe that only the wife is obliged to manage domestic responsibility.

The full-time housewife: image and reality

Some young working mothers told me that they respected full-time housewives, since they regarded full-time housewives as women who can put up with what they themselves cannot. As Hirokawa-san (31) said:

> "I respect full-time housewives because they can cope with small children all day long. They have no place to get rid of stress stemming from mothering and few chances for social participation. It must be tough being a full-time housewife. If a woman can fulfill herself that way, fine, but I can't."

As Fujiki-san (33) said:

> "I think full-time housewives are great, since they devote themselves wholly to housework and mothering. Before giving birth, I cleaned the house only once a year. I didn't know that the cleaning was supposed to be done every week. Now I have some teaching assistants who also help me with the housework. [Fujiki-san ran a small private tutoring school (*juku*) at home]. My 5-year-old daughter will be surprised when she discovers that her friends' mothers always do housework (laughs). My husband does some housework, though I don't ask him to. He never complains about my not doing it."

These younger mothers neither admired nor criticized full-time housewives. Rather they felt that full-time housewives were women with different values from their own. They regarded full-time housewives of their generation as women who voluntarily chose such a lifestyle, not as those who are forced to take on a restrictive lifestyle, as was the case with women of the older generation.

However, it seemed that even full-time housewives in the younger generation were not interested in spending every day doing housework chores. As Hirai-san (35) told me:

> "I like being a full-time housewife very much. I want to make the most of my mothering. I don't need outside work to fulfill myself. Luckily my 3-year-old daughter is obedient, so I want to keep her at home as long as possible. My husband respects my decision, so it's up to me if I choose to be a full-time housewife or not. We don't share housework;

rather I order him to do this and that, such as cleaning the bath. My husband takes care of himself, like making a cup of coffee. He doesn't need a wife's assistance as much as other husbands do."

As Maeda-san, another full-time housewife, said:

"My husband often cleans the bath and does the laundry, especially when I say I feel tired, because I repeatedly ask him to do these things. A man doesn't do anything unless he's ordered to! My husband often reads my face, and does some housework stealthily. I don't think it is a wife's duty to take good care of her husband all the time."

These women organized household chores in their own ways, and as "managers" of the household, delegated housework to their husbands. They left the workplace not because they wanted to play "traditional" housewifely roles, but rather in order to spend more comfortable lives as mothers. They were well attuned to the ways in which they can raise their children and enjoy mothering, and not interested in housework as a form of obligation. While their older counterparts identified full-time housewives as being subordinate to their husbands due to their total financial dependency, young full-time housewives appeared not to share this idea.

Changing attitudes towards university-educated full-time housewives

As society has begun to accept university-educated mothers continuing full-time work, the reaction to young educated mothers' decision to be full-time housewives has also changed. As Maeda-san told me, "My unmarried friend said that she can't imagine a university-graduate woman becoming a full-time housewife, spending time chatting with other housewives all day." As Orita-san said, "I was told by women of my mother's generation that if I stayed home, I'd be wasting my ability. Junior college graduates are engaged in 'women's work' in a bank, for instance, but university graduates can work under the same conditions as men. So they told me that I'm over-qualified to be a full-time housewife."

Perhaps these women were the first generation to be asked why they left the workplace after giving birth, rather than why they did not leave the workplace. While the older generation felt that society did not allow them to have any option other than staying at home when they were mothers, these younger women were advised by women around them to keep working. Unlike the older generation, however, they seemed not to feel pressured by such external expectations. These young mothers understood that it should be they themselves who decide whether or not they should work outside the home.

Child-rearing and children's education

Mothers' involvement in community activities

When the older mothers were young, they tended to stay at home with their children. They had little assistance in bringing up their children in the community. Some of the mothers knew other young mothers in their neighborhood, and might sometimes leave their children in one another's care. According to my informants, however, there were no mothers' circles or mother–toddler groups around them.

Ochiai points out that there was a tendency for urban Japanese families in the 1960s, especially families with infants, to turn to their kinship networks for help rather than to seek mutual support from within their neighborhood network (2000: 95–127). In the 1980s, however, kinship networks, which consisted mainly of parents, siblings and parents-in-law, became weaker as the number of siblings decreased. Because parents had fewer siblings, their children had fewer cousins to play with; thus mothers needed to expand their networks to obtain child-rearing support (ibid.). Subsidized by the central government, in the 1980s local governments started to organize classes for pregnant women to teach them how to breast-feed, and bring up children (Arichi 1993: 111).

Young mothers whom I interviewed were involved in community activities not only for their children, but also for their own pleasure. A mother's involvement in community starts from her participation in local governmental services such as the above-mentioned "classes for mothers." These activities are aimed not only at providing guidance for new mothers, but also at promoting friendship between them.[7] As their children grow up, mothers are involved in a variety of community activities, such as mother–toddler groups and PTA activities in preschool and primary school. Mothers' personal networking also expands through child-related activities, and they often gather just to have fun. One full-time mother, Yanai-san (36), told me that she loves going out every day. She spends busy days joining mother-child activities in the community and playing tennis with other mothers. Mothers like her spend lots of time with other mothers participating in the same group activities, enjoying chatting, as well as exchanging information concerning child-rearing.

Generational conflict and investment in children's education

The young mothers whom I interviewed were keen on education for their children. A few decades ago, the term "education mother" (*kyōiku mama*) was used to criticize the excessive focus on education that Japanese mothers placed upon their children in order to send them to prestigious high schools and universities; but in recent years mothers' devotion to their children's education often starts even before children's entry into primary school. For example, her daughter was just 3 years old when I interviewed Hirai-san, but it had already been arranged that she would spend busy days with piano and ballet lessons. Young mothers seemed to be keen on their children learning English, playing a musical instrument, and practicing physical exercise such as swimming from a very early age: they were interested in investing in their children's education to develop their abilities and talents. Young mothers give their children material and mental support to encourage them to do well in school, as those of the previous generation did. However, these new mothers also believe that extracurricular learning activities other than studies at school will have a beneficial effect on their children's growth, and will enrich their lives in the future.

From the older mothers' point of view, however, young mothers' enthusiastic attitude toward their children's education may reflect more their own pursuit of self-satisfaction than a genuine interest in their children. As Yoshioka-san told me:

> "Younger mothers these days indulge their children too much. They don't ask their children to help with housework. When I was a child, we helped with housework chores before going to school and after we came back from school. Younger mothers today don't do that; they're only eager to have their children study many things at private tutoring schools. It's too much of a burden for the children."

Nakai-san criticized young mothers for making education for children a matter of "outsourcing," leaving their children's education with private tutors or sports instructors. Older mothers tended to believe that a child should be educated at home by his or her parents in order to become a good member of society; they felt that too many learning activities will only make a child feel frustrated and exhausted.

Despite the older generation's criticism, the young mothers I spoke with enjoyed investing time and effort in their children's education in a great variety of ways. When a mother has sole responsibility for the care of her child at home, as was the case for the stay-at-home mothers whom I interviewed, she may gain a sense of autonomy in making crucial choices about raising her child. For younger mothers, child-rearing is more a personal venture than it was for their mothers – it is an investment detached from larger society.

Pluralism and autonomy in mothers' lives

Women's attitudes toward their personal lives have changed over the past few decades. Underlying this is the fact that women's views about being "self-centered" have changed from negative to positive.

When they were young, the older generation of women did not strongly resist the idea of women's monopoly over domestic responsibility; they fulfilled themselves by achieving their socially expected roles at home. However, they also felt that they were somehow victims of society, not allowed to have any option other than becoming a full-time housewife. Because of this, several mothers took part in social activities in order to change a society which they viewed as forcing women to stay at home. After her children grew up, Miyagi-san organized a women's group with other female university graduates to offer women in her community opportunities to study women's issues:

> "There were few women who entered university in the past, so we thought that we should pass down what we learned to the next generation. I was told once that 'university-educated women of your generation have a responsibility to society,' and I agree. Young women these days are more interested in themselves than in society, thinking only about how they can have a comfortable life."

These women all held the idea that paid work is an important factor in releasing women from a subordinate position. Thus, older mothers had an ambivalent feeling toward their own domestic role; they justified their status of being full-time housewives through their knowledge that they had had no other choice. They expected their daughters' generation to handle both mothering and housework, and full-time work outside the home, rather than following their own path of becoming full-time housewives. These older mothers wondered why currently some young mothers want to leave paid work, to live as they themselves had lived, despite the fact that they are no longer forced to do so. These older mothers agreed that if a woman wants to become a full-time housewife, her will should be respected. However, they often had a negative view of young full-time housewives today. As Nakai-san said:

> "A variety of childcare facilities and other arrangements for childcare are available these days. Even so, some young women choose to be full-time housewives. They have only one or two children, and spend much time on their own pleasure. The meaning of being a full-time housewife has changed, from a housewife who has no alternative choices to a housewife who shows off her husband's large income."

Younger mothers' desire for autonomy in their lives tends to be seen as "selfish" (*wagamama*) by the older generation of women; these older women think highly of altruism and serving others, and see the younger women as giving top priority to their own preferences and interests.

Women's strong sense of obligation toward a housewifely role has indeed weakened, as the number of full-time housewives has decreased. Full-time housewives among wives of salaried men decreased from 74.9 percent in

1955 to 62.0 percent in 1970, and to 46.6 percent in 1995 (EPA 1997: 12). Especially after the 1970s, mechanized household chores no longer required the full-time attention of housewives, and full-time housewives were often labeled as women enjoying their excessive free time. Housewives needed to find some way to spend their spare time and to broaden their horizons, it was claimed, in order to overcome their "disgraceful" reputation for being "lazy": they did not need to stay at home all day long any more and gradually began to seek activities outside the home for their personal fulfillment.[8] Housewives' lifestyles became diversified: some took part-time jobs, some went to classes of various sorts, and some engaged in volunteer work. Mothers began to think about how they could fulfill themselves through activities they choose, rather than only in devotion to their family.

It has become possible, as we have seen, for mothers to pursue a career and climb the ladder of professional success if they have strong motivation and sufficient childcare support. However, full-time mothers of the younger generation stay at home if they see that choice as more conducive to their own fulfillment. Young mothers today can exercise a large degree of individual control over child-rearing, educating their children as they choose. They all agree that they do not want a completely child-centered life. They are not satisfied with only staying at home with their children, and they want something else – activities which stimulate their interest and enable them to lead a full life.

Young mothers have thus begun to think of themselves as creators of their own lives. During my field research, I frequently heard the phrase *jibun rashii* in conversations between the younger generation of mothers. *Jibun rashii* means "like oneself": living in a way that suits oneself, expressing one's "self" (*jibun*) as one truly is. This expression also implies emancipation from external pressure imposing fixed social roles, such as that of "mother" or "housewife." The notion of *jibun rashii* encourages women to determine their own lives – to choose their own sense of how to live. For the younger generation, a "self-centered" attitude toward their lives does not mean "selfishness," as the elder generation of mothers saw it; rather, it signifies self-fulfillment.

Conclusion

A "generation gap" can clearly be seen in the changing attitudes of university-educated mothers. The most significant aspect of young mothers' changing situation over the generations is that they have gained a degree of autonomy in their personal lives. While older mothers left the workplace upon marriage or childbirth whether or not they wanted to, the younger generation can choose to do so, based on individual preference.

Young university-graduate stay-at-home mothers' high opinions of the motherly role and their active involvement in mothering activities may seem to indicate that they spend their lives centered around their children. However, while the older generation of mothers accepted the idea that self-sacrifice symbolizes motherhood, younger mothers control mothering carefully, holding a sense of their own needs and seeking ways to enjoy their mothering role.

The idea that children should be raised not only by their mother at home but also in the community, and that mothers need social childcare support, has begun to be shared in Japanese society. The older generation's desire to realize a gender-equal society encouraged their daughters' generation to continue working outside the home, and the increasing number of working women has contributed to changing governmental and corporate attitudes toward women. Childcare support services have become much more accessible, and a variety of child-related activities are available in order not to let a mother and her child be isolated at home. A mother is still regarded as the primary agent of child-rearing (and mothers themselves agree), but support from society is now available; and it is up to the mother to decide what kind of support is necessary and how to manage mothering and other activities in negotiating her personal life.

Young mothers' increased autonomy in their lives makes them not at all reluctant to ask their husbands to share housework and responsibility in bringing up their children, even if they are not engaged in full-time work. As women's idea of domestic responsibility as their housewifely obligation has weakened, socially fixed roles of men and women have also been changing: men today are expected to play a domestic role to some degree, and this may contribute to changing the entrenched idea of gender-specific roles – "men at work and women at home" – in Japanese society. The younger generation of mothers is redefining women's roles (and men's roles), because of their diversification of lifestyles in seeking life courses which suit their own needs and desires, rather than fulfilling socially expected gender-specific roles as did their elders.

These changing approaches toward motherhood will no doubt continue to affect the coming generation. Yamamura (1971) argued that the "traditional" Japanese mother–child relationship was characterized by emotional reciprocity – a mother's devotion to her child and self-sacrifice makes her child feel *on* (a debt of gratitude), which motivates the child to repay his (or her) mother by studying and working hard. Such an emotional relationship may not exist for younger mothers: if mothers do not sacrifice themselves for their children, then children will have to find their motivations for study and work by themselves, rather than through their relationships with their mothers.

The children of these young mothers will be shaping the Japan of the future. Mothers today are not satisfied with their children simply being good members of society; rather, they expect them to develop their own special abilities. Children are raised and socialized to be someone special, not simply to play socially required roles. In other words, they are not "allowed" to follow the older generation's path. The pressures that come to bear on a child's passage to adulthood are shifting. Possibly, some will enjoy living as they desire, while others will feel great pressure in seeking what they really want in life, and will hesitate to become adults until they find out who they are: not in terms of a social role, but in terms of their own "real" selves.

Notes

1 A university in this chapter means a four-year university (*daigaku*), not a two-year junior college (*tanki daigaku*).
2 The names of the mothers in this chapter are pseudonyms.
3 Parents need permission from the local governmental office to send their children to a day nursery, *ninka hoikujo*, even if the nursery is privately owned. If the number of applicants for admission into a nursery exceeds a certain fixed number, the governmental office gives priority to parents who have more urgent need, such as single mothers, low-income families, and families without a grandmother living nearby.
4 Central and local governments' strong anxiety about the sharply declining birth rate has caused an expansion of public childcare support systems for mothers in recent years.
5 This service is not aimed at making a profit, but is run on a voluntary basis. Hence requesting mothers pay only 500 yen (approximately US$4.20) per hour from 7 a.m. until 8 p.m. on weekdays, and 600 yen per hour at other times.
6 In the case of one private firm, for instance, a professional baby-sitter costs 1,600 yen per hour (approximately US$13.30) from 9 a.m. to 5 p.m.; 300 yen per hour is added to the service from 5 p.m. to 8 p.m. in the evening, and 500 yen per hour from 8 p.m. until 9 a.m. the following day.
7 The local government provides a variety of childcare support services in order not to let mothers feel isolated, because isolated mothering is regarded as a potential cause of child abuse or over-protection by mothers (Sasagawa 1996: 42).
8 According to Imamura, who did her research on housewives in a suburb of Tokyo in the late 1970s, housewives felt guilt about engaging in outside non-paid activities, because a housewife's "reluctance to spend household money on herself is correlated with her role as manager of the [family] finances" (1987: 89).

References

Arichi, T. (1993) *Kazoku wa kawattaka* [Has the family changed?], Tokyo: Yūhikaku.

Brinton. M. (1993) *Women and the Economic Miracle: Gender and Work in Postwar Japan*, Berkeley: University of California Press.

Economic Planning Agency (EPA) (1997) *Heisei 9-nenban kokumin seikatsu hakusho* [White paper on the national lifestyle 1997], Tokyo: Ōkurashō Insatsukyoku.

Fujimura-Fanselow, K. (1995) "College Women Today: Options and Dilemmas," in K. Fujimura-Fanselow and A. Kameda (eds) *Japanese Women: New Feminist Perspectives on the Past, Present, and Future*, New York: Feminist Press.

Imamura, A. (1987) *Urban Japanese Housewives: at Home and in the Community*, Honolulu: University of Hawaii Press.

Jolivet, M. (1997) *Japan: the Childless Society?* London: Routledge.

Lam, A. (1992) *Women and Japanese Management: Discrimination and Reform*, London: Routledge.

Lebra, T. S. (1984) *Japanese Women: Constraint and Fulfillment*, Honolulu: University of Hawaii Press.

Maeda, M. (1997) *Hoikuen wa ima* [The day nursery today], Tokyo: Iwanami Shoten.

Mifune, M. (1996) "Kōgakureki josei no kazoku to seikatsu" ["Highly educated women and their families and lives"], in N. Toshitani *et al.* (eds) *Kōgakureki jidai no josei* [Women of the highly educated generation], Tokyo: Yūhikaku.

Ministry of Labor (MOL) (2000) *Heisei 11-nenban josei rōdō hakusho* [White Paper on Women's Work 1999], Tokyo: 21-Seiki Shokugyō Zaidan.

MOHLW, Ministry of Health, Labor and Welfare (2002) *Heisei 13-nenban josei rōdō hakusho* [White paper on women's work 2001], Appendix, Tokyo: 21-Seiki Shokugyō Zaidan.

Ochiai, E. (2000) *Kindai kazoku no magarikado* [A turning point of modern families], Tokyo: Kadokawa Shoten.

Okano, K. and Tsuchiya, M. (1999) *Education in Contemporary Japan: Inequality and Diversity*, Cambridge: Cambridge University Press.

Sasagawa, A. (1996) "Japanese Mothers: Their Role and its Meaning as Social Ideology," unpublished MA dissertation, Oxford Brookes University.

Tanaka, Y. and Nishimura, Y. (1986) "Shokugyō keizoku ni oyobosu gakureki kōka" ["The effect of education on continuous work"]," in M. Amano (ed.) *Joshi kōtō kyōiku no zahyō* [The position of women's higher education], Tokyo: Kakiuchi Shuppan.

Uno, K. (1993) "The Death of 'Good Wife, Wise Mother'?," in A. Gordon (ed.) *Postwar Japan as History*, Berkeley: University of California Press.

Yamamura, Y. (1971) *Nihonjin to haha* [The Japanese and the mother], Tokyo: Tōyōkan Shuppansha.

Epilogue

Are Japanese young people creating a new society?

Bruce White and Gordon Mathews

Assessing this book's chapters

Are Japanese young people creating a new society? It is remarkable how profoundly the different chapters of this book disagree on this question. If the reader has read to this point, she or he will already be well aware of the very different viewpoints the book's chapters put forward. Of course every new generation in the world today to some extent creates a new society, to fit the changing circumstances of the world in which it finds itself; and of course Japan has always been changing – the idea that "young people will finally bring change to the world of their conservative elders" ignores all the extraordinary transformations that have taken place in Japan over the past centuries. However, postwar Japanese society has been structured in particularly rigid ways, demanding, broadly speaking, a standardization of behavior and the sacrifice of the individual to the collective. Now that that society no longer offers the rewards it once did, discontented young people may serve as agents for its transformation. But is this in fact happening? Are young people creating a new Japan, or are they being molded to fit the rigidity of a social system created by their elders?

Let us consider each of this book's chapters in turn, to assess how they answer this question. Sakurai (Chapter 1) offers the view that the generation of protest in the 1960s, while dormant in subsequent decades, has raised a new generation that may finally create a Japanese society that can embrace rather than reject the world beyond Japan. This seems plausible, especially given his discussion of the Internet and its impact. However, Sakurai pays little heed to the fact that it is the generation of protest in the 1960s that became the stereotypical "father devoted to his company/mother devoted to her children" of subsequent decades; this generation became "the older generation" against which today's young people may struggle. Will today's young people, in their evolution through the life course, really be any different from their parents?

Kotani (Chapter 2) examines how, cocooned in their comfortable world of mass media and consumer goods, young people today feel no anger at an adult society that is shutting them off from a viable future – they, in effect, "fiddle with their mobile phones while Japan slowly burns." He asks, "Why don't youths protest?" However, he does not consider the fact that societal change may come about not through overt social and political action but through millions of individual choices – if enough young people choose not to live lives like their parents, then Japan will indeed be transformed.

White (Chapter 3) offers, in effect, an ethnographic validation of Sakurai's argument in Chapter 1. It is remarkable that the openness to the world that Sakurai claims is a hallmark of the young White does not find among the urban intellectuals discussed by Sakurai but among youths in a rural Kyushu hamlet. This makes their argument doubly convincing – perhaps Japanese young people really are open to the world in a way that their elders never were. However, it is notable that White's chapter does not deal with organizations, and the immersion of individuals within them (we know the occupations of none of the people he portrays): when and if the young people he depicts become company workers and parents, how much will their youthful attitudes shape their behavior and how much will those attitudes become irrelevant?

Part I thus sets the stage by offering two very different interpretations of whether or not Japanese young people really are creating a new society. Part II turns to youth in their teenage years. Ackermann (Chapter 4) considers secondary school students and how they respond to the ubiquitous social pressure working to mold them into proper, self-sacrificing adults. They respond, he demonstrates, by creating their own world, particularly through *keitai* (cell phones), a world largely beyond adult surveillance. He emphasizes that these youth are not rebellious, but are simply seeking to preserve themselves. His analysis parallels that of Kotani; but rather than being passive consumers, the young people he describes seem more like beleaguered survivors, struggling to maintain their own identities against an adult world that seeks to dominate them.

Miller (Chapter 5) depicts one realm in which some young people do indeed exert an exquisite, flamboyant control over their lives: their own bodies. Cosmetic surgery and the elaborate costumes of kogals enable some young people to mold their bodies in ways unimaginable to their elders – "they don't even look Japanese!" older people may remark. Miller's analysis clearly links to that of Sakurai and White: they also argue that the bounds of Japanese ethnicity are becoming progressively less important. Miller adds the realm of appearance to this consideration, illustrating how, increasingly, "anything goes" – ethnicity too is now no more than a fashion accessory. What we cannot know from her chapter – as from Sakurai, and White's as well – is what will happen to the young people whom she portrays. Is this a fashion flirtation before they become mothers, fathers, and office workers, little different from their parents? Or does their appearance reflect a change that may be more enduring?

In Chapter 6, McVeigh examines how university students experience "guidance." He argues that through this "guidance," students are trained to pass over "the generation gap" and become adults, not much different from their parents. The Japanese adult social order is so powerful and pervasive, he maintains, that youth cannot possibly change society. When McVeigh's own survey results indicate that young people feel a degree of autonomy in their choice of university, he dismisses this as false consciousness – young people may think they have free choice, but really they are guided and controlled, he tells us. Perhaps he is right; but his data seem more equivocal than his conclusions. McVeigh continues the argument of Kotani and Ackermann, making an even stronger claim that young people have no choice but to reproduce the Japanese adult social order: meaningful resistance is impossible.

In examining individuals largely free from organizations, White and Miller argue that young people may be creating new lives and identities in a changing Japan; in examining individuals within organizations, Ackermann and McVeigh argue or imply that such change is unlikely. To the extent that individuals are emphasized, change by youth of the Japanese social order may seem inevitable; to the extent that organizations are emphasized, change may seem impossible. Part I, dealing with the historical background of generational conflict, and Part II, dealing with young people in their teens, thus offer two very different views: are young people creating a new society (Sakurai, White, Miller), or are they doomed to be swallowed up by the society of their elders (Kotani, Ackermann, McVeigh)? By looking at young people in their twenties and thirties who are now making irrevocable choices about their lives, Part III offers the beginnings of an empirical testing ground for this divide.

Mathews (Chapter 7) examines two groups of young people: those who have entered full-time employment, and those who have spurned or been rejected from such employment. It is noteworthy that the latter, working in temporary jobs, seem happier than the former, despite making less money and having more precarious futures; the latter can preserve their dreams, as the former, seemingly owned by their companies, cannot. Mathews asks but cannot answer the central question these "outsider" young people embody. Are they doomed to be losers, having been permanently excluded from the Japanese adult social order? Or might they turn out to be agents of that social order's transformation?

Nakano and Wagatsuma (Chapter 8) look at the other side of the family/work divide: not young men and women spurning careers but young women spurning families. They examine three pairs of mother–daughter relations, in which the daughter is unwilling to marry and follow the path of her mother. Nakano reveals the complexity of "the generation gap": it is not simply a matter of mothers wanting their daughters to marry, while their daughters seek careers. Rather, both mother and daughter conceive of their lives within the shifting discourses of "individual choice" and "familial responsibility." The former is emphasized over the latter in a Japan where social roles seem to be losing considerable constraining power, and in which free choice has become progressively more salient as a value.

Mori (Chapter 9) considers Japanese who graduated from American universities, and what happens when they return to work in Japanese companies. In the late 1980s and early 1990s, these returnees were viewed as "functionally useful yet morally objectionable," since they were seen as having lost their "Japaneseness" – their ability to work smoothly within the Japanese corporate order. Over the past decade, however, these returnees have come to be seen as increasingly necessary in an era of globalization. Furthermore, unlike earlier decades, in which young and old Japanese corporate workers alike saw returnees as outsiders, today, young corporate workers educated in Japan have become allied with these outsiders against their elders. The struggle is no longer "Japanese versus outsider" but rather "young versus old" – young Japanese have themselves become "foreign" to their elders, Mori tells us.

Finally, Sasagawa (Chapter 10) looks at the different ways in which young full-time mothers conceive of child-rearing as opposed to older mothers. She finds that whereas older women became full-time mothers because they had no choice, younger women actively choose that role. However, they carry out this role in a very different way from their elders: whereas older mothers sacrificed themselves to their children, younger mothers raise their children as a way of attaining self-fulfillment. The same behavior across the generations – giving up work to devote oneself to one's children – may have very different motivations, Sasagawa finds, and different implications as well. Whereas earlier generations of young people struggled for success in the world to repay a debt of gratitude to their mothers, young people tomorrow, raised by today's self-oriented mothers, may instead see the world as a maze within which to find themselves.

Part III is less dramatic in its fissures than Parts I and II: its chapters seem largely to agree in their analysis of incremental change in the worlds of work and family. What we do not know is the significance of the changes they describe. While Mathews and Nakano/Wagatsuma refuse to speculate as to the ultimate significance for societal change of the young people they depict, Mori and Sasagawa do indeed imply that what they depict is a matter of historical transformation – young people may truly be creating a new Japan, they seem to say. However, all this remains open to question.

Reviewing the question: are Japanese young people creating a new society?

Let us now consider in a more thematic way the question asked in the title of this epilogue. We will divide our analysis into three parts: (1) how young people may see their lives as offering more choices and alternatives; (2) how young people may be interacting with each other and with their elders in new ways; and (3) how young people may be challenging the legitimacy of institutions.

How young people may see their lives as offering more choices and alternatives

Young people, as many of the chapters of this book show, are moving away from the rigidity of the postwar social order, into a world of greater choice as to how to live their lives and conceive of and express their identities. The chapters in Part I set the notion of expanded choice into a history of generational change in Japan. For Sakurai in Chapter 1, the range of choices that young people experience today comes from a series of generational shifts accompanying improved access to education and a large-scale rebalancing of class relations since the 1950s. Kotani (Chapter 2) sees this history of generational change as having been cut short in the era of Japan's economic success. While previous postwar generations fought for improved choices and freedoms, a resignation that "society cannot be changed" has set in since the 1970s. Despite seeing a weakening of the generational change dynamic in society, Kotani argues that youth have more "flexible and adaptable models of understanding" than their elders. White (Chapter 3) suggests that young people's communities are where they express their diversity and gain access to choices. For White, Japan's young people find choice in a variety of stylistic and consumer-driven "communities" offering them an individualized and diverse approach to building society at large.

Part I, then, depicts a range of alternative lives and identities as coming from a series of generational transitions that have cumulatively worked to break down a rigid social order. Since the 1970s, overt generational conflict may have faded; but the newly arising diversity of young people's lives may help to explain why that social order has lost much of its power without overt generational confrontation. This greater freedom of choice for young people than in generations past is due not simply to the fading legitimacy of the adult Japanese social order, but also to a globalization of consumption and information, connecting an internal with an external diversity, and causing some of the boundaries and borders of Japan to become porous.

If Part I shows young people's increased access to choices and alternatives, Part II considers how much these options really are available, particularly to students still under the thrall of "adult supervision." Ackermann (Chapter 4) sees that such choice both is and is not available. Adult society exerts pressure on the young to conform to an ideology of an ideal, harmonious society which restricts choice; but young people also belong to their own generationally contextual world which operates under rules that necessitate choice: *keitai* (mobile phones) allow youths to choose which groups and relationship networks to maintain and which not to maintain. In Miller's Chapter 5, we see the inherent diversity of youth "communities" or "subcultures" feeding the media industries in what becomes a youth-driven "loop" of diverse fashions, styles, and trends. Young men and women are thus able to draw on a huge variety of options to present alternative ethnic and gender identities. McVeigh (Chapter 6) is more skeptical: Japanese conservatism subliminally orders the decisions and identities of an "alienated" youth. He does see young people as "materially richer" and thus able to travel and consume in new ways: but this means little in his view, in that the adult social order has effectively deprived them of the ability to make choices that really matter.

If Parts I and II have in varying degrees stressed access to alternative options and identities, Part III presents these considerations in empirical examples of young people making life-determining decisions from a diverse set of options. In Chapter 7, Mathews finds that the majority of his *furiitaa* informants insist that they chose for themselves their irregular employment. This may be partly a delusion, he notes; they may be mostly dreamers doomed to be unfulfilled. However, the fact is that many do dream, as their elders for the most part apparently did not – this fact in itself implies greater choice. Nakano/Wagatsuma illustrate how new generational understandings have interacted with the discourse of women's freedom of choice. Young women now think of their lives as offering a variety of alternatives that their mothers never had, and mothers and daughters alike accept this as the way of the world today. Mori (Chapter 9) explores how young people are now able to choose to study abroad without the stigma that once would have followed them upon their return to Japan. Sasagawa (Chapter 10) puts access to choice at the center of her examination of the pursuit of self-fulfillment for young educated mothers. Sasagawa helps us to add to Nakano/Wagatsuma and Miller's understanding that access to choice has established itself in gender roles. Indeed, several chapters of this book convincingly suggest that women, more than men, may be the primary bearers of generational change in Japan today, since they, more than men, can escape the pressure of having to fulfill narrow adult social roles.

Being able to plausibly envision alternative life courses and choices thus forms a central difference between young people and their elders in Japan today. Compared to their elders, young people operate from a diverse range of possibilities, and it is this generational difference that most separates their views of life in Japan. Let us now consider how this envisioning of a greater access to alternative lives and identities leads to particular forms of social interaction which may be both reflecting and producing change in Japanese society.

*How young people interact with each other and with their elders
in new ways*

The chapters in Part I stress that interpersonal interaction between young people has taken new and diverse forms. Sakurai (Chapter 1) sees the Internet as a key access point through which younger people interact without the constraints imposed by publishers or the mass media. While Kotani (Chapter 2) argues against a vision of a more empowered interactive youth – he maintains that new media enable them to avoid rather than interact with the world – he does portray some young people as becoming more involved in volunteer activities and thus in "helping to change the world." White (Chapter 3) sees youths' "exposed" communities as providing a diverse network of stylistic connections with others. Youth interaction crosses geographical borders, connects with a diverse popular culture, rallies around common "interests," and has an open, globally connected membership. Part I thus gives examples of how youth are interacting with one another in ways that seem specific to the diverse contexts of their generation as opposed to the more rigid social worlds of their elders.

Part II explores the mechanics of these new interactions and how they are formed *vis-à-vis* elders and society at large. Ackermann (Chapter 4) considers how youth interactions are modeled on and formed in response to the pressures of the adult world. Through their use of language, and of mobile phones, high school students create an alternative social world that at once invades their privacy and increases the power they have to shape interpersonal relations, as a refuge from the social pressures around them. If Ackermann focuses on responses to pressure, Miller (Chapter 5) represents the creative and empowering contexts in which youth interaction takes place. Through fashion, her kogals and other young people manipulate "sincerity, mockery, and kitsch" and draw upon a wide variety of societal interpretations (bodily, ethnic) in structuring and expressing their interpersonal interaction; she, like White, emphasizes how young people may form their own communities of the like-minded. McVeigh (Chapter 6) does not examine interaction between youth, but rather their commentary on an adult order they seem often to view in positive terms. One wonders: Are Miller's bold fashion adventurers and McVeigh's often meek college students altogether different groups of young people? Or might they overlap – behaving in wholly different ways in different social environments? And what might this mean for the possibilities of young people creating a new Japanese society?

In Part III, by looking at older young people who are faced with life-shaping decisions, we attempt to gauge the extent to which the youth communities and identities seen in Parts I and II may influence young people's interactions with older generations. Mathews (Chapter 7) finds that discontented young corporate workers seem unable to successfully communicate with corporate-minded elders who, to their minds, may embody an intolerable rigidity. Like Mathews, Mori (Chapter 9) sees interaction in companies between the young and old as problematic – young Japanese-educated employees have become allied with returnees against older employees, who represent the corporate norms of the past. Nakano and Wagatsuma (Chapter 8) find a more integrated relationship between young and old. They show how young daughters conduct a variety of negotiations with their mothers, and make choices about work and love in consultation with parents as well as with peers. Sasagawa (Chapter 10) depicts inter-generational conflict. Older mothers may see educated young stay-at-home mothers as "selfish" in their pursuit of fulfillment, illustrating how the young and old may view self-sacrifice and independence in ways that clash. This reflects new interpersonal approaches of the young against the collective models of interaction held by the old.

These chapters show a variety of examples of how young people are interacting with each other and their elders in new ways. If Japanese young people are indeed changing Japanese society, then they are doing so not only in terms of a plurality of life choices they envision and exercise, but also through a greater variety of interactions with others than their elders ever imagined (Chapters 1, 3, and 5). That young people may be adopting new forms of interaction could be a sign that they have a new-found ability to incite change. However, these capacities for creating change may be blocked when it comes to interacting with the institutions of the adult social order.

How young people are challenging the legitimacy of institutions

Two of our chapters deal explicitly with school, the first institution of the adult social order that young people encounter outside the family. In Part II Ackermann and McVeigh both look at how teenagers deal with social pressure in schooling. Their chapters put forward two somewhat different perspectives. Ackermann (Chapter 4) sees indirect social pressure – categories, guidelines, and codes that seek conformity – as exerting considerable force for conformity, which youth in part are able to ward off, largely because such pressure is seen as irrelevant to their own lives and social worlds. The young, in Ackermann's portrayal, are attempting at least inchoately to deactivate the power that their elders have over their lives. McVeigh (Chapter 6) on the other hand, sees youth as unable to move beyond the pressures they encounter in education, the pressures of the adult social order molding them to be like their parents. If McVeigh is right, then Japan seems doomed as a vital society: the world is rapidly changing, rendering the Japanese adult social order of thirty years ago unable to deal adequately with the world of today, and yet this is what the young people he describes are being indoctrinated to follow. Part III, however, indicates in different ways how this may not be the case: young people, by changing or spurning the institutions they must interact with, may perhaps be creating a new Japan.

Mathews, Mori, Sasagawa, and Nakano/Wagatsuma all examine what may be the beginnings of this process. The young workers described by Mathews in Chapter 7 may see their companies' employment structures as anachronisms that have "survived from the past, but cannot survive much longer." In an era of economic downturn, lifetime employment and seniority-based pay and promotion cannot continue, and therefore young people's flexible approaches – to become a *furiitaa* or freelancer, or to become a regular employee to learn all one can before moving on – may represent appropriate survival strategies. In taking these approaches, young people are also challenging the status quo. They are – through the combined effect of many individual choices – in effect "helping to destroy the Japan that their parents and grandparents built." Whether they succeed or fail may depend less on the efforts of the young themselves than on the fate of the Japanese economic system.

Mori (Chapter 9) illustrates this process from a different angle. His returnees have taken the risk of being educated by universities overseas, a risk that until recently had made them unemployable by Japanese companies. Today, however, in a Japan pushed into globalization, these returnees hold an important value for organizations, and can no longer, as in past years, be dismissed as "non-Japanese." In turn, the returnees may choose to work for a company that eschews standard Japanese employment patterns; or they may shake up the more conservative companies that employ them by questioning their elders' stereotypes of gender or of leadership. All in all, these young returnees, like Japanese young employees as a whole, are making countless individual decisions and engaging in interactions that cumulatively may work to bring about wider social and institutional change in Japan.

The family is of course also an institution; according to Nakano/ Wagatsuma (Chapter 8) and Sasagawa (Chapter 10), it is one which has already embraced discourses of individual freedom. Nakano/Wagatsuma's unmarried daughters may avoid the institution of family in their futures, at least beyond their own natal families, while Sasagawa's young mothers reconstruct family in a self-centered way – they put personal fulfillment at the center of their decisions, and elder mothers often cannot understand this. The consequences of this shift may have far-reaching and unintended implications – the parents advocating "*tomodachi oyako*" ("parent and child as friends") described by Kotani in Chapter 2 did not intend to create the generational passivity he discusses, and the children of today's fulfillment-seeking parents may turn out to be very different people from those that their parents imagined. Nonetheless, change in child-rearing patterns seems clear, at least within the small subset of mothers described by Sasagawa, and from such change in the intimate institution of family, other institutions may eventually be transformed as well. All this indicates that a familial environment may be more conducive to inter-generational communication and transformation than a corporate one. This may be one reason why young people quit their companies so readily (Chapter 7) and yet so readily remain with their families (Chapter 8).

Finally, the nation-state may be seen as an institution of identity. Sakurai, White, and Miller, in Chapters 1, 3, and 5, illustrate how young people put forward reinterpretations of Japanese ethnicity as alternatives to conceiving society at large. While Miller's young people offer alternative presentations of Japanese ethnicity by remaking the body, White's young people attempt to integrate their cosmopolitanism into their parents' homes and communities. In both cases, ideas and peoples that have been historical "others," from Koreans to African-Americans, are embraced as part of a broader and more diverse "Japaneseness," and this presentation may delegitimize a homogeneous status quo. Sakurai sees these and other efforts as already influential in doing away with conservative conceptions of Japaneseness – in finishing what generations of elders have tried and failed to do, in finally breaching a Japaneseness walled off from the world at large.

In illustrating the subtle ways through which young people's concerns are legitimized and old institutional frameworks delegitimized, this book's chapters have revealed areas in Japanese society that are under increasing pressure to adapt to new and diverse youth-driven values. Some institutions, such as the media and popular cultural agencies that perpetuate the youth market and further diversify Japan, are already under the sway of youth values (Chapter 5), at least to the extent that they are shaped by as well as shaping the desires of youth. Others, such as educational institutions, continue to put pressure on young people to conform to old established norms (Chapters 4 and 6). Still others, such as family and company, are between both poles, with families, as noted above, being apparently more amenable to generational communication and change than companies.

Ultimately, the question is whether young people, in all their diversity and cosmopolitanism, will be able to displace the old values inherent in the institutions of the adult social order with their own. Will they transform, or themselves be transformed by these institutions? Both will happen, we predict; but it seems clear that the growing diversity of the young will continue to erode the conservative institutions of the postwar Japanese social order. The ultimate success of young people in changing that order depends on a host of macro-economic and global factors, but it also depends on the vitality and persistence of the young themselves in the years and decades to come.

Conclusion

In the postwar period, each Japanese generation of youth has become largely subsumed by the adult social order into which it has entered, but has also shaped that social order. Today, however, more than in previous generations, a pivotal moment of historical generational change may have arrived. In the ways the young people we have seen in this book perceive society as offering them a variety of options, in the ways they form generational identities and interactions enabling them to live out these alternatives, and in the ways they begin to displace ideas fundamental to old institutional orders, we see considerable potential for change in Japanese society.

The change we envision will probably not come about through organized protest or even conscious generational solidarity, but rather through a vast array of individual choices and micro-interactions. That this accumulation of change is occurring in the intimate and individual settings of people's lives points to the importance of ethnographic and anthropological approaches in understanding change in a complex society like Japan. Revealing the subtle ways in which contemporary change is produced in Japan has implications beyond Japan; in an era where organized protest may be giving way to diverse individually-led changes in a range of contemporary societies, there is clearly a need to understand emerging identities and generations in new ways. Social change may not occur in the ways we have learned to recognize from historical examples. In interpreting the often unfamiliar worlds of younger people, the danger is that we conclude that no observable change is happening, or that only negative changes are occurring. In an amusing reflection addressed to those who too readily seek to label the young as the bearers of societal maladjustment, Castiglione wrote in 1528:

> and truly it seems against all reason and a cause for astonishment that maturity of age, which, with its long experience, in all other respects usually perfects a man's judgement, in this matter corrupts it so much that he does not realise that, if the world were always growing worse and if fathers were generally better than their sons, we would long since have become so rotten that no further deterioration would be possible.
>
> (1967 [1528]: 107)

The young people we have seen in this book in many ways represent a divergence from the identities, life choices, and worldviews of their elders; it may indeed be that these young people will create a Japanese society offering more personal opportunities and diversities than that of the recent past. This book has not, of course, shown this conclusively; but it has shown that the fault lines and adaptations to generational relations and worldviews in Japan can reveal the complexities of its social transformation over time. The detailed ethnographic study of generational succession and change is essential for understanding not just Japan but all contemporary societies, in all their ongoing transformations. We have not been able to answer whether young people in Japan are creating a new society. But by looking at Japan's changing generations, we have perhaps come closer to understanding the nature and intensity of the changes that challenge them, and challenge us all.

Reference

Castiglione, B. (1967 [1528]) *The Book of the Courtier*, London: Penguin.

Index

Printed in the United States
132847LV00002B/16-30/A